in repair

LORI LITTLETON

IN REPAIR

Copyright © 2024 by Lori Littleton

All rights reserved. No part of this book may be reproduced in any form or by any electronic or mechanical means, including information storage and retrieval systems, without written permission from the author, except for the use of brief quotations in a book review.

This is a work of fiction. Names, characters, businesses, places, events, locales, and incidents are either the products of the author's imagination or used in a fictitious manner. Any resemblance to actual persons, living or dead, or actual events is purely coincidental.

ISBN 978-1-0689221-0-7 (hardcover)
ISBN 978-1-0689221-1-4 (paperback)
ISBN 978-1-0689221-2-1 (ebook)

*For Chloe, Addison and Ashton
Don't ever fall into the box of mediocrity*

Sweet are the uses of adversity
Which, like the toad, ugly and venomous,
Wears yet a precious jewel in his head;
And this our life, exempt from public haunt,
Finds tongues in trees, books in the running brooks,
Sermons in stones, and good in everything.

—William Shakespeare
As You Like It, Act 2, Scene 1, 12-17

one

MAY 2016

I WAS ALREADY a bundle of nerves on the morning of my big Toronto meeting when my sons spilled orange juice at breakfast. After mopping up the mess with paper towels, I left them in the kitchen while I dashed to find them dry clothes. When I arrived in Aidan's room, I was reminded that the toll from working at a shoe store filled with customers all day long, every day, was showing up at home. I had neglected the laundry that week, and the basket in Aidan's room was overflowing. Dismayed, I turned to his dresser and pulled his drawer open so fast it fell out. I grabbed a shirt and pants from the top of the heap. Aidan usually kept his room tidy, putting away his toys in labelled bins and storing them on his bookshelf, which was also neat and arranged by largest books at the back, smaller ones up front. But today, the drawer toppled a stack of books, and strewn clothes covered a variety of plastic figurines and metallic cars all over the floor. I sighed and told myself we would deal with the mess later.

The boys giggled as I shuffled them into the bathroom to get cleaned up and changed. I dashed into Jacob's room, which was just as chaotic as Aidan's. This wasn't a total surprise—Jacob enjoyed a mess. Today he'd tossed his stuffies all over the place, and his bed quilt lay crumpled over the side of the bed and onto the floor. I searched for something clean for him to wear and, at the bottom of a molehill of clothes, found the outfit he'd worn to Beavers earlier that week. It was clean. My children believed that if they wore an article of clothing for more than three minutes, it was dirty. And, most of the time, I'd concur. But this morning, I didn't care if the shirt had a stain on it, Jakey was wearing it.

I ushered the boys out of the house and down the walkway. I loved spring in St. Catharines, especially that magical time when the magnolia trees on our street bloomed, pale pink bursts that later rained all over lawns. My boys didn't often fight, but seeing them walk together, backpacks bobbing, chatting about how they couldn't wait to get home that night to continue exploring their "jungle" hideaway, melted my heart. And, despite feeling rushed, anxious and worried about what I was doing most days, I was happy. I captured the picture in my mind.

They boarded the schoolbus and I waved goodbye and then hurried home to throw on a new work outfit, a scarf with an array of pinks, and some makeup. I was almost out the door when I realized I'd forgotten to brush my hair, so I backtracked. I braced myself as I checked my map app, but it was showing traffic was moving at a brisk pace. It would take me about an hour or so to reach downtown Toronto. Of course, en route, we had a slowdown on the Gardiner Expressway and I arrived with just a few minutes to spare. I was grateful when a close parking space opened up at the front of the nondescript conference centre. That bought me enough time to slip into the ladies' restroom to give my reflection a last-minute once-over before scurrying down the hall and into the meeting room identified for Heusten Shoes. Feeling plush carpeting underfoot, I noted the mahogany oval table with a dozen leather chairs around it took up most of the space in the room. Coffee, tea, baked goods and fruit were laid out on a similar, smaller table near the back of the room, opposite a whiteboard with a projected image of the company's logo. Several people milled about the refreshments. I dropped my bag into the chair furthest away from the projector and whiteboard and went to get a tea.

I watched the drops of milk swirl in my cup. The ribbon of white cut a river through the darkness. I blew steam off the surface and was reaching for a packet of sugar when I heard his voice. I froze. When he spoke again, my head snapped up and I scanned the people to my right. At the very corner of my vision, I saw him, standing alone next to the conference room window.

His brown hair was less voluminous, and wavy, no longer corkscrew curly. But I knew it was him. Stuart. My heart pounded, my breath falling into a little staccato beat as he continued speaking into the phone cradled at his left ear. His right hand stirred sugar into a coffee mug. Black. He hated cream. His voice. His laugh. I closed my eyes, eavesdropping, trying to remember the last time I'd seen him. April 2000, at the close of our second year of university. It hadn't been a good time.

When I opened my eyes, I saw my new colleagues, with heaps of fruit pieces and cheese on small Styrofoam plates, moving toward their seats. I crept toward mine. Stuart laughed into his phone, the lines beside his eyes crinkling in tandem. His beautiful smile. I watched him from the corner of my eye as he ended his call, gave one last stir to his coffee, and then tossed the stick into the garbage.

He strode to the front of the room just as I placed my bag on the floor and slipped into my chair. My breath quickened. I couldn't face him, but I was trapped. If I stood up and tried to leave the room, he'd see me. And if I stayed put, he'd eventually notice me. I rubbed my palms on my pants, trying to reassure myself that I wouldn't need to speak to him. Just catching a glimpse of him made my head feel fuzzy, as though I had just awoken from a nap stolen after staying up far too late and then rising early in the morning. As my wrists brushed against my thigh, the bracelet my husband, Rob, had given me at Christmas jingled softly.

After I lost my job at the end of last November, Rob and I made the painful decision to cut back on our Christmas spending, eliminating all non-essential gift-giving. At first, I envisioned my boys in tears and full of complaints as we lived out a Dickensian Christmas scene. But they didn't notice anything different this year, and I chalked that up to my wrap-happy attitude, where everything, including socks and underwear, got separate packaging in an effort to extend the gift opening as long as possible.

On Christmas morning, Aidan, my oldest, and Jacob were rapturous, declaring, "This is exactly what I wanted!" each time they opened a gift. They deposited each item on their piles before searching for something else. The cutbacks meant Rob and I didn't buy for each other, vowing instead to get a sitter and go out for dinner in January. However, as the boys pulled the final gifts out from under the tree, Jake found a small box. Aidan rushed to his side to read the tag.

"It's for you Mommy," he said, handing it to me.

The tag simply read, "You are the backbone and heart of this family and my life, xo R."

I looked over at Rob, who was sitting in his favourite chair, next to the fireplace. We almost didn't buy that chair. When we moved into our Magnolia Street home, we purged the ragtag bunch of couches, dressers and chairs we had accumulated over the years and purchased grown-up furniture. Rob had lobbied for the dark brown leather chair, and we entered into a pretty heated stalemate. Rob envisioned himself napping in it, while I thought it would look too big and bulky in the living room, especially at Christmas when the room housed a tree.

"Open it! Open it!" the boys chanted.

I ripped open the wrapping and discovered a robin's-egg blue box. The colour was so distinct. I knew what was inside.

"I thought we said..." I said, as Rob interrupted me.

"I had already bought it and didn't want to return it. Besides, you deserve it."

It was the Tiffany bracelet I coveted. A shiny silver piece of art, with intricate links and a heart tag, which I discovered while shopping in Toronto a couple of months earlier. The boys began hopping up and down.

"We went with Daddy to pick it out," Jacob said, as he and Aidan began to talk over each other.

"In the big city with the big tower," Aidan said.

"And then we ate crêpes," Jacob said.

"I love it," I said, hugging both boys.

Rob came over from his chair and I kissed him. "Thanks."

He opened the clasp and the beautiful piece fell into place on my wrist.

"You're welcome," he said, nuzzling my ear as I inhaled his musk shower gel scent, a mix of strength and security.

Now, as my thoughts returned to the conference room, I forced myself to stop squirming and to still my hands. Stuart shrugged out of his jacket and placed it on a chair off to the side of the table. The action was as familiar to me as pulling on my socks. He must still run. He had that lean runner's body. His crisp, white shirt was tucked into his pants and his belt buckle wasn't bulging like so many other men his age. Rob was also trim, an avid cyclist during the summer. Our two sons and I pitched little chairs at the side of the road to cheer him on when he raced. At the last fifty-kilometre competition, Rob teared up when he crossed the finish line, and it was more than adrenaline that had caused his flood of emotion. Aidan had made a little sign that shouted GO DADDY! and featured a picture of a man the size of a mushroom riding a bike that was bigger than a house.

But comparing these two men was dangerous.

When Stuart finished organizing the papers in front of him, he looked up at everyone seated around the table—a dozen of us in total, all managers or assistant managers hired to help an American shoe store expand into Canada. Stuart didn't see—or recognize—me at first glance, but as he welcomed everyone to the day-long meeting and thanked us for coming, his face did a second tour of the table, spending more time on everyone as he went around. When he reached me, our eyes locked. His eyebrows shot up, his eyes widened and he twitched his head.

And then he smiled.

"Caitie," he said.

I felt a tug in my stomach from long ago. Now, hearing him say my name, it felt as though all the air had been sucked out of the room. I wanted to be witty, to say something cute, but was so unnerved at seeing him I barely coughed out the word *hello*, feeling my cheeks burn with both delight at hearing his voice and embarrassment at being the centre of the group's attention.

"Let's take a minute and go around the table and introduce ourselves," he said, not taking his eyes off me.

So much came back to me in that instant, the intensity of his gaze, the way he looked at me when our faces were close, his cologne—Eternity for Men, a scent I adored—and how he'd held me, one hand firm on my back, the other behind my neck. I also, for a second, remembered that final, heartbreaking month.

My colleagues started introducing themselves. Many had worked in the retail sector for a long time. One man had celebrated his thirty-year anniversary the month before. Most managers sounded excited to be with Heusten Shoes, viewing their current positions as potential springboards for greater opportunities.

"I'm Caitlin, or Caitie," I said, glancing at Stuart when it was my turn. "Until recently, I worked as a graphic designer, but I got downsized and started looking for a new career."

"Welcome, Caitie," Stuart said, his blue eyes staring at me. "I'm thrilled to have you working with us, and I look forward to getting to know you better."

Oh dear.

The morning dragged on. We watched videos on the (short) history of Heusten Shoes, the company's five-year plan, which sounded a tad overambitious, and some infomercials detailing the latest shoe trends. At the coffee break, Tom, a manager from Sault Ste. Marie, cornered Stuart to ask him managerial what-if scenario questions. Tom was *that* guy, the one in every class who asked too many questions and assumed we were interested in hearing his every opinion. No matter how inane the question was, Stuart remained calm, his patience infinite. I wanted to throttle Tom by the one-hour mark, but every time he asked a question, Stuart said, "That's a great question, Tom," or "How interesting," and Tom would sit up a bit taller and look around the room as though he was a king surveying his fiefdom.

Stuart was energizing, just as I remembered him, and the entire room hung on his every word. At the start of the lunch break, I was in a stall in the ladies' room when I overheard two women discussing him, their voices muffled occasionally by running water or the hand dryer.

"He's gorgeous," said one of the women whose store was in downtown Toronto. "And he seems to really care about what you're saying when you ask him a question. I don't see a ring on his finger, so I might try to meet up with him sometime for lunch, you know?"

"He seems to know that lady," said her friend, though I couldn't remember her name. Her voice belonged to the woman sitting to Stuart's left, who wore a yellow jacket with a black camisole underneath, making her resemble a giant bumblebee. She spoke once in a while but tapped her pen on her coffee cup non-stop. "You know the blonde one who's sitting at the back with David from Etobicoke? He knew her name when he first saw her. But I think she said she was from Niagara, not Toronto. They must know each other from somewhere else."

I waited until they exited the bathroom to leave my stall, wash my hands, pat down my hair, and take a few breaths. I certainly did know Stuart from another time. During the morning session, I'd had trouble concentrating when he spoke. My mind had wandered. I had run the highlight reel of Caitie and Stuart in my head, all the events bookended between meeting and that final phone call.

A few times, while other managers spoke, I caught him watching me. I knew his walking behind my chair as he circled the room wasn't by accident. I felt his magnetism every time he stopped near me, even if he was two feet away. And I couldn't stop staring at him. He caught me a couple of times but just smiled. I looked away, flustered and embarrassed, worrying he knew what I'd been thinking. I twirled my engagement ring and wedding band. Unless he was an idiot, which I knew he was not, he could see I was married. But those women were right—I didn't see a ring on him.

I couldn't explain why, but I found wedding bands sexy. Every time I saw Rob across a room from me, I stole a moment to look at his ring. To me, it said "I'm yours" and to everyone else "I'm taken." No symbol was as universally understood as the wedding band. Stuart wasn't wearing one. And he didn't have a white line where his ring should have been, in case he'd just returned from a Caribbean vacation and misplaced it.

I exited the bathroom and, standing directly across the hall, was Stuart.

"Let's go have lunch," he said, beaming. "I can't believe you're here. I mean, they emailed me the group list this morning and saw your name but I thought, 'No, there's got to be another C. Morissette.'"

"Won't the others think you're favouring me? I'm not good at corporate politics, but aren't we all supposed to be treated equally? If you're the boss and you're eating lunch with me, what will that say to the others?"

I wasn't concerned about how eating lunch with a superior could be interpreted. I was trying to come up with other reasons to not have lunch with Stuart. Our history gave me pause. On some level, I still hoped he desired me. Over the years, I'd thought of Stuart, especially when a Backstreet Boys or Spice Girls song came on the radio, transporting me back to the late nineties. I'd wonder what he was doing, who he loved. I Googled him once. I saw he was friends with a friend of a friend on Facebook, but I couldn't bring myself to poke him (gah!) or send him a friend request. It wasn't as though I'd pined for him the past dozen years or so. Until today, I'd thought my feelings for him had been resolved.

"I don't give a crap what the others think. You *are* my favourite, and they *should* construe something from me having lunch with you," he said, touching my arm to direct me out the front door of the hotel. I felt his warmth after he removed his fingers. "But if you're worried about being watched, we can head to a place just down the road. I gave everyone an hour and a half. We'll have loads of time to catch up."

We got into his Lexus, which was immaculate and devoid of car seats, stuffies, Ninja Turtles, candy wrappers and juice spills. I thought about the first time I'd gotten in a car with him. It was the night of our first date, when he showed up at a party I'd gone to with someone else.

"Caitie, you're stunning. You've hardly aged," he said as

we closed the doors and clicked our seat belts into place. "God, it's been, what, fifteen years, hasn't it?"

"Sixteen. The last time I saw you was at the apartment before you left," I snapped, my cheeks aflame. I glanced over at him and saw him pause for a second. I looked away, out my window, and began speaking to my reflection. "Um, sorry. Honestly, I've dealt with what happened. I've just wished you the best. I don't want to drag up our not-so-great history. I don't want us to get off on the wrong foot, so I'll understand if you'd rather eat alone."

"Are you kidding?" he said, as I turned back to look at him. His eyebrows knitted. He looked as though he wanted to say something else but then turned away from me and looked ahead. As he reversed the car, his arm reached around my headrest. That was a change. When he used to drive us around, his hands were glued to the steering wheel. Stuart swung the car into the street.

"I know things ended badly. And it's entirely my fault they did," he said in almost a whisper. "I didn't handle anything well. Look, I don't want to rehash everything. I'd really just like to catch up with you."

We drove to a Mexican place—my favourite, which Stuart remembered. We ordered drinks—for me, water, for him, iced tea—and our talk became comfortable. We checked off the things people ask about when they're becoming reacquainted. He'd been married to a woman named Erin. They'd met in line at a Starbucks while he completed his master's degree at the University of Toronto. Their daughter, Paisley, lived with Erin. Stuart had visitation Tuesday nights and every second weekend. I imagined a blue-eyed, curly-haired little girl with perfect, tiny white teeth. A pang went through me. I loved my boys but would never have a daughter.

"It took a while, but we get along very well now, Erin and I. I went to her second wedding about three months ago."

"What was that like?"

"Most people think it's weird, but it's fine. And you? Looks like you're married."

"I am. His name's Rob and we met in university after you and I, um…" I grabbed my glass of water to take a drink. "We have two sons—Aidan, who just turned six, and Jacob, who's four."

There was a pause and then Stuart said, "You told the group you worked as a graphic designer? I knew you'd be successful. You worked hard in university and were so focused."

After I detailed my resumé for him, he asked why Heusten Shoes.

"Well, there's not a lot out there, for starters," I said. "But then, I was interested in doing something completely different. I'd never thought about retail, but I'm learning a lot and I enjoy the people. It's nice to work with a company that's expanding. With all the computer programs out there, people think they can design on their own. They even admit what they do isn't half as good as what I could do, but at least it's cheaper."

Stuart laughed. Then he became serious.

"When we…" he started.

I didn't take my eyes off him. My heart pounded in my chest. I waited to hear what he was going to say.

"When we were together, did you ever think we would have kids?"

"That's a cruel thing to say, Stuart," I said, exhaling. Were we going to talk about it so soon?

At the look on my face, he retreated. "I'm sorry, Cait. I shouldn't have asked you that. I don't know what I was thinking. Seeing you has gotten to me. It's like the late nineties all over again."

He paused and looked at me. His eyes narrowed and the corners of his mouth turned ever so slightly upwards. I toyed with a fork, every once in a while bringing my gaze back to his face instead of staring at him, which was what I wanted to do. My head felt heavy. Memories and thoughts swirled around like a swarm of bees. When he spoke again, I looked up.

"I have to say this because, for all I know, you'll go home and quit and sue me for sexual harassment. So, before I lose my chance, here goes. I feel terrible about what I did all those years ago, and every once in a while, especially when I see a Cate Blanchett movie, I think of you." He held my gaze, and I felt that pull in my stomach. "For years, I wanted to find you just to tell you how sorry I was for being such an asshole. I'm really, truly sorry. Maybe that's how you ended up in my training session today, for the sole purpose of me being able to apologize to you. And if that's the reason, then I'm grateful."

I realized I'd been holding my breath. Why Stuart left the way he did remained a mystery to me. I agonized over why things had gone so spectacularly wrong. I assumed I was the reason they had. And that I was—at least somewhat—to blame. And though I still didn't know why, at least I had an apology. Redemption. But seeing Stuart, hearing him speak, being close to him again, made me remember the way he'd push my hair out of my face, how soft yet strong his fingers felt as we held hands while strolling down the sidewalk in the summer, how we danced at our proms, how we made love. I was hit by too many uncomfortable feelings. I wanted to be alone to process this.

"I appreciate it, Stuart," I said. I looked away, unsure what else to say. And I wasn't a person often stumped for words. "Maybe we should start heading back now."

He looked at me one last time and signalled for the cheque. He brushed off my offer to pay my half, and I accepted. The mood shifted between us, but not in a bad way. Images of us together for those three years kept resurfacing. In this moment, I could sense something was off with him, just as I always could. He never needed to speak; his mood was something I could always sense, as though he emitted wind currents only my weather system could interpret.

We drove to the parking lot at the conference centre in silence. I wanted to ask him so many questions but felt raw, as though I had ripped off a bandage I'd been wearing for a long time. He parked the car.

"Caitlin," he said, putting his hand over mine, which I had placed at the side of my seat. "I'm truly happy to see you. I'm glad you're doing well and that you're happy. I hope I haven't caused any weirdness between us. Part of my job is to observe the stores, and you're in my area. I'm already looking forward to seeing you again. I mean, in a business sense."

And with that, Stuart opened his car door and climbed back into his corporate costume, the one he wore for the next four hours. I decided to stay to the end of training, even though I knew he wouldn't rat me out to my boss if I left early. I wanted to connect with the Hamilton store manager because their store was the next closest to mine. But also, a part of me was enjoying the memories that kept returning. I thanked Stuart again for lunch and walked toward the front doors, where Tom accosted him. With a smile, I dashed inside, heading once again to the ladies' room.

    I splashed water on my face and looked in the mirror, trying to corral my thoughts and feelings back into their proper pens. I felt hot. My body ached a bit. I took a few deep breaths. And then I balled my fists; I became angry. Not because of the unknown reasons that had ultimately ended our relationship and not because of the heartache I endured when he left, but because he had stirred up something I had tried to keep hidden for more than a decade.

    Up until I married Rob, I had believed Stuart and I would parent together.

two

MARCH 2016

I WAS in my fourth month of job searching when I stumbled upon the listing for Heusten Shoes. I hadn't had to look for a job in more than a decade and was struggling with the overwhelming fear I would never find another place to work. After university, I began working in graphic design, hopping from job to job until finally landing a position as a senior graphic designer at an award-winning design and advertising studio called Legandcy in 2006, which is when we moved to St. Catharines.

Located in what had once been a Tudor-style home right in the heart of downtown, the boutique was run by Meredeth Lejeune and Cyril Brown, a couple who were not only business partners but life companions as well. The Leg (as we termed it) had grown steadily in the first few years after I was hired, and then it exploded and we hired five junior designers. Most of the new business was from

Toronto-based companies. Not only were The Leg's rates much lower than slick city firms, but in this digital age, the hour-long drive (if traffic was good) between St. Catharines and the provincial capital was reduced to a two-second click of the mouse.

But I noticed things had been changing over the past year or so—even if I didn't want to admit it. All of a sudden, clients seemed to be swayed by the burgeoning offering of affordable, do-it-yourself website templates and phone apps. Why sit around in design meetings with me (even if they were virtual), which costs money, when a client could just plug information into boxes, select stock images and launch a website? It didn't matter if, at The Leg, we could create something unique, a brochure or webpage that broadcast a company's values or a marketing package that was guaranteed to be memorable. "I just need to have my name out there," I had heard from several clients. It all came down to the bottom line. Thus, I found myself without work. As a 37-year-old mother of two young boys, the idea of not having a paycheque, something I had received like clockwork for what felt like forever, was worrisome. But it was the loss of my career, something I tied to my identity, that I was really grieving.

In the weeks following being let go from The Leg, I spiralled through denial to worry to acceptance and optimism, only to find myself back at the start. One of my favourite pastimes became revisiting the glory years of my early twenties, a time when I thought the world was my oyster and I was guaranteed to have a successful career for the lone reason that I wanted one. My original goal, though, was not to be a graphic designer but a novelist.

After high school graduation, I headed to the University of Ottawa, where, I figured, I could learn to become both more independent and a brilliant English Literature major. Ottawa was a six-hour drive from London. I figured it was far enough away to create some independence from my family but not too far away that I couldn't go home for a weekend if I was homesick. In my first class—CanLit, a core class full of Margaret Atwood and Mordecai Richler wannabes—I met my best friend, Siobhan. It was 1998 and I was nineteen. I'd scoped out the building the week before class began so I wouldn't have trouble finding the room. I didn't need added stresses that first morning so I woke up early, afraid of being late, terrified of being labelled a slacker. A half-dozen or so people milled around outside the classroom when I arrived. Once the doors opened, people clamoured for a seat near the front. I stayed in the middle. I didn't want to seem too keen, yet didn't want to appear to be dawdling at the back of the auditorium either. There was a stage at the front of the wood-panelled room and, when I sat down on a padded chair, I felt like I was sitting on bare wood. As classmates filed in, I realized I didn't know a soul.

A red-headed girl rushed in a couple of minutes before the class was set to begin and plopped down beside me, flustered.

"Christ, this is a big room," she said, an Irish lilt to her speech. She looked around. "I'm Siobhan. I came here from Victoria—well, you can hear that I'm originally from Ireland, but we moved to Victoria when I was eight—to get as far away from my family as bloody possible. You?"

"I'm Caitie," I said, smiling. "I'm from London. Not London, England, but London, Ontario."

We exchanged small talk for a few minutes. I was

relieved to discover she lived in my dormitory and I now, at last, knew someone in my program. Everyone on my dorm floor seemed to be in medical sciences or an engineering student.

The professor arrived on stage to a round of applause. The auditorium was almost full.

"Good morning," he said, in a gruff voice. He wore jeans and a sweater. A pair of glasses rested atop his dark, messy hair. I pegged him at fifty. "Welcome to the University of Ottawa. You are here to receive one of the finest educational experiences in English Literature in Canada." People interrupted his introduction with further applause, though it seemed to only humour him. "Congratulations on being accepted. Your high school marks were impressive. To be sitting in this room now, you needed at least an eighty-four per cent average. You're all overachievers. But now I want you to take a look to the left and then look right. Two of you won't be back next year."

Siobhan laughed, while I followed his instructions. As I glanced around, some people smirked, likely thinking there was no possible way they wouldn't return next year. Others had wide eyes, knitted eyebrows or hunched shoulders. I added up all the hours I'd studied for my final high school exams and how much money my family and I had spent so far on my education, not to mention how my boyfriend, Stuart, had followed me to Ottawa so I could chase my dreams. I worried I might not be good enough.

"Relax," Siobhan said, as I turned back to her. "We've got this."

Now, more than a dozen years later, on mornings when the job search felt most bleak, I thought about my early novel-writing dreams. I still loved to read and usually hit my

Goodreads goal for the year by October. Writing a novel was on my bucket list, along with travelling around Europe. But as a carefree twenty-something, I had done neither. I could hardly expect Rob to support my novel-writing whim now, when we had things like property taxes, credit cards and a mortgage to pay—not to mention two boys to take care of. If I found steady work, I could carve out spare time to write my novel. I thought about digging out the couple of manuscripts I'd started in university and I had tried to finish before the boys were born to see if I could get any traction with them. The plots and writing quality might be weak, but that would give me focus and a goal to work toward.

Despite feeling overwhelmed most mornings, and after procrastinating by cleaning every speck of my kitchen after the boys left for school, I forced myself to continue sending out resumés. I applied to every design job I unearthed and sent out oodles of freelance queries. Slim pickings. Some industry friends gave me leads to follow, and I pursued them the way a dog does when it smells a scrap of food while on a walk—with relentlessness followed by dejection. I got a couple of offers, designing a logo for a sports team, a menu for a local restaurant, and a business plan for a woman who wanted to open a bakery, but I knew I would need more if I wanted to launch my own business.

After a couple of weeks of rejections, I branched out, looking for jobs that might offer a similar pay to my former salary. When I'd started job searching, I assumed everyone my age who was looking for work had been let go from careers. But it struck me that perhaps most of my fellow job seekers were not in the same boat as I, the *S.S. Laidoff*. Instead, they were trying to navigate a ship into the slipstream, to find something that excited them. I came across hundreds of postings, but what I wanted in my heart was the listing that read: "Indispensable, will never let you go because you're too valuable." Everyone was expendable. All positions could be replaced.

One Tuesday, as I read through another bunch of form emails thanking me for applying for yet another office administrator position—the prospect of each on par with mortician—the phone rang. I grabbed it, hoping it was Siobhan calling to commiserate with me. But a British, not an Irish, voice sounded through the line.

"Hello, this is Melody Samuels calling from Heusten Shoes. May I speak with Caitlin Morissette?"

"Hello, this is her," I said, as my palms began sweating. I rubbed them on my thighs and searched for a pen on my desktop, which was strewn with printed-out emails. Over the weeks, I had developed a job search system. And it included printing out every form letter I received so I could follow up with them in a week or two.

"I'm calling because we're opening a new store at the Outlet Collection at Niagara, and we liked your resumé. Would you like to come in for an interview?"

The swanky outlet mall was just ten minutes from my house. I did a fist pump and willed my voice to remain calm.

"That would be great, Melody. Thank you." I jotted down the details. "I look forward to meeting you."

I hung up, jumped off my chair, and punched the air. An interview! Finally! Then I stopped and sank back into my chair, stunned as I realized I had attached so much of my sense of self-worth to my job search process. A year ago, I would have scoffed at the prospect of managing a shoe store. And, when it came to shoes, I was a minimalist. I had five pairs of shoes: one appropriate, black pair for work that went with everything; one pair of high heels, also black, in case Rob and I went somewhere fancy; the obligatory rain and snow boots; and one pair of running shoes because I had high hopes of getting back in shape. Would I need to become a shoe expert before my interview? I texted Siobhan.

After university, Siobhan had landed a job at a small community magazine as a writer, and then worked her way up to editor at *Capital LIFE*, a lifestyle and human interest magazine. She left the magazine after a huge blowup with the publisher, whom she had been dating, and got hired as editor of a glossy magazine called *High Life* that had nothing to do with cannabis and everything to do with condo living in Toronto. She had always been a solid friend to me, an accepting, safe space when I was figuring things out, and a voice of reason when I was fed up with Rob for walking past the basket at the bottom of the stairs and leaving me to bring it up—again.

She came across as tough and brash but I knew how tender she could be. She took the boys for overnight visits to her condo in Toronto to give Rob and I some alone time, always returning them the following day with the exclamation that I had (once again) saved her from any thoughts of having children of her own. And she was currently in the longest relationship of her life to Mike, a guitarist who travelled across North America half the year with his band. His absence, she exclaimed, was the only reason why they were still together because she needed her "space." "God, Caitie," she would say to me, "the man is so emotional!" Because he liked to buy her flowers. But I knew she kept petals from the bouquets in a box in her closet. She also anointed me *Caitie-cat*, a special pet name used only by her.

IN REPAIR

> Got a job interview Thursday

SIOBHAN
> Thank Christ! Good news. What is it?

> Heusten Shoes

> WTF? You're going to work in retail? You hate people

> I don't hate them that much. I just hate stupid people. What do I wear?

> Wear your heels and a skirt. Oh, and don't wear one of your black shirts. Wear colour!!!

> Got it! Thanks

> Oh, brush up on some interview questions. This isn't 2005

> What do you mean?

> Google job interview questions. Don't lose it. XO

Oh, holy God.

Siobhan wasn't kidding. The lexicon of job interviewing was a foreign language I needed to learn. I scrolled through articles about how to give perfect interview answers. If everyone who's hiring knew people were just rehearsing what to say, then what was the point? Couldn't employers tell they weren't getting genuine answers? I decided to attack the interview questions one by one and come up with answers I could memorize or at least deliver in a confident manner.

Why do you want to work for this company? Real answer: I

don't. I want my old job back, but I'll take this in the meantime. Expected answer: Heusten Shoes represents a wonderful challenge in an exciting field, one that's expected to grow rapidly in the next five to ten years.

Do you enjoy working in a group? Real answer: Not on your life. Expected answer: Yes! I believe each individual brings a unique set of experiences to the table, thereby complementing one another and ensuring the successful completion of whatever task we're working on.

How do you react to instruction and criticism? Real answer: I hate it and would tell you to go fly a kite. Expected answer: We can learn a lot from being criticized, which is, truly, someone's way of showing us how to grow and be the best contributor possible.

Where do you see yourself in five years? Real answer: Not here. Expected answer: I believe Heusten Shoes is a great opportunity and I can see myself helping to open another store and perhaps managing that.

The morning of the interview, my stomach flip-flopped as I attempted to put on mascara. The boys brushed their teeth, alternating between spitting in the sink and asking questions.

"Mommy, if you work at the shoe place, do we get free shoes?"

"Will this mean you won't be at the cool house?"

"Do you make the shoes or just sell them?"

I couldn't figure out why they were so excited. Though thrilled to have a job interview after months of nothing but rejections, I wasn't looking forward to the prospect of stacking shoes for a living.

"Maybe the boys are excited because I've been so down-in-the-mouth since leaving The Leg," I said to Rob as he washed his face after the boys ran out of the bathroom. I heard their voices, loud and animated, in the kitchen, while I took the straight iron to my blonde shoulder-length hair and applied pink lip gloss.

"They're excited because you've gotten dressed up and they think you're secretly going to take them to McDonald's," Rob said, chuckling, as he patted his face with a towel before bending down to plant a kiss on my forehead. He touched my shoulder and then looked into my eyes. "I'm proud of you."

As I drove down the QEW toward the outlet mall, I sang along to the radio. This job, if I got it, would be a temporary detour from my real future, but at least I would be contributing to our household economy and not just drawing from my severance pile. Plus, this would get me out of the house and meeting new people. Siobhan told me I was taking on the pallor of a disgruntled housewife. The work might even inspire me to do that thing—that unknown—that would make my heart sing. Maybe this might even be that thing.

I parked my car, dropped my keys into my purse and went off in search of Heusten Shoes. I didn't usually spend much time at this mall because its stores were out of my league—COACH, Kate Spade, ESCADA and Burberry just sounded posh. I preferred to shop in the smaller, indoor centre that offered more common stores and was closer to my house. To be honest, I wasn't a big shopper at all. I romanticized the idea of browsing in boutiques, picking up a new shirt or pair of earrings, but when it came down to it, I was a functional, get-what-you-need-and-get-out shopper.

The window outside Heusten Shoes boasted large

turquoise OPENING SOON announcements to rally interest among mall browsers. On my way through the mall, I felt a tremor of excitement that I might become part of this opulent atmosphere. Siobhan had insisted I research Heusten Shoes before my interview, and so I knew the company's headquarters were in Dallas and that, in the past year, they had opened a few stores in Canada, paving the way for an ambitious expansion plan expected to take place this year.

I hoped Heusten Shoes would do better than other companies that were hightailing it out of the Canadian retail landscape, especially after I counted three other shoe stores while hurrying through the corridors. Then I chided myself. Why did I care about the future of Heusten Shoes? I told myself that I shouldn't worry whether they'd be in business in five years. I didn't plan on being there that long. This was temporary. I repeated this phrase to myself as I reached for the steel door handle.

Inside, I halted. Cables snaked from the ceiling tiles to what would be the checkout area. Shelving units were scattered around the room, and it resembled the boys' untidy playroom. There were stacks upon stacks of unopened boxes.

"Hello?" I called. I jumped at the sound of my voice, which echoed.

A second later, a well-dressed man emerged from the backroom. He wore a dark blue suit and a blue, pinstriped shirt with a red tie. He was a bit shorter than me. He wore glasses atop his head and his heels clicked when he walked toward me. He had a distinct receding hairline and looked like he was trying too hard. He smiled, though it seemed to pain him, and held out his hand.

"I'm Trevor Murdock," he said. "I'm the store manager. You must be Caitlin."

"Right. Well, Cait, actually," I replied, shaking his hand. "The only person who calls me Caitlin is my mother, and it's usually followed by a sigh."

He didn't laugh but allowed for a small smirk. "Well, I'm called Mr. Murdock, and I prefer to call my employees by their legal names, not their nicknames or short forms. You can come here to the back. It's the only place we have an actual table set up. The workers will be here shortly, so hopefully we can go over everything before they arrive because they're very loud," he said.

As Trevor spoke, I felt beads of sweat pool under my arms and in the small of my back. I followed him to the backroom and took a couple of deep breaths, running Siobhan's mantra through my mind: *You're a champion. You're overqualified for this job. They would be lucky to have you.*

The backroom was smaller than the retail space. But it was just as messy, with boxes piled together in rows of three and shelving leaned against the wall, waiting to be brought out to the front and installed. There was a card table like the one Rob had stored in his university apartment for his weekly poker games, and the chairs were the folding metal type. I hoped I wouldn't tip over as I sat down. The refrigerator made some interesting gurgling sounds every few minutes.

"The fridge is new," Trevor said, by way of explanation, "but I think the workers damaged it last week when a ladder fell on it. Let's get to it. I'm looking for someone to be my right-hand man, or woman." He sat down in a folding chair opposite me. I placed my bag on the floor but wasn't sure if I should take off my coat, so I kept it on and dropped my gloves on top of my bag. Trevor picked up a mug on the table and sipped from it, glancing at a clipboard and tapping a pen against it. He stilled the pen and then spoke.

"I've been with the company for two years, training in Dallas. I'm originally from this area, and I contacted them when I learned of their expansion plans. I wanted to be involved with a company that was going places. I have a retail background and have been a manager for about fifteen years now. I'd like to get someone in here next month to help with the store set-up, learn the system and be ready to go when we open on April 1. No fooling." When he saw my expressionless face, he said, "That's a joke."

"Ha, of course," I said, feebly.

"I saw on your resumé that you worked at Legandcy? Why were you let go?" he asked.

"Apparently, work had been slowing down and so it was either myself or the owner's niece who had to go. It's a 'family business,'" I said, using air quotes.

"That's too bad. Well, I don't play favourites here. If you're hogwash, you go. If you're good, you stay," he said, putting his glasses on. "I have a stack of two hundred resumés for the assistant manager's position. I can only imagine how many resumés I'm going to get for the sales associate positions, but I'm not going to post those for another two weeks. Why don't you tell me a bit about yourself?"

As I gave a summary of my resumé, I started to relax. I understood what he was doing and could read him like a book. He was impatient, tapping his foot on the linoleum floor, but trying to look interested in what I was saying. He reminded me of Jacob, who paced in front of the television as he waited for *Paw Patrol* to come on. We went through some of the questions I was familiar with from my Googling and got some surprises like, "How long would it take you to make a meaningful contribution to our company?"

After about thirty minutes of questioning, Trevor put down his clipboard and pen, which also settled his foot. He looked at me as though trying to discern the one thing that bothered him. I'd once gotten the same look while going through the checkout at the grocery store. The clerk was sure I reminded her of someone. I told her, "I'm very famous. You've likely heard of me." Then, donning my sunglasses, I grabbed my bags and left the store in what I tried to pull off as a mysterious air. But Trevor's inquietude was because he couldn't decide whether to hire me—whether I might be too much trouble due to my inexperience.

"You can start two weeks from next Monday," he said, after what felt like ten minutes. "You'll get two weeks' vacation and you have every other weekend off. Your shifts will rotate from opening to closing, so I hope that's not a problem. Depending on how well the store does, we might be able to hire another manager, which means we could all have a semi-regular schedule. Your pay is set, but you're entitled to an annual bonus, and pay increases every six months for the first two years. After that, it's on merit. You can think about it for a day if you need to, but I'm offering you the job now."

I didn't hesitate. "I'll take it."

"Caitie, I didn't know you liked people," Rob joked when I called him to say I'd taken the job at Heusten Shoes. I told him retail was unlike anything I'd ever done, which was a pep talk for me as much as for him. *Not everyone could do this job*, I told myself. Plus, it bought me time to figure out what I wanted to do with my life. I could always write on the side.

Rob was executive director of an advertising agency called Cre8tive. He had started working there as a junior account manager when we moved to St. Catharines and advanced through the company every couple of years. He was steady. He worked hard, paid close attention to detail and had—in my opinion, his best quality—genuine curiosity of and care for his clients. He never forgot a birthday and never failed to send a gift to welcome a large client's new baby or celebrate a retirement. I was never surprised when he was promoted.

When I had lost my job at The Leg, Rob suggested he could see if they could afford to hire another junior designer so I could have something, at least on a temporary or contractual basis, in my field. The look I must have given him, which communicated I would rather have eaten glass than have my husband as my boss, induced a silence in him so profound the idea had yet to be resurrected.

A few days before the store opened, Trevor called a staff meeting. On the way there, my mind drifted back to my first day of university. I'd felt the same way then as I did now, hopeful for the future and believing I was part of something big, but also scared I wouldn't live up to expectations. Just outside the store's door I paused, calming my nerves. The OPENING SOON signs remained in the windows, though a date two days away had been added. I opened the front door and took a moment to admire the showroom. It was beautiful. There was a sleek new cash area, the wall behind it had been painted a refreshing turquoise, the company's signature colour, and glass tables displayed the season's latest shoe styles. A dozen people mingled about, most of whom were under twenty-five. I introduced myself to some of my coworkers I hadn't yet met and started to get to know them by asking them about themselves, their families and, for those in school, their studies. Then, Trevor strode into the showroom and I stood to the side along with everyone else, giving him the stage.

Everyone was grinning, including me. I was thrilled to see something grow from just Trevor and me to a team. Even though I found him to be a control freak and uptight, I understood what corporate had seen in Trevor. He'd put together more than a roster of staffers. He'd assembled a squad that had already juggled dozens of tasks and nearly impossible deadlines to open the store on time. In that moment, we were united.

Trevor had been sketchy about my duties when he hired me, but after the store opened, my responsibilities became clear—do whatever he didn't want to do. This included but was not restricted to hiring, firing (yes, we fired two people that first week), scheduling, ordering stock, calling the heating or air conditioning people (depending on the day and how the sun was positioned in the sky), as well as helping customers, overseeing staff, and training. Because my hours varied from day to day, I was no longer there for the boys after school, and I hired a teen who lived on our street to tend to them until either Rob or I arrived home. Thank God the boys adored her as much as I appreciated her reliability.

Caleb, a twenty-year-old computer engineering student with a severe bowl cut and Buddy Holly glasses, was my favourite co-worker. He never complained about his shifts and had a happy-go-lucky demeanor and a wry sense of humour. On the rare days we grabbed lunch together in the backroom—corporate had replaced the card table and metal chairs with a wooden table and chairs straight out of the IKEA catalogue—I looked forward to hearing about his classes and his girlfriend. If asked, I suggested restaurants and attractions he could take her to and ways to surprise her. If he came to work with a big smile on his face, things were going well. But I never asked for details. Siobhan said if I did, he could sue me for sexual harassment.

Trevor informed me about a month after the store opened that I was to attend a managers' meeting in Toronto later that week. For the rest of my shift, he peppered me with "Caitlin, if they ask you this, what will you say?" or "Do you know our growth projections for the coming year?" and other mind-numbing questions every time I moved into his sight line. How hard could this be? I would show up, listen to the information and come home. But Trevor was so on edge that, after his twentieth question, I started to worry that my job would be on the line if I didn't make a good impression.

When I look back on the morning of that Toronto meeting, I wonder what would have happened if I hadn't gone. As I cleaned up that orange juice, I had thought about calling in sick, telling Trevor I just couldn't make it. I could have used the extra hours to clean up the house, to put away all the laundry that had accumulated. I could have got the groceries and surprised Rob with a nice risotto. I could have taken a pause and thought about whether I was enjoying working at Heusten Shoes, if it was a career path I wanted to continue on. I had no inkling that I was about to have a grenade lobbed into my already chaotic and messy life through the reappearance of Stuart. That questions I had wanted answers to for so long would be within my grasp. That I might open myself up to all kinds of hurt. That my life, the one I had built with Rob, would face a stress test. Despite all of this, I would have still gone.

three

SEPTEMBER 1996

THE FIRST THING I noticed about Stuart was his corkscrew locks.

I was on a city bus, travelling to my first tennis lesson. I was seventeen and dating Mark, a dean's honour-roll member whose best feature was his floppy brown hair and who was hell-bent on studying economics at university. I had no idea what economics was, aside from home economics, which was the lamest class offered at our downtown London high school, Catholic Central.

I had signed up for lessons with my best friend, Grace, who went to a different school, the non-denominational London Central, located a couple of blocks from mine. We enrolled because we had fallen in love with Andre Agassi. We never missed one of his matches, scouring teen magazines and taping posters of him, smiling and poufy-haired, on our bedroom walls. We figured that, if we got good enough at the game, we'd end up at a high-ranking tennis tournament. We'd bump into him and one of us would become his girlfriend. We kept that dream alive until he married Brooke Shields, and then he just seemed old. Of course, I had wished it would be me.

Grace was stunning. And, like her name suggested, she was poised. Tall, with long brown hair that she'd wear in a braided ponytail, Grace had blue eyes and a thin build. Boys stared at her. But she was no shrinking violet. Brassy and confident, she was also someone who never forgot a friend's birthday or failed to call when she thought you were upset.

On the day of my first lesson, I waited outside my school for the city bus that would take me to the London Tennis Centre. After my stop, the bus would wend its way past Grace's school and she'd hop on, but today I would be solo because Grace's family had extended their European summer vacation by a week. My brother, Matt, had ridden London's complex warren of bus routes for years, but my sole previous bus experience was the direct route to the mall and back. My palms sweated and I kept looking down the street to see if the bus was coming. If I ended up on the wrong bus, it could take anywhere from a half hour to an hour to get straightened out.

When the bus arrived, I exhaled, climbed aboard and found an empty seat near the back that faced another row of seats. I took a book from my backpack, flipped to a dog-eared page and read. When the bus pulled away from the stop outside Grace's school, I happened to glance up just in time to witness a tennis racquet, poking out of a backpack, nearly hit a frowning grey-haired man, when the bus lurched. The racquet's owner apologized to the man he had almost careened into, and caught me watching. He gave me a sheepish grin. I chuckled and then stared. This boy wasn't Andre Agassi, but he was beautiful—not cute and not Adonis-like handsome. His smooth skin had no traces of acne and his blue eyes deepened when he smiled.

The boy wore shorts and a polo shirt. It was the second week of September, but we were still enjoying warm weather. I'd been confident when I left school in my pink shorts and a white top—preppy, but not too over-the-top. Some of my friends, in an act of teenage rebellion, wore spaghetti-strap tank tops to school—to reveal their bra straps—but I was too afraid of what my mother would say, so I stuck to T-shirts with sleeves. My mom was a high school principal and she busted girls for dress code violations all day long. Matt told me to pick my battles, and I was smart enough to know that dress code wasn't one I was going to win.

The boy stopped at my seat and smiled. I wondered what he thought of my outfit.

"Can I sit here?" he asked.

My eyes skirted around the other seats to make sure he was speaking to me. At my school, nobody dared speak to anyone they didn't know, lest the person you tried to talk to was lower on the social scale than you.

"Go ahead," I said, flicking my hand toward the empty seat across from me.

"You're heading to the Tennis Centre?" he asked as he sat, dropping his bag to rest at his feet. He held the offending racquet.

"How'd you know?" I said.

He didn't laugh or make fun of me, which was what

most of the boys at my school would have done. He smiled, pointing to my racquet, which stood up on the seat next to me, its handle resting on the window.

"Of course," I said, shaking my head and rolling my eyes.

"I'm Stuart," he said. "I'm heading there, too. First time? I've never seen you before."

"You're right. I'm just starting lessons. I'm Cait, but spelled C-A-I-T. My mother wanted my common name to be unique in some way."

"I like it," he said, smiling.

We continued chatting during the bus ride and, after that day, Grace, Stuart and I sat together during our twice weekly trips to the tennis centre. I started to look forward to spending time with him, whether it was on the bus or on the court. A few weeks later, I broke up with Mark, whom I had been dating for a couple of months. He didn't seem too bothered—just shrugged and gave me a hug. He reserved crying for times like the day he got an 85 on his mid-term calculus mark.

My thoughts about Stuart went from occasional to constant. I asked Grace about him. She told me he wasn't dating anyone but she heard lots of girls at her school talk about him. That didn't surprise me. But I wondered how many of those crushes were based on more than his looks. Stuart was more than congenial—he got along with everyone at tennis—he had class. Whenever we spoke, his eyes remained on my face and didn't travel down my neck and onto my chest. Sometimes, I was caught off guard when he'd ask how a test of mine went, amazed he had listened and remembered.

Though he seemed distant some days, as though he had

a lot on his mind, he was never snarky or sarcastic, like so many guys. Mark acted like the biggest baby sometimes. He once crossed his arms and refused to budge outside the movie theatre until I agreed to see *Independence Day*. I had been dying to see *Jack* because I was a huge Robin Williams fan. Stuart addressed our coach as "Sir," and I respected that. Sometimes, while in line waiting to hit forehands, I'd let my mind wander, thinking about how it would feel to have his arms around me or to run my hands through his hair. A couple of times, Stuart caught me watching him. Rather than make fun of me or give me the stink eye, he'd just smile. I snapped my head away so he wouldn't see me blush.

As the weeks passed, my crush on Stuart deepened. I couldn't wait for my lessons. I got to know him better. He was eighteen, in Grade 13 or what we called OACs, one grade ahead of Grace and me, though I would turn eighteen in January. He lived near the University of Western Ontario with his mother and his sister, Nicole, who studied kinesiology at Western. He had another sister, Emma, who had already graduated from Western and was living somewhere in Alberta. His parents had divorced when he was eight, and his father lived in the United States with his new family, which included six-year-old fraternal twins. Stuart loved his little brother and sister and wasn't jealous of his dad's new family.

"Caitie, my parents were miserable when they lived together. At least now, I have the chance of having at least one parent who's a relatively nice person." I assumed he meant his mother.

Aside from Grace, Stuart and me, there were four other players in our class—all boys under the age of fifteen. Our coach was a former pro whose claim to fame was playing in qualifiers at the US Open.

At the beginning of October, a guy from my math class called my name while I was waiting at the bus stop.

"Hey, Cait, wait up," he said, striding across the lawn.

Terry was a class clown with a mop of unruly hair and big brown eyes. He'd garnered a reputation as a player—a serial dater—though I found myself, along with most girls in our grade, attracted to him every so often. I knew it was best just to avoid him, though, especially after he dumped Mary Cordoso at the spring dance and was seen making out with Angela Martin the next day.

"Hey," he said, as he reached me. "I wanted to talk to you."

"About what?" I glanced down the street to see if the bus was coming.

"Going to the formal with me."

"What? You want to go with me? What about Angela?"

"Old news," he said with a quirky smile. "I think we'd have a lot of fun, and Phillip's having a party after. So?"

Though I had promised myself I would never date Terry, I knew he would be a lot of fun at the dance. Plus, Mark had already started dating someone else and the relief of not having to go solo was too overwhelming for me to decline.

"Okay, sounds good. You'll pick me up?"

We exchanged numbers—on paper—and made tentative plans. He jogged back to the school but turned and waved when my bus pulled up. I continued to smile even after the bus pulled away, and I shook my head. I felt confident most days, and my prior dating experience had included a few boyfriends, but I was not at the top of the popularity list at my school. Football players held top rank and most of them, in a perfect cliché, dated cheerleaders. I wouldn't be caught dead cheerleading. Terry was in the second tier, and I supposed I was, too. In the past year, I'd come out of my shell and become more involved in school activities. It was easy to get swallowed up in a school of two thousand students.

"What happened?" Grace asked me as soon as she and Stuart sat down in our usual back-of-the-bus seats. My cheeks hurt.

"Terry Di Stefano asked me to go with him to the fall formal!"

Grace squealed. She didn't know anyone at my school apart from a few of my friends and Mark. We'd double-dated toward the end of my relationship with Mark, but she called him boring and told me I needed to find someone else because she'd barf if I went all the way with him. Grace lost her virginity the year before to a football player at her school, which was the worst team in the city so it wasn't a status score for her. He was more like a decent-enough guy to get some experience with. She was now single.

"Ooh! Find out if one of Terry's friends needs a date," she said, smiling, her eyes dancing. She scrunched her nose up. "That way, I can check him out—see if he's good enough for you."

"For sure!" I started running through Terry's friends, trying to figure out if I'd heard whether any of them already had dates. I would ask him the next day.

During the bus ride, Stuart remained quiet. Grace and I blabbed on about the latest dress fashions and how she would style my hair. She peppered me with questions about the after-party, which was the real reason people went to our school dances.

We reached the tennis centre and Stuart trotted ahead of us into the lobby, where the adult club players lounged while waiting for a table at the trendy club restaurant or to finish conversations begun over the net during matches. Grace and I passed through the waiting area, which featured dark wood panelling, a vending machine, and Agassi, Seles, Graf and Lendl posters. We continued through a door that led to the stairs to the women's change room.

"Is Stuart okay?" I asked Grace when we got into the room. I put my bag down on a bench and searched for an open locker. "He seems a little quiet."

I took off my school clothes, replacing them with shorts, a sports bra and T-shirt. I hurried, not only because I was embarrassed about my small chest, but because the room was frigid and I didn't want to be unclothed for a second longer than necessary.

"Um, yeah," she said, giving me a quizzical look. She stood in her bra and tennis skirt. Grace never felt the cold nor any discomfort with her body. "I don't think he's crazy about the idea of you going to the dance with Terry."

I flushed, excited to think Stuart might be jealous. At times, I caught him looking at me, and I wondered if he felt even the tiniest bit interested in me. If he'd gone to my school he would have been considered tier-one material, so I assumed he wouldn't want to be with someone like me. I was attractive, maybe even pretty, but not gorgeous. I liked my personality but I was more serious than a lot of other girls my age about doing well at school and having other interests beyond parties and boys.

When I zoned out in class, or while I lay in my bed at night, it was Stuart I thought about. I liked everything about him—his blue-eyed, intense gaze, his laugh, his kindness, and most of all, his hair. I imagined what it would feel like to wrap my finger around a curl, which made me smile and feel ridiculous at the same time. Every time I saw Stuart, he smiled as though he'd waited all day to see me, and our conversations were natural, never stilted or blundering. It was like I'd known him my entire life, not just a couple of months.

I fantasized about asking him to take me to my school dance. He wouldn't have any trouble making friends. People gravitated toward him. I dreamed about how his arms would feel around me, his face close to mine, as we danced. But I kept my feelings about Stuart to myself. I didn't want even Grace to know. I couldn't stand the humiliation if he turned me down or, even worse, told me he'd go with me as friends. I worried I was reading him wrong, and that could make things awkward at our lessons. So I said nothing.

"What do you mean?" I asked, nibbling the skin beside my thumbnail.

"Caitie, I can see you like him. And I see the way he looks at you," she said as my blush deepened. She stopped folding her school clothes, holding a turquoise T-shirt in her hands, and sighed as she dropped one hip. "Listen, Caitie, I think Stuart's great. He's nice to everyone, he's hot and totally popular. He's a great friend, but I don't think he'd be a great boyfriend."

"Well, maybe it's better to be friends first," I said, slightly miffed. To avoid snapping at Grace, I stuffed my clothes into my gym bag, unzipped my racquet bag and pulled out my racquet. I twirled it in my hand as Grace finished dressing and began to tie her shoelaces. "Why do you say that, anyway? It's not usually the kind of thing someone says about a guy."

"At our last semi-formal in the spring, he took Jessica Keaton, a super-popular girl in his grade. She's really pretty and her dad is high up at that insurance company downtown. You know—the one with the really nice lawn? Anyhow, she's got money. Stuart also has money, did you know that?"

I shook my head. I didn't care whether Stuart's family had money or not.

"Anyway, they go to the dance. She's thinking she's going to be his girlfriend now because they've been out a few times. My friend saw them kissing at lunchtime. But at the dance, they have a big fight and she leaves. I didn't catch the entire conversation because I was in a corner with Jeremy—you know, the football player. But my friend heard Jessica telling him that his reputation suited him: great guy, lousy boyfriend. She said he never paid enough attention to her, that he was too wrapped up with his family, that kind of thing. Personally, I think she might be too high maintenance for him—or anybody, for that matter—but there you go. And we'd better get going, too."

I followed Grace out of the change room, replaying in my mind two things she'd said. The idea of Stuart kissing someone bothered me and I ordered my brain to swat the image away. But when she'd said, "I see the way he looks at you," I melted.

The lesson seemed unending. My backhand was out of sorts.

"Cait! Follow through!" my coach yelled. "What the hell's the matter with you?"

I wasn't sure. I'd been excited after talking to Terry. And after hearing what Grace had said, I felt like I was floating.

Stuart wasn't his usual self. He was distant when I tried

to talk to him and he seemed to be avoiding me. Usually, when we stood in line together waiting to hit balls, we would joke with each other. Occasionally, he'd touch my arm, or push my shoulder to let me know he was teasing me. Today, he was silent and inaccessible.

"Go talk to him," Grace whispered to me as we waited to hit forehands. "See what's his problem."

With just a few minutes left in our lesson, I found Stuart alone, piling tennis balls on his racquet in one of the corners of the court. I trotted over and started doing the same.

"Stuart, you okay?" I asked, bending down to pick up some balls.

"I'm fine."

"Well, you don't seem fine. Did I do something to upset you? Or did Grace? I know she likes to bust your chops," I said, standing up, my racquet full of balls.

"No, Caitie, I'm fine." He paused and stood up to look at me before bending back down to scoop up some more balls. Then he jolted up, startling me. The balls I'd gathered fell off my racquet and back onto the court, and my racquet slipped out of my hands. "No, you know what? I'm not okay. I wasn't sure about anything until the minute you mentioned you'd be going to that dance with that guy, and now I can't stand it."

He bent back down. My breathing became shallow and quick as he began foraging for the fallen tennis balls, placing them on my racquet, which lay on the court beside him. My heart thumped in my chest. I bent down to bring myself close to him.

"What are you saying?" I whispered. And when he looked at me, I felt a fluttering in my stomach. My pulse quickened and I held my breath. I'd never felt the way I did now, with Mark or anyone else I'd dated. It was like an electrical current passed between us.

"Don't tell me you don't feel it," he whispered.

I couldn't breathe. I just nodded, not trusting my voice.

"I want to take you out. Can I call you?"

four

MAY 2016

"DID HE CALL ON YOU?" Trevor asked when I returned to the shoe store the day after the training. He was squinting and his mouth was clamped together. He looked like he needed to run to the bathroom before he crapped his pants. "You were on time, right? Tell me you were on time. I know Toronto traffic can be a headache. Caitlin, did you talk to Mr. Taylor at all? He's the executive vice-president of Heusten Shoes Canada. It's kind of important that we make a good impression on him. All our jobs are on the line. He can be pretty serious, too, if he wants to be."

"Trevor, calm down," I said, and his nerves must have been sky high because he didn't force me to use his proper name. "It's fine. We got along very well. We ate lunch together. I kind of know him."

Trevor looked like he'd tried to swallow something and it had gotten stuck in his throat. "You had lunch with him?"

"Yes, we had lunch and he thinks the store is doing just

fine and that you're a great manager." Out of the corner of my eye, I saw Caleb's shoulders shaking with laughter. He knew what I really thought of Trevor and that I would never give him a compliment unless it was completely necessary.

"Oh, thank God," he said, exhaling a long breath. He pushed back his thinning hair and adjusted his glasses. Then, in an instant, he switched gears, whirling around on his heel and clicking off toward the backroom. I, too, released a sigh of relief that he hadn't asked me any other questions, such as how I knew Stuart or why he would have picked me, out of everyone there, to take to lunch—the one benefit of working with a narcissist.

"Caitie, you like to rile that guy up, eh?" Caleb said as I started laughing.

I'd called Siobhan on my way home from Toronto. She knew Stuart. She'd witnessed first-hand the aftermath of Stuart leaving me.

"I'll kill him," she said. "Oh, God, Caitie, what are you going to do? Is he your boss? I bet we could sue him."

One of the reasons I loved Siobhan and was fiercely loyal to her was because of how well she took care of me after Stuart had left. I'd cried until I felt hollowed out, and my head always felt foggy, confusion an overriding emotion. I don't remember much else from the days after I found his clothes and books gone, along with his brief note. But I do remember Siobhan's support, her warm hand holding mine, her gentle, soothing voice encouraging me to eat as she spoon-fed me ice cream. Tears pricked my eyes every time I remembered how she tucked me into bed, the bed I'd shared with Stuart, telling me I was loved, that I would love again.

"I'm surprised he's working at Heusten Shoes. Didn't he go to school for 'I'm a big, huge important person?'"

"Be nice. He finished his undergraduate degree in Boston and then decided to do an MBA at the University of Toronto. He worked a few corporate jobs and was headhunted for Heusten," I said, repeating what he had told me at lunch.

"I'll bet he was. Lucky cad. The rest of us, who didn't leave behind our beloved, had to slough it out in crappy barely-eking-out-a-living jobs. Of course the golden boy was recruited."

"Siobhan," I said, with a sigh. "He did some shitty things, no doubt. But it was a long time ago. I made my peace with what happened and I don't want to think about how crushed I was every time I see him." As Siobhan started to say something that sounded like, "There's no fucking way you should have to see this guy," I cut her off. "Listen, it's fine. I'm kind of excited to see him again, you know? He's still charming—told me I was beautiful."

Siobhan didn't play by normal dating rules. With Mike, she was currently in the longest relationship of her life, one that remained monogamous. She had cheated on almost every other prior boyfriend, sometimes dating two or three people at the same time. Her radar for infidelity was better tuned than most people's, which was why I heard the warning in her voice when she said to me, "Be careful, Caitie-cat."

To Rob, I said I bumped into an old friend from university. When Rob and I met, he knew I was fresh from a lengthy and serious relationship and wasn't looking to get involved with anyone. We disclosed certain elements of our pasts to each other, more to be responsible and respectful than for any other reason. I'd kept the depth of what Stuart and I had been a secret. I felt it was no one's business, not even Rob's. I didn't want to know about the girls he had dated or slept with before me so I figured he didn't need to know the details about my previous love life either. Once we'd committed to each other, the past no longer seemed to matter.

It was a hot Wednesday morning in July when the store door opened and Stuart walked in. I hadn't seen him since May, and sometimes I wondered if I'd dreamed up the entire scenario of eating lunch with him.

That morning, I'd gone for a run. I'd resurrected this habit a month earlier because I wanted to spend as much time as I could outdoors, soaking up the warmth before winter returned. The boys were out of school and being watched by Julie, the teenaged girl who lived on our street, when I worked. On my days off, we went to the beach. I cherished this time with my boys, watching them wade into the water and run back out again, chased by a tide. Their sandcastle-building skills also improved. We'd spent an hour crafting the last one, which featured a moat, three turrets and a large courtyard.

Aidan and Jacob were still asleep when Julie arrived at eight, so I slipped on my running shoes and went for a brisk, five-kilometre run along the trail near our house. By then, it was already hot, my shirt sticking to my body. I dripped with sweat, my cheeks red with exertion. I'd been a long-distance runner in high school and university. Then, when Rob and I moved to St. Catharines, I became a semi-regular member at the all-women's gym downtown until Aidan was born. One reason we moved to the Niagara region was for work. The other was because Rob's family also lived here and we knew they could provide a helping hand if, and when, we had kids. After I became a mom, I just couldn't find the time—and sometimes the energy—to work out after a hectic day at The Leg, not to mention cooking, cleaning, doing laundry, tending to an infant and, later, two small boys, as well as reconnecting with Rob.

When Stuart came into the store, he looked fresh, though the noonday sun was searing. He smiled at me and I felt my stomach pull the way it did on roller-coaster rides when the car drops into the steep decline. He walked over and leaned close to me. His hand held my elbow.

"It's nice to see you again."

He smelled good, though it wasn't the cologne he used to wear.

"Good to see you as well," I said, looking into his eyes, my pulse racing. "Are you here to see Trevor, I mean, Mr. Murdock?"

"I'm here to see you, but Trevor will have to do. He's the one who must answer all the questions."

I went to the backroom to fetch Trevor, who came out, clickety-clacking, all aflutter.

"Mr. Taylor, how nice to see you. You already know Caitlin. This is Caleb. He's a part-timer and goes to university."

Stuart raised one eyebrow and smirked. "Nice to meet you, Caleb. Yes, Caitie and I know each other from a long time ago. Let's go for a coffee," he said to Trevor.

As soon as the pair was out of the store, Caleb asked me how I knew Stuart. I told him we went to university together. The answer seemed to satisfy him because he didn't ask me anything else, just went back to his till as shoppers arrived.

I was eating my lunch in the backroom when Trevor barged in, almost breathless and wearing a strange smile on his face. I started to speak, but in his excitement, he cut me off.

"Mr. Taylor wants to see you, Caitlin," Trevor said, beaming. "I can't understand why, but he asked if I could spare you for a little while. I said, 'Of course.' He's giving us a great review. Store's doing immensely well."

"That's great," I said, stuffing the last of my salad in my mouth, resisting the urge to roll my eyes. "Did he say how long he wanted to speak with me?"

"No, doesn't matter. You can take the rest of the afternoon off, if you need it," he said.

My mouth snapped open. In high school, Trevor would have been the one who sucked up to anyone he thought mattered, while at the same time ratting out the kids who were smoking on school property or kissing in corners at the semi-formal dance.

I closed my mouth, wiped my fingers with a napkin and collected my containers into my lunch bag. I started to wipe the table clean, but Trevor hurried me along, saying he'd do it. I ducked into the bathroom, reapplied my lipstick and then went into the busy showroom. Trevor must have gotten great news to allow me to leave—that, or he was afraid of Stuart.

"You wanted to see me?" I asked Stuart as I walked toward where he stood.

"You have no idea," he said, smiling. He opened the door for me and we were hit with a blast of humidity so thick my hair felt as though it had gone instantly limp. I touched it to see if I was right.

"You look beautiful," Stuart said.

"You know, Stuart, you could get in trouble for this flirting," I said, chuckling. "You're still charming."

"Do you think I speak to every woman like this? I'm actually insulted," he said, glancing sideways at me. His intensity was unnerving, lessened only by his jovial manner. We walked along the outdoor corridor, which was shaded and which featured beautiful bright flowers in planters about every third store. Unconsciously, I moved my arm as though to entwine it with his, the way I liked to walk with Rob. My motion could only have lasted a fraction of a second, but he caught my hesitation as I pulled my arm back.

"You can, you know," he said, with a shy smile. "I wouldn't mind."

"Sorry, it's kind of automatic," I said, my cheeks burning.

"I remember."

"Hey," I said, making him stop to look at me. "Where are we going, anyway?"

"I was hoping we could play hooky. My work is all wrapped up and I told Trevor I needed to prep you on some new forms they're getting the stores to use. He sold your talents immediately. 'Caitlin is impeccable at ensuring the systems flow at this store,'" he said, doing a spot-on impression of Trevor. "'Caitlin is one of our most valued employees. She won't let you down.'"

I laughed. "What'd you say to that?"

"I told him I knew you wouldn't," he said, becoming serious. "Caitie, I don't need you for anything business-wise. The forms are in my car. You can just take them home and read them. To be honest, I haven't been able to stop thinking about you since I saw you in Toronto. After we had lunch, I wanted to call you. I want to get to know you again. I understand that it's entirely inappropriate. I know you're married. But I want to get to know you. I can't begin to explain what it feels like to see you again after all this time."

He paused, considering what he was going to say next. I waited, feeling frozen to the pavement.

"Caitie," he said, before sighing. "I'm not sure you even want to be friends again, and if you don't want to spend any time with me, you're free to go and there won't be any hard feelings. But I'd like to take a tour of Niagara Falls and I'm guessing you know where all the best places are."

In my mind, I took out a piece of paper and drew a line down the centre. On the left side, I jotted down reasons why I should continue to spend time with Stuart. Those reasons included curiosity, a need to find out why he left, the feelings I felt when I looked at him, and, even though I didn't want to admit it, I was flattered that he wanted to be with me. On the other side, the column that outlined why I should just go home, were three names: Rob, Aidan and Jacob. Despite that, I nodded and smiled.

We climbed into Stuart's car—me, again, envious of the immaculate space—and drove to Niagara Falls. I pointed out various facts about the area as we drove down the busy highway and up the Niagara Escarpment. In the city, I directed him toward a little hideaway parking lot I'd discovered a few years before. By stopping here, it meant we had a bit of a walk ahead of us to get into the tourist area, but I felt like I won every time I didn't have to pay the exorbitant parking fees in Niagara Falls.

We walked along the dirt pathway, high-rise hotels to our left. The roar of the falls acted as a backdrop to our conversation, and the sun warmed my skin. I smiled nonstop and kept sneaking glances at Stuart. My thoughts skirted to Rob and the boys, but then they returned to being with Stuart. I basked in his attention, feeling like I was the centre of his universe. I felt like I was twenty again. When we were younger, I loved spending every moment we could together. I was desperate to ask him about our final months together, to know, once and for all, what made him run, but I knew it was too soon.

We walked along the busy tourist trap. As a general rule, I avoided the Fallsview area most of the year, more so in summer, when the sidewalks were lined with people wanting to see one of the natural wonders of the world. When you lived in the Niagara region, the waterfall was more of a nuisance, a burden to visit. But its majesty wasn't lost on me and, every once in a while, I marvelled at the site.

Playing tourist with Stuart was fun. He admired the falls, and when we stopped at a lookout point, I studied him. I saw traces of his boyish features. I'd never tired of gazing at Stuart when we were together. I loved his beautiful face. Women passed us, admiring him.

"Caitie," he said, not looking at me. He continued staring out over the water. "I'm so glad I found you after all this time."

And then, just as he would have done all those years ago, he turned and looked at me, and I felt the intervening years vanish. He reached his arm over me, his fingers trailing down my arm, and he laced his hand in mine before pulling me to him, enveloping me in his arms.

five

OCTOBER 1996

STUART WAS distant after our tennis conversation. And he didn't call until the night before the dance. By then, I had spiralled through the usual teenage trifecta of doubt, insecurity and second-guessing but kept myself busy with schoolwork and student government. I organized a fundraiser where our student council delivered cookie-grams the morning of the dance.

It turned out that Terry's friend, Tristan, needed a date and Grace was now coming. He was popular, a complete jock, and hot. In other words, he was firmly ensconced on the first tier. Our foursome would meet up with Heather, my best friend at Catholic Central, along with her date for dinner before the formal, and head to the dance and then to the after-party.

That Thursday, the day before the dance, Grace and I blew off tennis, knowing we wouldn't be able to concentrate. Instead, we shopped for the finishing touches to our ensembles. I decided to wear a red, fitted chiffon dress with a flowing hem that stopped just above my knees. It was sleeveless—not the brightest choice for mid-October, I later realized. I was wearing my hair up, with a few stragglers cascading over my ears. Grace and I perused the stores at the downtown mall after school to complete our outfits—"Accessorize, Caitie!" Grace said, laughing—and I bought silver earrings and a matching bangle.

I had been hanging up clothes in my room when the phone rang. I rushed to answer it, thinking it was Grace, who'd already called four times. We'd rehashed our plans during the first three calls. The fourth was to let me know she'd stolen some vodka from her parents' secret stash.

"Grace, if you call me one more time, I'm going to uninvite you. I'm up to my ears in clothes," I said, laughing into the receiver as I looked at the huge pile on my bed.

"It's Stuart," he said.

"Oh, hi! How are you?" I felt the fluttering return. Next, I felt guilty, as though I was cheating on the possibility of Terry. I wasn't even sure I liked Terry, but I knew Stuart was special.

"You missed tennis," he said, his voice neutral.

"Yeah, um, Grace and I went shopping because we needed accessories for our new dresses. Um..." I said, unsure what to say next. I shoved a hill of shirts onto the floor and sat down on my bed, coiling the phone cord around my finger until it hurt. I looked down. My index finger was turning an angry purple. I unwound the cord.

"I'm sure you'll look great and it'll be a fun night," he said.

"You know exactly what the evening's going to be like," I said. The throbbing in my finger helped throw off my self-consciousness. I spent only a few hours a week around Stuart, but during those times I felt like I was my authentic self. When I spoke to guys at my school, I demurred, not wanting to sound too aggressive or too self-assured. With Stuart, I was just me. I spoke my mind. I told him how I felt; I gave him my opinions. He accepted that. He accepted me. And it was exhilarating.

"There'll be girls crying in the bathroom because their dates aren't paying enough attention to them or someone acted like a jerk at dinner," I continued. "And there will be more of the same at the after-parties because everyone will have had too much to drink. But I know you don't want to hear about this. What did you call to talk about?"

"Where's the party?" he asked.

"Terry's friend's house," I said, feeling conflicted, second-guessing being so open with him. One of the things I liked about Stuart was his talkative, energized nature. Tonight, on the phone, his tone was even and impossible to read.

"No, I don't mean whose house," he said, laughing. "Tell me where it is. I'm going to come."

"Um, I'm not sure that's a good idea," I said, flummoxed.

"I'm not coming to crash it—I'm coming to take you out. Don't worry; I'll make sure you're home before you need to be."

"I'm staying over at Grace's," I said, my voice squeaking.

I could almost hear the smile in his voice as he said, "Well, then, that's perfect."

The next day, I couldn't concentrate in class. During math, not my favourite subject, we gossiped about the dance, recapping who was going with whom and wagering on who would get the drunkest. After forty minutes of trying to get us to focus, our teacher gave up and assigned an open-book quiz, which we continued to whisper through. After math, I shuffled off to geography. This teacher, loved for letting the odd swear word slip during his lectures, said he wasn't even going to try and teach. Instead, he fired up the reel-to-reel projector and we watched a *National Geographic* special.

"You can thank me by finishing your projects for Monday," he said, spooling the uncooperative film through the machine.

As the final bell rang, I sprinted to my locker, grabbed my bags, reviewed the evening's plans with Heather, and hurried to my bus. Heather was shorter than me, with mousy brown hair and braces. Though sharp-witted and intelligent, she was painfully shy. I was excited about the formal, but it was the promise of being alone with Stuart that made my heart race. In an uncharacteristic move, I failed to mention he was coming for me to either Heather or Grace. I didn't want to say anything in case he stood me up. The entire cloak-and-dagger operation seemed far-fetched, and I couldn't bear the shame if it turned out he'd lied. Plus, I didn't want to upset Heather, who'd become tetchy when I announced that Terry had asked me to go with him, confessing her months-old secret crush for him. I felt bad that I'd accepted, but she brushed off my apologies with a curt, "Don't worry." If I told her I was going to ditch Terry for Stuart, it would only have made things worse.

At home, I hurried to pack my overnight bag. I took my new dress out of my closet, along with my new heels. I ran down the stairs, skipping the final step, and dashed into the kitchen, where I found Matt making what looked like a four-course meal but for him was just a late afternoon snack.

Matt was a Western student, studying business with a specialization in finance.

"Hey, can you give me a ride to Grace's?" I opened the fridge and took out a soda. I cracked open the tab and took a sip. "You going out tonight with Sarah?"

"Yeah, we're going to the movies. I can take you in a few minutes; no trouble. Who're you going with?" When I told him, he gave me a disapproving look. "Hey, be careful. That guy's always looking to get experience, if you know what I mean."

"Gross, stop. I'm not interested in him," I said, surprising myself.

Had Stuart not phoned me, my giddiness and jumpiness could have been attributed to Terry. I might even have considered becoming his girlfriend, despite my initial misgivings about him. But my emotions were a mixed bag. Guilt and worry were fierce competitors. If Stuart didn't show up, the entire night would be a disappointment.

I wished all guys were like my brother. If he said he was going to do something, he did it. As a Catholic Central student, he had been quarterback on the football team. If his jock status hadn't landed him in the first tier of popularity, his pleasant disposition and generosity would have. I knew that some brothers and sisters—Grace and her brother, for starters—fought all the time, always looking for ways to get in little digs and hurl insults at one another. Matty was different. I'd broken my wrist three years earlier, trying to ride my bike over a railroad crossing but getting my tire caught in the metal groove. A kind motorist had seen what happened and drove me home, bent bike and all. The driver knocked on my front door while I waited in the car, and Matt ran out of the house, carried me inside and helped wash the tears, snot and blood away. Then he bandaged my arm before driving me to the hospital.

He and Sarah had started dating a couple of years ago. My family adored her and we assumed they'd marry. Matt wouldn't dump someone in order to make sure she was *the one*, by dating other people the way his former best friend had, or because some people believe that marrying your high school sweetheart is a recipe for a bad life. He followed his heart.

On the way to Grace's, Matt picked up Heather and as soon as we walked in the front door we bolted to her bedroom to get ready. This was no easy feat because Heather fretted about everything—her dress, her hair, whether someone would dance with her, whether she would have a boyfriend after tonight.

"You're so lucky," she kept saying to me. "Terry is so cute. And he asked you to the after-party, so he must like you! You guys will be going out after tonight. I just know it."

I rolled my eyes and told her to stop being so dramatic. Heather was going to the dance with Kevin Dorenfeld. Everyone in our grade knew Kevin fancied her—he sent her three cookie-grams that morning—and they'd gone out on a few dates. Heather claimed she didn't feel the same way.

"He's so sloppy when he kisses," she said. "Saliva everywhere. Feels like my face got a lick from my dog."

Once we were ready, we sauntered down the stairs and posed for photos while Grace's brother made kissing noises until Grace threatened to destroy his Nintendo Game Boy. Our dates arrived and we introduced them to Grace's parents and then grabbed our coats, bundling up to face the chill that had arrived a few days earlier. As we walked to the vehicle, we took turns teasing Terry about the minivan he'd borrowed from his mother, but he was too cool to care.

Then we were off to the restaurant. I tried to stay focused on what everyone was saying, but I zoned out a few times and didn't realize I'd been asked a question until Grace whispered to me, "Hey, are you okay?"

"Hmm? Yeah, oh, yeah, fine," I said, giving her a quick smile before staring out the window again, trying to keep my breath steady. I didn't think I'd be able to eat. I guarded a secret that could hurt several people. But that wasn't what bothered me. It was that I didn't care.

I ran through a variety of scenarios of how Stuart and I would leave the party together. Would we sneak out? I preferred that. Would he come in and try to get to know people and then offer to take me home? Too risky. As I ran through each scene, my stomach fluttered because I also allowed myself to think about what we might do afterwards. But I didn't have a lot of experience with boys and this also made me nervous. I assumed Stuart had a lot of experience with girls. If he liked me, would my inexperience make him change his mind?

A server with slicked-back black hair and a discreet stud earring in his left earlobe arrived at our large booth at the back of the restaurant. I ordered iced tea and then excused myself and went to the washroom. A couple of minutes later, Grace came in. I remained where I was, staring at my reflection in the mirror.

"You okay, Caitie? You seem a little distant."

"I feel, oh... I'm not sure I can talk about it." I took a gulp of air and sat down on the brown wicker bench in the sitting area. I massaged my temples and started to put my hands in my hair until I realized it would ruin my updo. I tried to calm all the thoughts in my head as I looked around at the gilded mirrors and baskets holding washcloths. Terry had done well, picking an upscale restaurant that most of us who worked part-time at fast food joints couldn't afford on a whim.

Grace sat down next to me.

"Are you worried about whether Terry likes you? Personally, I think he does," she said.

I agreed. When he'd arrived on Grace's doorstep, he took his time admiring me before saying, "You look hot," and handing me a corsage adorned with a single white rose. It was understated, yet elegant. I would have chosen the same thing.

I nodded and looked at her. "Ah, up until yesterday that would've been the reason I'm acting so strange," I said, still unsure if I should say more. Of course, Grace knew I liked Stuart but she had no idea how enamoured of him I was. On the phone the night before, we'd talked for two hours. We disclosed tidbits about our families, what school was like and, most scintillating for me, our exes. I knew that was always how relationships started—by removing any doubt that you were involved with anyone else.

Until I'd met Stuart, my ability to describe why I liked a certain guy consisted of whether I thought he was cute, nice or smart. And while Stuart was gorgeous, I was attracted to more than just his looks. He was mature, he listened to me and he made me feel important. I didn't want to tell Grace this. It sounded ridiculous, even to me. And though she was my best friend, I knew she'd roll her eyes and tell me that maybe now I'd finally get laid. I was also conflicted about what Grace would say about being on a date and heading out on another at some point during the same evening. I knew Grace didn't obey rules, but even in my limited experience, I was sure that what I was doing was pretty low on the scale of admirable dating principles.

"I like Terry," I said. "Well, at least I did until yesterday when Stuart phoned."

"Stuart called you?" She burst into a smile.

"You were right. He doesn't like the idea of me going to the dance with Terry. And, um, I kind of agreed to have him pick me up at the party." I looked away from her excitable face.

"Why didn't you tell me this before now?" she asked. I returned my gaze to her. Her eyebrows were knitted, her mouth a little circle. "Any of the ten times we spoke yesterday would have been a better time than right now, between ordering drinks and dinner, when your date is out there waiting for us."

"I know," I said, squeezing my hands together. "I didn't want to tell you because I'm pretty sure Stuart feels the same way about me as I do about him. And I'm afraid of that. Plus, I'm sitting here, talking to you, while a guy is spending a crapload of money on dinner for me—a guy who, until a day ago, I might have been interested in. And he has no idea what I'm up to. He has no clue that I'm planning to ditch him for Stuart tonight. Am I a terrible person?"

"No, you're my hero," she said, laughing while hopping from one foot to the other. "Now, tell your face that you're going to have a good time with Terry at dinner and the dance. Who knows? Have some fun with him. When we get to the after-party, I've got your back. We'll figure out a way for you to meet Stuart. Do you guys have a plan to hook up? No? Okay, well, we'll figure it out. Oh, God, this is going to be great! But I want full disclosure."

Fortified by my talk with Grace, I tamped down the emotions that kept swirling inside me and enjoyed dinner. I thanked Terry for the wonderful meal after he paid and, when we stood up to put on our coats, he pulled me close and kissed my cheek. Grace winked at me and mouthed, "Have fun," before allowing Tristan to help her into her coat. Despite being uncomfortable with Kevin's obvious infatuation, Heather looked like she was also enjoying herself.

On the way to school, Terry pulled into a nearby park, opened the trunk of the minivan and got out a cooler filled with beer. He handed one to each of us but popped the cap off mine before handing me the bottle. We downed those and then another round and then got back in the van. Terry made a show of not drinking the second, letting us know he was our responsible DD. When we arrived, I was buzzing. We waited in line at the gym doors, on which hung a sign that spelled out WELCOME TO HEAVEN SENT FALL FORMAL 1996 in silver lettering. We handed in our tickets, hung up our coats and then headed onto the dance floor.

Despite the school's kissing ban and the teachers stationed all over the gym to look for hands that were too low, bodies that were too close or lips that were locked, smooching was on full display. When I slow danced with Terry, I tensed, spending the entire time making sure we were never face to face just in case he tried to kiss me.

After the dance, Grace and I hugged Heather goodbye in the parking lot and watched as she walked hand-in-hand with Kevin to his friend's car. We piled into the van and headed off to the party. I spent the entire fifteen-minute drive to Phillip's house fretting about what would happen once we arrived, but I underestimated how many people would be there. As soon as we walked through the front door, the throng of people inside swallowed us up. Phillip's parents were vacationing in Aruba, so no one was home except his older sister, a Western student who'd invited a throng of her friends to join in the festivities. There were wall-to-wall people in every room.

Grace whispered to Tristan for him and Terry to get us drinks and they wandered off to find the throw pile for our coats as well as the spiked punch. Grace grabbed my arm and tugged me back outside. She kept hold of my arm and I followed, silent, wondering where we were going. A few seconds later she stopped. Stuart stood five feet away.

"Hey, I saw you as soon as we pulled up," she said. "She's all yours."

"Hi Grace, you look nice. Are you having a good time?" he asked, giving her a crooked smile.

"Yeah, it's been great. Listen," she said, turning toward me. I forced myself to stop staring at Stuart and look at her. Part of me couldn't believe he had actually come—for me. "I'll cover for you. The house is packed. No one will know you're missing. I'm going home for two. If you don't show, I won't worry, but if you're coming to my house, make sure you're back by two, okay?"

"Okay," he said, staring at me as I returned my gaze to him.

"Well, all right then," she said, giving me a hug and a peck on the cheek before whispering, "I do really like him."

It took me a few beats to realize she meant Stuart, not Terry, but by that time she was gone. I stood on the lawn in my new red chiffon dress, feeling young. I shivered and then did a mental eye roll—my jacket was somewhere in Phillip's house.

"You look very pretty," Stuart said. And before I knew it,

he'd walked over to me, placed his hands on my waist, his face inches from mine. "I don't even want to think about what you've been doing all night or if that guy's been holding you, but now you're mine."

He moved his hands up my back to the nape of my neck and pulled me to him. I held my breath, feeling my heart thump in my chest. Anyone I'd kissed up to that point now seemed like an amateur. The passion I felt—reciprocated in him—made me gasp. I didn't want to stop. His hands held my face before retreating down my back. When I had to come up for air, he pulled away.

"Let's go somewhere else," he said, taking my hand. Touching him felt so intimate, I wanted to cry.

A few of the windows at the front of Phillip's house were cracked open and I could hear blaring music. I trailed behind Stuart, my hand in his, until he stopped. He pulled off his coat and put it around me.

"It's okay; I have another in the car," he said. "I grabbed it and a blanket, just in case."

He put his arm around my waist and we walked to his car, which he'd parked across the street, in full view of Phillip's front door.

"I didn't see you when we pulled in," I said. "I'm surprised Grace saw you."

"I saw you guys arrive, but didn't want you to think I was stalking you so I kind of hid. I saw you. I saw you holding his hand."

"I was making a backup plan," I said without thinking, just as we reached the car. When I arrived at Phillip's, I'd still had a buzz from the alcohol, which proceeded to full-blown intoxication when I kissed Stuart a few minutes before. But as soon as those words were out of my mouth, I sobered up. He was about to open the passenger door for me when I spoke.

He froze. "What do you mean?"

"Well, I wasn't sure if you were really going to come," I said, deciding to be honest. He moved closer to me, his face, again, inches from mine.

"Caitlin, I will never lie to you."

He pushed his body against mine as he kissed me again, hungrily. I was heady when we broke apart, not wanting to stop but worrying we'd get caught by some nosy neighbours. Stuart opened my door and shut it once I was in. He went around to his side and got in, put on his seat belt and started driving. The radio played, Bryan Adams singing about making it a night to remember. We were silent.

"Where are we going?" I asked.

"You'll see," he said.

Then he lapsed into silence, which was a good thing. Scattered thoughts flew around my brain, flitting from wondering what Grace would tell Terry, and what he must be thinking, to replaying what had just happened and where Stuart and I were going. A few minutes later, he turned right and drove into the University of Western Ontario's gates, its stately buildings illuminated by spotlights, its sidewalks dotted by a few students rushing home after a night of studying. As we neared the building housing the student centre, we saw more people milling about. We drove on, following the main artery out the other side of the grounds.

We wound our way down a few side streets until Stuart pulled into the driveway of a red brick, ranch-style home. Two tall trees adorned the front yard, both of which were nearly barren. A tended garden, now filled with dying chrysanthemums and bushes, curved from the front of the house to run the length of the front yard. An avid gardener lived here.

"This is your house," I said, as he turned off the engine. "What are we doing at your house?"

"My mom's gone for the weekend and my sister is at her boyfriend's."

We were alone. My stomach jumped as we exited the car and I followed Stuart to the front door. He opened it and we walked inside. It was as though he'd opened the cover of a book I didn't want to stop reading. I wanted to see every inch of the house, to imagine him growing up there. I wanted to see where he ate breakfast, his favourite colours, how he filled a space, where he slept. He stood behind me as we entered the foyer. He helped me shuffle out of his coat and he brought his lips to the nape of my neck. I felt his breath and closed my eyes. Afraid we might get carried away, I moved ahead so we no longer touched.

"I want to know everything about you," I said.

He opened a closet door and hung his coat on a hanger.

"You know I'm eighteen—my birthday's March 26 so I'll be nineteen soon. I go to Central and am graduating this year. I mostly like playing tennis but I love to ski. You know my parents are divorced. I have two older sisters: Emma, who lives in Alberta, and Nicole, who is unfortunately still here. She goes to Western," he said. I rolled my eyes. He smiled.

His house was exquisite. The living room, to the right of the foyer, was painted a soft, robin's egg blue, with a large, blue cloth sofa and accent chair. Long, dark blue curtains covered two windows, and soft, beige threads carpeted the floor. I could see dark wooden cupboards in a cheery yellow kitchen from the foyer. This was a woman's house.

I trailed Stuart into the kitchen. He went to the refrigerator, opened it and asked me over his shoulder what I wanted to drink.

"On better thought, I'll make tea," he said, closing the door and smiling at me. "I don't want to impair your thinking any further."

I was both embarrassed and worried by his comment. I was a teenage drinker, imbibing only while out with my friends, that kind of experimental, let's-see-what-trouble-we-can-get-into drinking. But I was rarely drunk.

"Don't worry," he said, catching my conflicting emotions. "I know you're not hammered. I was only teasing you."

I sat at the oak dining table, waiting for the kettle to boil. Stuart brought over sugar, spoons and milk before going back to pour the water into two stylish white mugs and allowing the tea to steep in front of us. He sat down next to me, looking at me with that intense gaze I was beginning to feel comfortable with. I felt like he saw only me when he looked at me like that, like he only wanted to know what I was thinking or feeling.

"I can't believe you're sitting here in my kitchen with me after midnight, and we're alone in the house," he said. "It's strange. This is the first time we've been by ourselves and I didn't take you out on a proper date. I'm sorry."

"Why didn't you?" I asked, sipping my tea.

"I wasn't sure I could handle a relationship right now," he said. Then, he hurried to clarify his words when he saw my face shift. "It's not that. I didn't know if I could be the sort of boyfriend you deserve. There's a lot going on here at my house."

I surveyed my surroundings. "Like what?" I asked.

"Well," he said, drinking from his mug. He sighed and stared ahead. "Things aren't going that well, actually. It's like my mom never wants me to go anywhere or do anything. She's always asking me where I'm going, who I'm going with and when I'll be home. And Nicole? She's just as bad. Honestly, you'd think a girl in university could care less about what her little brother's doing, but not my sister. She's on me like white on rice. 'Stuart, you should be home to help Mom,' is her favourite expression when she's going out with her boyfriend. When she is home, she and my mom fight like crazy. Emma gets it. When she's here, which is usually just at holidays, she's always on my side. But she lives two time zones away so... Am I boring you? I'm sorry. I don't talk about this with anyone, really. It sounds too pathetic."

"Not at all. My parents drive me crazy, too, so we've got something in common," I said, glad he felt he could confide in me.

"I feel like my mom expects me to be the man of the house, you know? I'm supposed to be strong and the one who sort of protects everybody, but I'm the youngest," he said. "I guess I can understand because she's on her own. And she got really weird after my dad remarried. She hates Gloria, my stepmother—even now—and refuses to acknowledge my half-brother and -sister. A few years ago, I asked her for some money so I could send them Christmas presents and she wouldn't give it to me."

My experience, albeit limited, told me you spent a first date at a movie theatre so you didn't have to talk, though the dark room would still provide ample opportunities for making out. That had been the case when I first went out with Mark. We went to the usual movie, followed by a quick kiss in the car when he dropped me off at home. I thought tonight would be the first and only time I went out with Terry—my twinge of guilt this time mixed with the hope that he didn't even know I was missing because he threw off the DD cap and was now drunk—and with other guys I'd dated, they spent most of the getting-to-know-each-other time talking about how great they were and selling me on the idea of being with them.

I was surprised, yet comfortable, with Stuart's openness. I knew our relationship would be built on complete honesty and truth, cutting through all the teenage bullshit of facades and expected behaviours. With Stuart, it felt like we had somehow passed all the non-essentials and the required small talk.

I stood up, moved his arm away from his mug and sat down on his lap so I faced him. I traced the outline of his face and drank in his stare. He brought his hands up to my face and kissed me, a slow, gentle kiss that became fierce. His lips were soft, his tongue searching for mine, his hands in my now-freed hair.

"I want to take you to my room, but not tonight," he said, as we moved to the living room. We lay together on the couch, alternating between making out, touching each other, and talking. At one point I glanced at my watch. I sat straight up.

"Stuart, I've got to go. I need to be at Grace's." I rearranged my clothes, touching my tousled hair. My lips felt swollen.

"Cait, I'm not asking you to stay, not because I don't want to. I do. But this is new. I don't want to move too fast or put pressure on us." He got up and went to the closet to grab us coats. He wrapped one around me, pulling me close to him.

Terry's minivan pulled in just as we arrived at Grace's house.

"You don't have to walk me," I said, putting my hand on his as he went to unlatch his seat belt. I shimmied out of his coat, leaned over and kissed him. When we broke away, I saw Grace waiting on her porch, holding my coat over her arm. She waved goodbye to Tristan, who had driven her home in Terry's minivan. I wondered why but was relieved. Then, I turned my attention back to Stuart.

"Cait, spelled C-A-I-T," Stuart said, "I can't wait to see you again."

I reached Grace's porch, where she stood with a huge grin on her face, and then turned and waved to Stuart. We watched as he drove away and then Grace unlocked the door. Once inside, we sped-walked to the bathroom she shared with her brother. Her parents had their own ensuite, which I thought of as the height of sophistication. My entire family shared a small bathroom and, most mornings, this caused fights between me and my mother.

Grace bounced on her toes as she brushed her teeth and hair, giving me knowing looks in the mirror. When we finished, we went into her bedroom, which, with its matching white wood bed frame, dressers and bookcase always seemed so grown up to me. I still had my little desk from when I was in elementary school and some stuffies I couldn't bear to get rid of yet.

"Spill," she said, a wide grin covering her face, as we sat down on her bed.

With other guys we'd dated, this was the routine—a full debriefing that could go on for hours and included details of every moment, word and touch. But it didn't feel right this time. Not only was I exhausted from, and confused about, what had happened, I couldn't talk about how he'd touched me, how he felt as my fingers explored his skin, how we kissed. It was familiar, yet exciting; unbelievable, yet expected. And though I was confident that the reason he'd taken me to his house tonight wasn't because he was bored or hoped to sleep with me, I was afraid, doubtful a relationship would follow. I had never met anyone like him, nor had I wanted to be with someone so much. I skimmed over the details but gave her enough, in appreciation of the risk she'd taken on to allow me to be with him.

"Oh my God, Caitie! Are you a couple now? You must be," she said, squeezing my hands in hers before she got off the bed and changed out of her black velvet dress and into her pyjamas.

I stripped off my dress and threw on my flannel pyjamas. Then I hunkered down under the Laura Ashley duvet on her queen-sized bed—another thing I loved about her room, no twin bed forcing guests to sleep in a sleeping bag on the floor.

"I'm not sure. We didn't talk about that," I said, laughing. "We were too busy. I think so? He seems to feel the same way about me, unless I'm reading him completely wrong. What about you and Tristan? And, oh my God, what happened with Terry? I feel like a piece of shit for what I did to him tonight."

"Don't worry about Terry. He came back with your drink but I told him you'd met some friends that you'd gone to catch up with and that you'd be back in a few minutes. He didn't seem bothered. I watched him drink his drink, as well as the one he got you. Then he got distracted watching the hockey game," she said. "He was really hammered when he found me again and asked about you. I made like you were mad because he was spending so much time watching the game, and you should have seen his face. He was so upset. It was hilarious."

My eyes went wide and I started to talk when she cut me off.

"No, don't worry, Caitie. Two minutes later, he was back watching the game. And that was the last I saw of him," she said, laughing. "Tristan and I spent most of the night upstairs in one of the bedrooms. I will not, however, skimp on the details for you."

As she went through the minutiae of her marathon make-out session, I only half-listened. I rewound my mental tape and replayed being with Stuart—seeing him standing on the lawn, feeling his body pressed against mine at the car and playing with his hair as we lay on his sofa.

"He's a great guy, not a dumb jock like I first expected him to be," Grace continued, climbing into bed beside me. "We're together, for sure, and we're going out tomorrow night. Are you and Stuart getting together tomorrow night, too?"

"We didn't talk about it. He didn't say anything," I stammered. That we hadn't made any further concrete plans allowed a tiny hint of doubt to creep in. "He just said he couldn't wait to see me again."

"I'm sure he'll call you tomorrow. I'll bet you're inseparable from this point on," she said as she pulled the covers over us and laid her head on my shoulder. "Eee! I'm so happy for you!"

When Terry called to apologize, I told him not to worry about it, and he asked if he could take me out for a proper date the following weekend. I accepted. Stuart was extremely confident and from what I knew of him, a person of his word, someone you could trust without question. I believed him when he said he would never lie to me. But my heart had been broken before. We hadn't spelled out the particulars of how our relationship was going to function, or even if we were going to have a relationship past that night. In the teenage dating world I inhabited, there were so many guidelines. I had thrown out the rule book at Stuart's home and just trusted my instincts. It felt right that night.

After Monday came and went and I still hadn't heard from Stuart, I wondered if I had misinterpreted his intentions and felt a bit the fool. I thought I knew him, but maybe he was like most of the other guys at my school. I was angry with myself as well as at Stuart but vowed to play it cool when I saw him at tennis.

When I boarded my bus the next day, my stomach was in knots. Terry walked with me to the bus stop and, though I enjoyed his company, I couldn't shake the niggling feeling that I was giving him a completely false sense of security because he'd lose to Stuart every time.

At the Central High stop, I forced myself to remain calm. Everything was fine, I told myself. I saw Grace and Stuart board the bus and my breath caught in my throat. I didn't relax until Grace sat down across from me with a huge smile instead of beside me.

Stuart plopped himself beside me, leaned over and kissed me, saying, "I missed you."

I was still angry but wondered if this was how grown-ups managed relationships. When I was mad at Mark, I gave him the cold shoulder or tried to pick a fight. This time, I held Stuart's hand when he reached for mine and laughed as

Grace recounted her hot Saturday night date with Tristan. As someone with a lot of experience with guys, Grace omitted any mention of how close Tristan and Terry were, and she waited until we were in the change room to begin prying into my phone call with Terry.

"Tristan seems to think you and Terry are going out next weekend. He even thought we could double date. What's going on, Cait?" she asked. "It looks to me like you're Stuart's girlfriend. He came and found me today at lunch to ask if you'd be at tennis."

"When Terry called Sunday I agreed to go out with him, but I'll have to find a way out of it now," I told her, finishing tying my laces and grabbing my racquet.

"But why did you agree to it in the first place? You had the perfect out that would make him feel like such an ass hat to get that pissed on Friday, even though he didn't know you weren't there. What would you have done if you were? Watched the boring hockey game while that idiot drank his face off?"

"Grace, hurry up, we're going to be late and I don't want Coach Adrian to make us run lines."

She planted her right fist on her hip and held her racquet like a cane as she stared at me.

"Okay! It was because I hadn't heard from him! You know what my past boyfriends have been like. I wasn't sure Stuart wanted to take it past that night, okay? I thought maybe he'd changed his mind."

"Oh, Caitie, he likes you—a lot," she said, walking over to me and putting her hand on mine. "I see the way he looks at you. I don't know why you're always so quick to think the worst of every situation. Just go with it. If you get hurt, so what? Maybe you'll end up hurting him. Did you ever think of that? Or maybe, just maybe, you'll both be happy for a very long time."

During our lesson, Stuart and I lingered around each other and we found ways to touch.

"Morissette, Taylor, separate courts!" Coach Adrian yelled at one point, which made me blush. When he got closer to me, he added, "I see the two of you and I've got an idea of what's going on. Leave it off the court. You're here to play tennis."

As the next few weeks went by, Stuart and I played by the teenage dating rules. I met his mother and sister.

"They seem normal, Stuart," I said to him afterwards.

"Yeah, that's how they get you," he replied. "The way a Stepford wife would."

He came to my house to pick me up and met my entire family. Matt told me he thought Stuart was a good guy, while Sarah, after giving him an appraising first glance, whispered, "I can see why you like him so much." My mother fawned over Stuart every time he arrived, trying to fix him sandwiches or a piece of pie. My father also seemed to like him. Stuart always addressed my father as *sir*.

Though we had become a couple only a few weeks beforehand, I felt like I'd known Stuart forever. I never tired of hearing about his thoughts and dreams, his childhood and what was going on at school or home, when he would talk about that. As we spent more time together, my qualms subsided, my self-doubt abated. Though he wasn't perfect, there was nothing I didn't like about him. He made me feel important, and when he looked at me with his intense gaze, I felt like I was the person who mattered most to him. Other boys I'd dated interrupted me, teased me about the way I looked and made thinly veiled jokes about getting naked.

Stuart was considerate, never joked about sex and always told me I was beautiful.

When I called Terry to tell him I wouldn't be going out with him the following weekend, he was pushy, trying to figure out why I'd changed my mind. I said I'd started dating someone else and he called me a slut. "That's a boy word," Stuart said when I later told him. I was falling in love.

We also spent time with Stuart's friends. I loved Brandon, who looked like a football player but was spectacularly uncoordinated. I wasn't so fond of Peyton, a snooty, privileged girl who spoke non-stop about an upcoming ski trip. She touched Stuart often and hugged him at every opportunity.

"Don't be jealous," Brandon said to me one night when we were at his house. "Stuart dated her a few times a long time ago, but he doesn't like her. She's doing that just to get on your nerves."

"It's a little weird, don't you think?"

"You're all he talks about."

Stuart and I were both swamped with school and family obligations in the weeks leading up to Christmas. I also worked extra shifts at my part-time job. Tennis lessons had wrapped up for the year but would resume in January. Without realizing it, a week had gone by without us seeing each other, though we talked on the phone almost every night.

A few days before school let out for the Christmas break, I was in the student council room and heard a knock on the door. I went to answer it and Terry sauntered in. His band would be performing in the school assembly the next day and he wanted to know when. I turned around to grab the list of the acts from a large table that had been pushed against the opposite wall. The student council room was the size of a closet—I could span my arms from one wall to the other.

"You really like that guy, eh?" Terry asked me as I turned back to face him.

"Stuart. And, yes, Terry, I do—a lot." I handed him the lineup so he could see where they had been slated. Though Terry was goofy and we'd been awkward with each other since the formal, I thought their band, set to play "Follow You Down" by the Gin Blossoms, was pretty great.

"Hey, Caitie, thanks for putting us last. I think you're awesome," he said, giving me a lopsided grin and thrusting his arm in an aw-shucks movement. "And, if you ever get tired of this guy, this *Stuart*, or if things don't work out, I'd like to date you. But I won't wait forever."

"All right," I said, laughing and rolling my eyes. "I appreciate it."

Terry and I were standing inches apart, so when I heard the door handle rattle, I jumped. I turned to see Heather come into the room. She gave me a quizzical look. Since the formal, Heather and Kevin had become inseparable, but it wasn't Kevin who was with her.

"Stuart," I said, my face breaking into a huge grin.

Stuart looked from me to Terry.

"Hey, Stuart," Terry said, smirking. "Good to meet you. I took Caitie to the fall formal."

"Yes, I know," Stuart said. "But she's not dating you."

I sucked in my breath. This was new. Stuart was usually affable and even-keeled, not prone to drama or anger. I found I loved this side of Stuart. He was jealous—but of what, I wasn't sure. We're now even, I thought, smiling on the inside, because as much as I tried not to let Peyton bother me, she did. I was, on some level, jealous of every girl who had hugged Stuart or kissed him or held hands with him, as irrational as that was. Heather's eyes widened, flicking between Stuart and Terry. The tension between the two was palpable. Terry looked over at me, still smirking.

"Caitie, I'm going to go. Thanks for *everything*," he said. Then he moved toward the door, in the process coming face-to-face with Stuart for a beat. Heather followed Terry out, but not before she turned back to look at me, her eyebrows raised, her lips upturned in a look of shock. I didn't say anything, too stunned to even formulate a sentence.

When the door shut, Stuart turned to me and smiled. He pulled me to him and when his lips found mine, I felt as exhilarated as I always did. "I had a break and since I hadn't seen you in a week, I figured I would come over here. I saw Heather outside and she sneaked me in."

"Everything okay?"

"Just busy. Things at home are the same. Nicole has finished exams, so she and my mom fight practically non-stop. Emma just got home last night and now the two of them aren't speaking to her either. My mom's always in a terrible mood this time of year," he said, rubbing his eyes with one hand as he held mine with his other.

"Was your mom always like this, Stuart?"

I complained about my family to Stuart, regaling him with tales about my mother's nosiness. But when I did, I felt like an idiot. Stuart was the one with real troubles. My mother seemed disinterested compared to Caroline, who wanted to know everywhere he went, who he was with and what time he'd be home. I was certain I'd heard the click of a receiver at least once when we were on the phone, as though she listened in on our conversations. Despite being so open about his problem with Caroline during our midnight chat at his house, it took a long time before he brought their issues up again, apart from the occasional, "Things are sometimes tough at home."

"It's hard to say because until I got to high school, I never noticed that my family was different from others—even for my friends whose parents are divorced. It wasn't until I noticed how Brandon's mom would just say, 'Okay, have a good time,' when we were going somewhere, or if she wanted to know what time we'd be back it was only because she wanted to have dinner ready. That's when I realized that's how it is at everyone else's house, and my home was the exception."

Stuart was a great conversationalist, but launching into a soliloquy was a rarity. When he did, I let him speak, not daring to break into his thoughts lest he think he couldn't trust me or that I didn't want to hear what he had to say. I did. He looked at me before continuing. I nodded, encouraging him.

"My mom was the same way with my dad. It's one of the reasons they got divorced. He calls me pretty often. And I have a phone card that I can use at a payphone to reach him in case I need to speak to him and can't get any privacy at home. I know she sometimes listens in on our conversations. But I'd rather hear your voice than hang up because of it. That's one reason why I don't like to talk too long on the phone."

"I'm sorry, Stuart," I said, my eyes full of worry.

"No, I'm sorry. I don't want to lay this all on you," he said, planting a kiss on my lips. "But I'm sure you'll understand why I've decided to go on that skiing trip Brandon and I were talking about last weekend. I leave Friday after school and I'll be back on the twenty-eighth. I'm sorry I won't be here for Christmas, but I'll see you as soon as I get back. Do you want your gift before I go—I could come see you tomorrow night—or when I get back?"

"Depends on what it is," I said, raising my eyebrows.

"Cait," he said, kissing me again. "Just say the word, and we will. I think about us that way all the time. But that wasn't what I was talking about."

"I'll wait until you get back," I said, pulling out of his embrace. I felt a bit of panic rise in my throat at the thought of being without him. I didn't want him to see my reaction, so I turned around and started tidying up some orphaned papers. "I can't believe you're going to be gone for eight days. I'll be stuck with my family the entire time. Well, Grace has promised we're going to go out. We'll probably find a party to go to, but she's kind of calmed down since she's been with Tristan. And I never see Heather anymore. She's always with Kevin. But, geesh, sorry! I'll miss you.

"If you wanted to stay here for Christmas, I know you'd be welcome at my house," I added. I turned back around to look at him, a sheaf of papers in my hand. He got up and moved toward the office door. "My dad would be thrilled to have you around, and my mom would fuss over you the likes of which you've never seen before. Matty and Sarah will be there—I swear he's going to propose. When I spell it out like that, it would actually be pretty great to have you there."

"I would love that, but it'd be worse for me if I was here and didn't spend Christmas with my mother," he said, leaning against the door. "I'd invite you to our house, but I can't stomach being there, so I know you'd have a terrible time. I mean it."

"Is Peyton going?" As soon as I asked, I wished I hadn't.

"I think she might be? Brandon's in charge of the guest list because it's his parents' cabin. Why?"

"It's just that she's constantly touching you. She finds any excuse to hug you. I hate it," I said, sounding pathetic and insecure and loathing myself for even caring about her.

"You're kidding, right?" he said, raising an eyebrow. "Listen, I have to go. I can't be alone in a room like this with you, which I'm sure we can lock, for much longer. But hear me when I tell you, it's you. It's always you for me."

six

FALL 2016

IN NIAGARA, summers pass quickly and this year was no exception. The boys took swimming lessons and spent a lot of time at their friend's house down the street while I logged overtime at Heusten Shoes. I also worked many weekends, which put a huge dent in our social plans. Rob, however, thrived at Cre8tive, and talk of a partnership was imminent, though that made life even more hectic because he also worked long hours. I was forced to call in his mother, Bridget, or Birdie as we called her, for reinforcement.

I cringed as I phoned her, expecting her to say no, that she was too busy to help.

"Of course I'll mind the boys," she said, and my jaw snapped open like the mouth of Aidan's toy hippopotamus.

And so the boys and Birdie developed their own routine. On Tuesday afternoons, she arrived at our house to take them to a fast food restaurant and then a movie. On Thursday mornings, she packed them up, along with towels, snacks and sunscreen, and took them to the beach and carousel at Lakeside Park. Rob's dad, Ken, and his wife, Sue, took the boys every second Friday for a sleepover, and Julie pitched in to cover the times when both Rob and I worked evenings.

Cre8tive had hired Rob just three weeks after we moved to St. Catharines. Since then, he'd worked his way up to executive director, moving through three promotions and pay increases, and he now oversaw a team of six. He loved his work and was good at it, so I wasn't surprised when talk of him becoming a partner resurfaced. The company's current partners, Ned Johnston and Ramona Mattick-Banks, had founded Cre8tive more than twenty years before. At last year's employee Christmas dinner at Ned's waterfront home, Ned and Ramona asked to speak with us after everyone else had left. They detailed Ned's exit plan and his interest in selling his ownership in the company to Rob, whom he had begun to think of as a son. Ned's own family was neither interested in design nor running a successful business.

I remembered Rob's face as we celebrated with a glass of Scotch. His eyes crinkled and seemed to shine; his laugh boomed. The ice cubes had clinked in my glass as I sipped my drink and thought, *He deserves this*. I was elated for him and when he looked at me, I saw gratitude and pride etched on his face. Since that conversation, Ned and Ramona had organized preliminary meetings between Rob and their lawyers to talk about costs and procedure.

By the fall, I settled into a comfortable routine at work. Some days, I enjoyed what I did. Though it was very different from being in design, the pace was similar and I liked the constant busyness. The major downside was

Trevor, who was becoming more insufferable by the day. He worried non-stop about profit margins and stock, which came from the warehouse either in droves, willy-nilly or sporadically. Some days, I spent hours in the backroom, trying to figure out if we had anything other than a size six in any shoe style. And Trevor, who was a stickler for order and precision, could be downright mean. One day, he made a new girl cry, after commenting on her facial acne. He also rankled Caleb.

"He told me I was too smart to work here," Caleb told me one day while we ate our lunch at the IKEA table in the backroom.

"You are," I said, giggling. But when I saw his face, I stopped. "You're brilliant, and once you get your degree, whatever it's about—don't even bother telling me because it sounds so complicated—you'll do great things."

"But he meant it as a put-down," Caleb said, not meeting my gaze. "Like, because he isn't as smart, he has to compensate by being mean."

"Ah, yes. Well, some men like him also have to compensate for many things, such as their height—or lack thereof. Just ignore him."

But I knew that was much easier to say than do. With his unyielding personality, Trevor required an inordinate amount of patience. Whatever I did wasn't good enough. He threatened to write me up for "fraternizing with the help," meaning being kind to anyone other than him. The schedule we'd discussed when I was hired was non-existent. There was no balance to when I worked. I was slated for an early morning shift one day and an evening shift the next. Once, Trevor had even "accidentally" scheduled me to work ten days in a row. He also made remarks about Stuart, trying to ascertain our past, though he guessed wrong every time. My secret was not that Stuart and I had worked together in another life and were plotting to have me replace Trevor.

I complained to Rob, but I could tell he was getting tired of hearing my work stories. I was, too. The last time I'd met up with Siobhan, she'd said, "If you're going to talk about your sorry-ass job, at least make it about Stuart. I don't want to hear one thing about Trevor. If you want, I'll call him up and ream him out for you."

"And then what would I do?"

"What are you talking about? You can do so much more than stacking boxes, Cait—so much more. Somewhere in that pretty little head of yours, you've allowed someone to let you think you can't."

My dissatisfaction with my work was causing tension at home. Rob wanted me to quit and work at Cre8tive. In theory, this made a lot of sense. They needed a junior designer, but the work would have been entry-level and my husband would then be my boss. That was a hard no.

Every day, I vowed to start writing again—my dreams of being a published author felt like puffs of cloud being carried along on a windy day. I spent most of my time at Heusten and was exhausted once I got home. I couldn't even muster the energy to turn on the computer. And then, I'd wake up every morning ruing the fact I hadn't at least attempted a word or two.

One gruelling day, I sold a pair of shoes with two right shoes. When the customer returned with them, laughing, about an hour later, Trevor was as sweet as could be until she left. He then berated me for being "such a disappointment."

"Caitlin," he sneered, after saying I couldn't take my

lunch hour as punishment for my folly, "you'll never climb higher if you can't even do this."

That night, I made it home in time to read the boys a bedtime story. Rob was working on a huge project for the provincial transportation ministry and his team had an impending deadline. I tucked them in bed, their little hands curled over their blankets, their eyes drowsy and their soft voices saying, "I love you." It almost made up for the shit show at work. I escaped down to my office once I knew they were asleep, but I just stared at the computer screen, tears running down my face.

I wiped them away and Googled *Stuart Taylor* on a whim, and the Internet spat back his beautiful face right away. I'd spoken to him on the phone a few times since we'd gone to Niagara Falls in July, and though he always asked if he could see me, I always said no, finding all kinds of excuses. I loved Rob. There was no question about that. He was a wonderful husband and I still enjoyed being intimate with him. I hated to admit, though, that our sex life had dwindled because of all the extra work lately—we were both too tired most nights, and Rob left the house by seven a.m., making sleep a far more desirable morning activity. But despite my love for Rob, I couldn't forget what it had felt like to be around Stuart that warm July day—the way his hand grazed my elbow, the way my cheek brushed against his when we embraced.

It was November, a day we projected to be busy because it marked the beginning of the store's annual half-off sale, and I was in a team meeting. Trevor was droning on about how we needed to be admirable in our duties to our customers and steadfast teammates to each other, when my phone vibrated for an incoming text message. Trevor hated being interrupted by a ringing cellphone. The month before, during a training session held on a Sunday night, Trevor had admonished a young mother when her cellphone rang.

"Are you stupid?" he roared at her.

She tried to apologize, saying it was her babysitter calling and she had just forgotten to put it on mute. Her son had fallen and cut his arm. I felt a little sick and a lot uncomfortable about the way he'd spoken to her. When she started to cry, I intervened to say we should take a quick break so she could call the sitter back, which earned me a terse directive following the meeting.

"Don't usurp my authority," Trevor had hissed at me after everyone left. Then he grabbed his wallet and keys and called over his shoulder, "You can lock up."

Now, with Trevor's attention elsewhere, I surreptitiously turned my phone over.

> **STUART**
> Hey, you in this morning?
>
> Yes, unfortunately listening to T yawn on self-importantly. Why?
>
> I'm nearly there. Bringing a couple mgrs with me. They're staying for a few hrs to work with Trevor. Want to skip out?

I felt a glow begin in the pit of my stomach that spread to my heart. A few minutes later, we heard the bell indicating someone had entered the store. Trevor looked annoyed at being interrupted but then propelled himself out of the backroom toward the front of the store. He'd been wrapped up in delivering a grand speech and hadn't noticed Caleb had fallen asleep. I nudged Caleb, who wiped the drool off his face, looking sheepish, while the others started laughing and imitating Trevor's self-importance. Though I should have reprimanded them, I didn't care enough. Trevor got everything he deserved and more. Plus, I was excited about Stuart's text and our impending time together. When I was with him, I felt like I was the centre of his universe, as though he once again had eyes only for me. I lapped up his charms and compliments.

Trevor returned, flustered, with Stuart and two other men, both around fifty, with slight paunches and dressed in dark business suits and navy ties.

"Well, team, today's our lucky day," he said, his chest puffed out, his shoulders back. "Richard McKinley and Gerard Sutherland are here from head office to help with the new Christmas display. Mr. Taylor, whom most of you have already met, is taking Caitlin off-site for some brainstorming and management activities. All right, everyone, let's get moving."

I gathered up my bag and slipped into my coat, grateful for the escape. I pulled on mitts and wrapped a scarf tight around my neck.

"So, where are we going this time?" I asked Stuart once we exited the store, a plume of icy air accompanying my words.

Christmas decorations had been installed the week before, and they made the mall, already upscale and modern looking, even more beautiful. Stuart wore a charcoal sport jacket with a crisp white shirt and dark grey tie, with jeans. He looked incredible. And, as we went outside the store, he pulled on leather gloves.

"Caitie, you look pretty," he said, looking at me. I looked down and was pleased to see I had worn my red, fitted coat, and not my ugly yet warm green ski jacket that I couldn't justify getting rid of simply because it was hideous. "Today, we're going where you want to go. We have four hours."

"Can't you get in trouble for being truant?" I asked him. "What are those guys going to say?"

"Do you think I care what Rick and Gerry think of me for taking you off-site for some training? I am the executive vice-president of Heusten Shoes Canada, and they work for me, first off. Secondly, my territory beat all sales projections by thirty per cent last quarter, and we still have the busiest season ahead of us. If I want to work with the woman who I think should be the next junior vice-president of the company, I don't think anyone would object, do you?"

"Really? You think I have that kind of potential?" I asked, trying to imagine myself as a corporate woman with my own office in a skyscraper in downtown Toronto. Siobhan would love it.

"If you want a job like that, I can arrange it, for sure. I remember how driven you were. It used to amaze me how hard you worked in every class and on every essay you had to hand in, while still finding time to work at that pub and have at least a bit of fun." We reached his car and he opened the passenger door for me, bending his head and planting a kiss on my cheek. "I've wanted to do that ever since you answered my text."

Stuart and I spent hours that day at a coffee shop on the outer rim of the outlet mall's property, talking about how our lives had unfolded after university. Neither of us skated anywhere near the frozen pond that represented our break-up. And, as much as I wanted to know, I couldn't (or wouldn't) break the ice by simply asking why he had left.

As Christmas neared and the busy holiday shopping

season ramped up, Stuart visited our store multiple times and I got the sense he was watching Trevor. To Stuart's face, Trevor acted the part of perfect manager. He certainly had the numbers to prove his store was not only doing well but exceeding all expectations. We were always busy. And when Stuart was around, Trevor spoke to us as a good boss would, praising our initiative and being patient when someone asked him to go over something. The real Trevor was condescending and cruel, and he created a fearful and mistrustful environment among staff. But he was also smart and knew when he needed to tone it down. He seemed to sense exactly where the line was and he would run up to it, stay along it for a while and then gently back off. When a part-timer was late because he had a flat tire, Trevor looked around to see who was listening before lowering his voice to tell the man it was disgraceful that a father couldn't adequately provide for his family. Then he suggested he might be able to earn extra money by working overtime.

 I debated whether to tell Stuart about Trevor. I didn't want to compromise our friendship or put Stuart in an awkward position. During our infrequent interactions, we rarely spoke about Heusten Shoes. If Stuart knew how much I disliked Trevor, he'd do something about it. And that felt too much like a high school student telling her daddy, the principal, that the math teacher was mean to her. I could fight my own battles. Rob had, thankfully, finished his project for the ministry, which helped the logistics of running our household. I worked overtime almost every night and I was even called in on my day off a couple of Fridays before Christmas when a part-timer quit without warning, saying she couldn't work for a dictator any longer. I couldn't blame her; Trevor was nearly out of his head with year-end figures and had taken on a manic sort of enthusiasm to get us to raise our numbers to increase our (his) bonus. But when he called, I considered quitting too. It was the night of Rob's staff Christmas party and I dreaded telling my husband I wouldn't be able to go. I had bought a new red dress just for the occasion and had lost fifteen pounds from my continued dedication to running. I hadn't felt this limber in years. It was as though my body, knowing it was finished bearing children, wanted to get back to being something I took pride in. I was even toying with the idea of signing up for a half-marathon clinic at a local running store in the New Year.

I knew I looked fantastic in the dress and I felt even better.

"It's because you know you could fuck him if you wanted to," Siobhan said while we shopped at the outlet mall. We had visited what felt like a thousand stores before we found the dress I was modelling.

"Siobhan!" I said, startled. "I'm not going to cheat on Rob. Jesus, I'm not even thinking about getting physical with Stuart."

"Are you sure?" she said, leaving me feeling a tad unhinged. "Caitie-cat, I'm your best friend. I knew you when you were with him, and I was there when he left. I remember what you went through. It's been the only time in my life when I actually worried about you. You weren't in a good place. I love Rob and your boys. I love those boys like they are my nephews. But you have unresolved business with Stuart. Besides, a little side fling never hurt anyone. And you say he still looks as good as he did in university?"

"Better," I said, blushing.

Before Trevor called, I'd been looking forward to

dressing up and spending the evening with Rob. Birdie was having the boys over at her house for a sleepover and gingerbread house-making adventure and they were excited beyond measure. I was full of dread when I called Rob.

"Don't be mad, but Trevor just called. A part-timer quit and the place is a madhouse. He said, and I quote, 'Caitlin, if you want to keep your job, you will come in tonight. I don't care what plans you've made. I'm nearly vomiting, I'm so sick and stressed,'" I related to Rob, imitating Trevor's inflections. Rob was quiet for a minute and I was about to repeat myself when he started talking.

"Caitie, I don't care if you quit your job. We don't need the money that bad, and it seems to be taking up a lot of your time," he said. "You just seem to be ready to rush off at a moment's notice for the store. Since you started working there, we've essentially stopped seeing most of our friends. And we haven't been out together in ages."

"So, it was okay that you worked late nearly every night because you had to finish the signage project for the ministry, but it's not okay that I have to work because it's nearly Christmas?" I asked, feeling anger rising.

"Well, it's not as if your job's all that important," he retorted. Then, realizing what he said, Rob tried to backpedal. "Caitlin, I'm sorry. That's not fair. I'm proud of you for working so hard. It couldn't have been easy to lose your job and then try to do something else."

"No, Rob, you're right, it wasn't. The fact is I feel humiliated most days. That should give you a clue as to how I really feel about my job," I said, stunned, trying to hold back tears. "You've never made me feel small—until now. I haven't had a chance to talk to you, but upper management has even hinted I might be in line for an executive position at head office."

"And who told you this?" Rob interrupted.

"Well, a manager who comes into our store every once in a while," I stammered. "Would that mean my work was worthwhile then? Listen, I've got to go. I'm going to try and forget you said what you did and, if I'm finished early enough, I'll text you and meet you. I was really looking forward to tonight."

"I'm sorry, Cait."

"I've gotta go. I'll talk to you later," I said, hanging up. I looked at the receiver, wondering if I should have asked him before what he thought about my job. When I left London for Ottawa at nineteen, I was taking the first step in what would be an exciting and successful life. I followed the plan and believed the middle class lie that if you got good grades and went to university, you'd get a good job and things would work out just fine. After university, each change I made felt as though I was moving up—I was taking a series of steps that would culminate in an illustrious career. It's how we ended up in St. Catharines. When I was hired at The Leg, I really felt that I had arrived at a great place. That I now found myself fetching shoes, ringing up purchases and smiling until my cheeks hurt was soul-sucking at times. And, until that moment, I had no idea Rob might also be slightly embarrassed by my work or that he thought what I did was trivial. I didn't view Stuart's path to Heusten Shoes as similar to mine. His role was important and the company depended on his efforts. I depended on the company's money and was ashamed of that.

When I arrived at the store, Trevor was nowhere to be seen. Caleb scurried between customers and the backroom, porting different sizes, colours and styles. Mateo and Keegan, a pair of new hires, worked cash, the line meandering throughout the entire roped-off area. I was trying to decide where I could provide the most relief when I saw two other sales associates come out from the backroom, carrying shoes. I threw my coat and my red dress, ensconced in its garment bag, in the backroom, along with my pewter, high-heeled shoes, which I'd bought with my discount, and my purse. I sped back to the front of the store and opened another till. I could almost hear a sigh of relief from Mateo, Keegan and the customers.

"Where's Trevor?" I asked Mateo.

"Sick in the bathroom."

"You've got to be kidding," I said, collecting a harried-looking woman's credit card and inserting it into the card reader. "He told me he wasn't feeling well when he called me in, but I thought it was just his imagination."

"I can see why you would think that. The man is melodrama personified," Mateo said, "but he's really sick. He's even called in another manager to relieve him."

We worked steadily for the next hour. Trevor staggered to the front of the store about twenty minutes after I arrived, begging off, echoing Mateo's words that someone would be in soon to help. And then, as dinnertime arrived, the crowds started to dispel. I sent Mateo and Keegan for a break and, as I started to help Caleb clean up, Stuart walked into the store. I straightened up, boxes perched precariously in my arms. He came over to me.

"He called *you*?" I asked him.

"Would you want someone else?" he asked, smiling a crooked smile. "You look lovely—are you going somewhere afterwards?"

"Actually, I'm missing my husband's office Christmas party right now," I said, as he took a couple of the boxes I was holding and followed me to the back. "I'm hoping to meet up with him later if I can get out of here early enough."

"We can try our best," he said.

We continued to be swamped with customers. By seven, when Stuart insisted I finally take a break, I checked my phone. Rob had sent me numerous texts. One said Ned and Ramona sent their regards; another, that dinner was about to start; and a third, with one word: *Sorry*. At that moment, I missed him and wished I were with him, my handsome husband.

Rob was wonderful at parties, a natural conversationalist. He was the guy you wanted at your table. When we first dated, I never worried about us going to a party where he knew only me, despite his initial shyness. After twenty minutes, he'd be engrossed in conversation with a gaggle of people, learning all about them. I felt a spike of anger, knowing I was missing out on a gourmet, four-course menu. Cre8tive skimped on nothing. Its Christmas parties were legendary and not in the vein of most office parties, where stories detailing how drunk everyone got and who made a fool of themselves on the karaoke machine were related for weeks afterwards. The Cre8tive Christmas dinner was a class act from beginning to end, and it was the best meal some employees would have all year.

> Miss you. Wish I was there. Place is a madhouse. I'll text you when I'm done but I'm thinking 11 at the earliest xo

> **ROB**
> We might hit the Merchant Ale House then. Come if you can. I understand. Sorry I was such an ass. Xox

> You have a nice ass, but you're not an ass. Red dress might be a bit much. Will let you know.

Finally, after the last customer left at nine-thirty, I surveyed the damage. Boxes were scattered everywhere. I told Mateo and Keegan that after they counted their tills they could go. They were so grateful they didn't complain about it already being late. I knew they were dating—the whole store was aware of it when they'd broken up two weeks before and Keegan came to work with puffy red eyes. We were relieved when they got back together earlier this week, if only because we wouldn't have a drama to deal with on top of the relentless busyness.

Stuart worked on some paperwork as I helped Caleb locate matching pairs to an endless stream of single shoes. At ten, I told Caleb and the other remaining staff to go so they could still have some fun. It was Friday and some of them, like Caleb, were studying for their finals and needed a break from hitting the books or time to sleep.

"I'll stay and help you," Stuart said.

"Thanks."

We worked in silence, trying to get everything into place as quickly as possible. I was still holding out hope that I'd be able to get dressed and meet Rob wherever he and his colleagues were headed. But being alone with Stuart also distracted me. He had taken off his jacket and rolled up his sleeves. Every once in a while, I'd catch a glimpse of his forearms, his muscles taut, reminding me of how they used to look as he held himself above me.

"I think we're done," he said, as the clock neared eleven. "I think we can go."

"Okay, I've just got to slip to the back for a few minutes and get ready to meet Rob," I said, scurrying off, but not without first noting the look that crossed Stuart's face. I grabbed the garment bag and headed into the bathroom, quickly exchanging my cotton bra for a lacier one that would tastefully hint from beneath the red material.

"God, Caitie, you could be a little adventurous," Siobhan had said when I asked her about the dress. She was right. I was a thirty-eight–year-old woman, not eighty. I pulled the dress over my head, brushed my newly highlighted hair into a tight ponytail, thankful it was ramrod straight, which was now the style, and quickly re-applied my lipstick. My makeup, which I had applied before I ran out of the house, seemed to have held. I checked my look in the mirror, gave a nod and then raced out of the bathroom. I grabbed my bag and coat and started walking to the front of the store just as my phone pinged.

> ROB
> Going to Merchant Ale House. Coming? Or too dressy?

> I'm waay too dressy. Super disappointed. Have fun! I'll head home.

Deflated and feeling cheated, I slumped the rest of the way to the front of the store. Stuart, who had turned off all the lights except for the emergency lights, waited.

"I wanted to make sure you made it safely to your car," he said, standing up from where he'd been sitting. He put his phone away and looked at me. "Wow, Caitie, you look amazing. Where are you off to?"

"Nowhere now," I said, my voice catching. I steeled myself not to cry. "I was hoping to meet Rob, but they've decided to go to a pub. I'm far too overdressed for that. I'd feel stupid, so I'm just going to go home."

"Oh, no you're not. You have a sitter?"

"Yes, my mother-in-law has the boys at her house. They've all likely gone to bed now. The kids wipe her out."

"Brilliant," he said, walking over to where I stood to take my bag, which carried my work clothes, and helping me into my coat. "Caitlin, that dress is stunning. I remember the first time I saw you in a red dress. You look even better tonight. I'm taking you out for a drink. You can't possibly go home without showing it off first."

"Okay, but let's go somewhere I won't bump into anyone," I said. Then, realizing what I'd said, I tried to recover. "I mean, I don't want to have to answer any questions."

"I knew what you meant. If you want, we can go to Toronto, but it might be easier to find someplace here. I'm staying at a hotel in Niagara Falls, actually. I figured I'd have to cover for Mr. Proper tomorrow as well and didn't want the burden of driving back and forth twice." His face was shaded and I was flooded with illicit feelings.

He looked at me expectantly, likely waiting for me to object, to further explain what I meant, that if I saw someone I knew, I'd be able to simply explain the drink away. But I could feel myself being pulled into Stuart's vortex, just as I always had. Since being let go from Legandcy, I often felt like a failure, that my life was unexciting and mundane. Stuart's attention was the elixir I needed.

"Let's go," I said, smiling.

We drove separately to the trendy, upscale bar attached to the Sterling Inn, a boutique hotel Stuart had chosen because of its proximity to the Falls. He said he was planning to walk down to the water to see what it looked like at night. I told him there was no way I was going to the Falls wearing a dress. The mist would be bone-chilling. The hotel's restaurant was sleek and modern, with red padded walls and cozy banquettes. Though the room was busy, it wasn't packed and we were able to find a banquette to ourselves toward the back of the restaurant. It felt oddly thrilling to be snuggled away with someone who was not Rob. I kept telling myself I was doing nothing wrong.

When the waitress arrived, Stuart ordered a whiskey smash, while I ordered a black current martini.

"You drink now?" I asked him.

"I like a cocktail once in a while," he said, "but I'm still not what you would call a drinker. Only on very rare occasions."

One of the things I had loved about being with Stuart was that although he didn't drink alcohol, he didn't care that I occasionally found myself on the losing end of a sober night. He never criticized me for it; the one time I forced him to pull over at the side of the road to be sick, he had held my hair out of my face. When we were together, it was refreshing to know he would never be like other guys, who spent their weekdays looking forward to getting smashed on weekends, and then, instead of getting out and doing things on Saturday, used the entire day to sleep it off and recover in time for the next go that night. Even now, I could hardly stand it when some of my friends' husbands got drunk every weekend. Rob and I laughed about how they stood around, fingering their rotund bellies like pregnant women, smelling of beer and leering at other men's wives.

"I always liked that about you," I said.

"I liked most things about you," he said, his gaze lingering on my face. "I can't get over how beautiful you are tonight. Look, I'm not sorry you're here with me, but I am sorry you couldn't have the night out you wanted, that you had to miss the party. I remember what a drag it was for Erin, my ex-wife, when the sitter would cancel or our plans got postponed. She stayed at home to raise Paisley and at first she enjoyed it but then grew bitter. The more unhappy she got, the more we fought, until it was non-stop and she said she wanted a divorce. By that time, I had worked my way up to CEO of Earth Threads, a small start-up clothing chain in Toronto, and had just got headhunted to work with Heusten."

"And now?" I asked, curious about this woman he had loved. I felt irrationally enraged and jealous as he spoke about her. And the absurdity of the situation hit me at the same time. I was the married one. I was going home to someone else tonight.

"She's remarried—I told you that, I think," he said. I nodded but didn't say anything. "She just opened a cupcake store. It's doing great and she seems much happier. I'm thrilled for her and I really like her husband, Gregg—with two g's."

"What was it like to get divorced?" I asked, drinking a mouthful of my cocktail. I felt the alcohol moving through my system, calming me.

"Awful. It felt like my world was ending. But not because

Erin and I weren't going to be together. We hadn't been together in a long time. The relationship had ended. That was just when the divorce showed up," he said. "But I miss Paisley a lot. And if I have to travel for business, sometimes Erin isn't able to switch weekends so I miss having Paisley at my place. Erin is great about visitation—she doesn't pull any of those tricks you sometimes hear about. I remember when we discussed getting divorced. It was at our kitchen table. It was a Tuesday night and we were having tea, like we would have done any other night, as though talking about the divorce was no big deal. She said she wouldn't play visitation games. She knew how devoted I was to Paisley, and she wanted that to continue. We went to see a lawyer together, split everything down the middle and walked out of a courtroom a few months later, uncoupled. But there's something incredibly sad about that as well. I sometimes wonder, had Erin been working, had she been busy outside the home, would we have stayed married? It still would have been the wrong decision, but it's so easy just to go along with things. It's easier, in fact."

"And now? Is there anyone special?"

"I've dated, but no, there's no one else," he said.

We continued talking about his life and a little about my family life. His father had retired, and his stepmother had sold her boutique, so they spent most of their time travelling and doing charity work in Boston. Emma now lived in BC and had four children. Nicole was married with a girl Paisley's age in a small town outside London. Stuart's mother still lived in their childhood house and they didn't see each other a lot. Stuart's half-brother was a lawyer in Boston, working at his father's old firm, while his half-sister was completing her PhD.

I told him about Siobhan and Mike. Grace had married an Englishman whom she met when she went overseas for a semester in university, but they didn't have kids. Heather was married and they lived out East with their two kids. Stuart steered away from asking about Rob, though he inquired about my boys.

"I'll walk you to your car. You never know who's out there at this time of night," he said, as he paid the bill. We gathered our coats and walked to the hotel's front lobby.

"I don't think I need to worry about a stranger walking by, Stuart," I said, playfully. "It's just you I need to keep my eye out for."

"That's true, Caitie," he said, taking my hand. Sitting with him in the banquette had transported me to the many times we had lain awake all night, talking. I remembered how we discussed our families and our goals and dreams, so many of which revolved around us, together. I linked my fingers with his and felt him pull me toward his side, a reflex awakened from a long slumber.

When we reached my car, I felt as though all the years we had been apart had evaporated. I felt as though I was in my early twenties, loved ferociously by the man who now stood beside me. I wasn't thinking about Rob or my boys. I was thinking only of how Stuart made me feel—wanted, loved, cherished and desired.

"Stuart," I said, nearly breathless. I turned to face him and I knew he was feeling the same thing I was.

"Caitie," he whispered, slipping his hand behind my neck, pulling me toward him.

seven

DECEMBER 1996

CHRISTMAS LIGHTS WHIRRED BY. The rush of wind on my face thrilled me. But each time I glanced over at Grace and Tristan and caught them holding hands while gliding, or embracing, I felt a pang for Stuart. We were skating at the outdoor rink in Victoria Park, in downtown London. Grace had begged me to join her and Tristan and, despite her best efforts to include me, I felt like a third wheel.

Stuart called from Brandon's parents' villa in Mont-Tremblant, Quebec, after they'd finished skiing the day before. I heard other voices in the background and tried not to let Peyton's bother me.

"We're having a great time," Stuart said, "but I miss you."

"I miss you, too. Matt and Sarah got engaged. All anyone's talking about is the upcoming wedding. You should see my mom. She ran out to the stores today just to get some wedding magazines. Forget the fact that it's the first time stores are open on Boxing Day and she was so against that. Just like she didn't agree with Sunday shopping."

"Tell them congratulations for me and I'll see you soon," he said, laughing, and he hung up.

When Sarah showed our family the diamond ring Matt had given her on Christmas Day, I enveloped her in a tight hug as I fought back tears. At that moment, I was so happy for my brother. I was also surprised when my thoughts flipped to Stuart. I couldn't help but wonder if I would be the one he gave an engagement ring to someday.

After hearing three days of wedding talk, I bolted out the door the morning of the twenty-ninth. Stuart was due home the night before. I grabbed the Christmas gifts I'd selected for him—a couple of books he'd wanted and a new wallet, the only presents still unwrapped under our tree—along with my parents' gift for him, which was Eternity for Men, and jumped into my dad's Volvo. I drove over to his house, giddy with anticipation and longing. Once I'd parked, I skipped up the walkway to his front door. I'd discovered who the family's green thumb was—his mother had filled with greenery two giant urns that stood sentry on the porch. The door boasted a garland wreath ablaze with red berries. The effect was something one might see in a designer magazine. I knocked on the door, smile ready. But it was his mother who answered.

"Caitlin, how nice to see you," she said. "Come in. Did you have a Merry Christmas?"

"I did, Mrs. Taylor. How about you?" When I entered the foyer, I could tell something was amiss. It felt like I'd interrupted something, but I couldn't quite put my finger on it. Stuart rose from the kitchen table.

"Cait," he said, grinning. He walked over to where I stood, immobile, and wrapped his arms around me. He kissed my cheek and whispered, "I missed you a lot."

"What's going on?" I whispered. "Should I leave? I thought I'd surprise you."

Stuart turned to his mother, who had moved into the kitchen to at least appear as though she was giving us some privacy, and announced we were going for a walk. She pursed her lips but said nothing. I put his gifts down on a chair in the living room and waited while he located his coat, gloves and hat.

We walked down his driveway in silence and Stuart took my hand in his gloved hand. I didn't want to force him to tell me what was going on. I figured he'd speak when he was ready. We turned right at the end of his street, and he picked up his pace. It was the cruel irony that is winter—a sunny sky tricking you into thinking it's beautiful out, but it's so cold that your nose hairs freeze as soon as you go outside. Thanks to my mom, I'd worn warm gloves and a hat.

We continued down the street, which would be resplendent and tree-lined in summer, and came to a wall constructed of old stone, just outside the university gates.

"Go in," he said, gesturing to a gap in the wall, which seemed to be a door of sorts. I moved ahead of him, having no idea where we were going, and stepped into a tiny, circular stone gazebo. Stuart followed me inside and pulled me to him, kissing me passionately.

"Well, hello," I teased when we broke apart.

"God, Caitie, I missed you. I thought of you every day. I couldn't wait to leave, actually, so I could come back to you."

"I missed you, too," I said, sitting down on a little wooden bench opposite the wall from where we entered the gazebo. I rubbed my mitts together to keep warm. Stuart sat beside me, placing his large, gloved hands around mine. "I don't want you to take this the wrong way, but couldn't we have just sneaked off to your living room downstairs? It's freezing. Why are we here?"

As Stuart spoke, my heart broke. He and Brandon had arrived home more than two hours late because of a snowstorm outside Ottawa. After seeing several cars in ditches, Brandon, who had driven most of the way, stayed under the speed limit.

"My mom was livid," Stuart said. "When Brandon dropped me off, she was staring out the living room window. She didn't wave. She didn't offer to come help bring in my bags. She didn't open the door and welcome us home. Brandon even asked if I wanted to go to his house to avoid her wrath. As soon as I got inside, she started on me for being late, how worried she was, how much like my father I'm becoming, so inconsiderate, so selfish. A good son would never leave his mother on Christmas Day to go skiing with friends, and on and on."

Not only was I saddened by what Stuart said, my cheeks flushed with indignation. He was the opposite of what his mother saw. He was so considerate and, as I'd heard my mother say several times, he was like Matty—her idea of a perfect son.

"I suppose it didn't help that I showed up," I said, leaning my back against his chest. He wrapped his arms around me, burrowing his face in my neck.

"I'm thrilled. Your timing was impeccable. She'd just started round two of how I am the worst son in the world.

Me leaving will take the wind out of her sails. Plus, when we go back, she'll be gone," he said, sighing. "She has a lunch party to go to. She won't want to be flustered when she shows up."

I enjoyed the feel of him for a moment, hoping I gave him some comfort, too, and then asked, "What is this place?"

"That's a good tale. Apparently, the guy who owned the house over there, you know the one you can see when you drive by the university on the way to my house? He built this gazebo for his young wife. They'd come out here when they wanted to be alone outdoors, and he built it out of brick so they could do as they pleased and no one could see them." He raised one eyebrow as he looked at me.

I giggled as we melded together. The cold burning sensation in my fingers, though, soon became impossible to ignore. I didn't say anything, not wanting to break the mood, but Stuart noticed me shivering. We got up and left the gazebo, walking with our arms around each other, retracing our steps. But when we rounded the corner to his house, I felt Stuart stiffen. His mother's car was still in the driveway.

"Shit," he said, dropping his arm from around my waist.

As we walked toward his front door, I told him I'd just go and see him later. Distracted, he leaned over to kiss me just as I saw a curtain move in the living room window. I waved as he opened the front door and he gave me a tight smile. It wasn't until I reached the end of his road on my way home that I realized he'd forgotten to give me my present and his gifts were still on the living room armchair.

Later that night, Stuart called to apologize. "I found the presents you brought after I got in, but I didn't open them.

And yours is still here," he said, with a sigh. "I'm really sorry for this morning. I thought the break would have been good for both of us. We're in such a routine of arguing and fighting that she doesn't know how else to treat me. It's exhausting. To be honest, I have no idea how to fix it. I keep my room tidy. I do my own laundry. My grades are okay—they're not straight A's, but they're good enough for university—and I'm always home when I'm supposed to be home. I don't even drink. Listen, Emma's gone back to Alberta, and my mom and Nicole are going to visit her sister in Kingston this weekend. We're supposed to be going to Brandon's party for New Year's, but why don't you stay the night?"

Grace asked every time she saw me why Stuart and I hadn't slept together yet. I couldn't explain why we hadn't except it hadn't felt right. I wanted to, and I knew he did, too, but I was nervous. He'd been with a couple of girls before me. One, he said, was mutual experimentation. The other was an ex-girlfriend he cared about, but she had moved away and neither wanted to put any effort into trying to keep it going. I was also afraid it would change everything. Grace said I was full of crap, that sex didn't change a relationship, but I didn't believe her. Since she and Tristan had started sleeping together, she wasn't as ready to make plans in case he might be available. She went to all his football games. And now that it was basketball season, she wasn't at just his games—she'd hurry over to our gym to make it in time for his practices, too. Before, we laughed at girlfriends who watched every practice and game on the sidelines with no clue about what was happening on the field or court. Now she was one of them. (Not that I mentioned this.)

Heather and Grace never tired of detailing every experience they had, but I couldn't talk about our intimacy. I refused to cheapen our words or touches or expose our secrets. I couldn't tolerate others knowing where Stuart was ticklish (his left shoulder blade) or how he got the scar above his right eyebrow. I'd asked him about it when we started dating, but he said he'd tell me only if we married. Eventually, I wore him down and he said he got it while snowboarding when he got hit in the face with a friend's snowboard.

"That's it?" I said, laughing. "Why are you so secretive about that?"

"I didn't want you to think I was a loser. I really just stood there and watched the board hit my face. Can you believe that?"

I could, and each time I thought of it, a warm glow radiated throughout me and I chuckled. I knew I was one of only a few people who knew these things about him and I kept those tidbits close to my heart.

"I'll tell my parents I'm staying at Grace's," I said.

"I'll pick you up at seven."

The next few days flew by. Grace was beside herself at my pending overnight stay at Stuart's, and we came up with a viable cover story. Being virtuous has its advantages. My parents wouldn't think I was sleeping anywhere but Grace's, and her parents would believe I'd gone home sick. We kept it simple because I didn't want to create any snags in the plan. I was a jumble of nerves as it was. I knew Stuart had zero expectations by inviting me to stay the night. But I knew I was ready.

On New Year's Eve, Stuart arrived with a bottle of wine for my parents. He wasn't legal drinking age yet, but for some reason, he never got carded at the liquor store. I told him it was because he needed to ask a staff member for their take on a good bottle of wine, and no one underage would be stupid enough to ask for help.

"Happy New Year, Mrs. Morissette, sir," he said, handing them the bottle. Stuart shook hands with my brother and gave Sarah a hug. "Hey, congratulations, you guys. Caitie told me your good news. That's awesome."

I watched all of this play out from the top of our stairs that led into the living room from our upstairs bedrooms. I had spent an hour getting ready, standing in front of my mirror, hoping Stuart would find me sexy. He told me I was beautiful all the time, but sexy is a whole different level. I wanted him to find me desirable. I wore a blue, skintight dress to show off my toned, athletic body. My hair was down and I wore little makeup because it was neither my style nor Stuart's preference.

He flashed me a huge smile as I reached the bottom stairs. The way he looked at me was the way I wanted him to look at me, with full-on longing and—even though we hadn't said it yet—love.

"Caitlin, do you have enough room in that dress?" my dad barked before my mom shushed him.

Matt gave Stuart a look that said, "I like you, but if you fuck this up, I'll hurt you," as Sarah winked at me and told me I looked beautiful.

"I'm speechless," Stuart said, moving forward to take my hand and kiss my cheek. "I'll be the most envied guy at the party tonight," he whispered, as he helped me into my coat. He took my overnight bag from me and said goodbye to my parents. It mattered to me that Stuart kissed me, albeit chastely, in front of my parents. We didn't hide how we felt about each other around adults. Our romance wasn't childish or immature.

Once inside Stuart's car, he turned to me as he put the key in the ignition.

"Holy shit, Cait, I don't think I want to go to the party. Can we just go to my house and fool around all night? Honestly, you are so gorgeous."

"As much as I want to, I won't be that couple everyone talks about when they're late because everyone knows what they've been doing—you know, like Dana and Scott," I said, laughing. "Drive, Stuart. Take me to the party."

And I was glad we went. Brandon and I had grown close, and I really liked their other good friends, Mackenzie and her boyfriend, Quinn, who went to Queen's University in Kingston, a five-hour drive from London. There, he studied engineering and did little else. Mackenzie amazed Grace and me. She was so mature, dating someone who was twenty. Their long-distance relationship didn't bother either of them.

"If he was here, I wouldn't see him any more than I do," she said. "Engineering's a bitch."

Peyton hugged Stuart a little too long when we first arrived and gave me a fake smile before turning away as Stuart kissed me, his way of sending her a message. I had forced myself to not ask Stuart about Peyton at all, and I didn't press for details when I found out something had happened during the ski trip.

"You don't need to worry about Peyton, Cait. Stuart really put her in her place one night," Mackenzie told me the day before, when I called to see what we could bring to the party. She was the evening's social convener. "Just get Stuart to bring some vodka. Maybe he'll get carded."

Despite the wonderful spread Mackenzie had organized, I couldn't eat much and I didn't want to drink either. We counted down to 1997, yelled "Happy New Year!" and then hugged others around us. Stuart and I became separated by the throng of people, but a few minutes later, he looked at me from across the room. He made his way toward me, shaking hands and hugging everyone, wishing them "Happy New Year" and fending off the "no, stay longer" calls. I said my goodbyes and went down a hallway to find Grace to let her know we were leaving. She hugged me tightly, kissed my cheek and told me to "have fun, but don't let him come too soon," before trekking off to find Tristan. I was walking back down the hallway when Peyton stepped out of the bathroom.

"I loved him, and he loved me. If you think he's going to stay with you forever, you're kidding yourself," she said, slurring her words. "Eventually, his mother will be too much for him to handle. He'll pull away and leave you, just like he left me."

I knew she was lying about them being in love. One night after we'd eaten dinner at a Chinese restaurant downtown, Stuart insisted I tell him what was bothering me. I wrung my hands together. I didn't want to pry, but curiosity and, to be honest, insecurity, had gotten to me. I begged him to tell me the truth about Peyton. Their relationship, if you could call it that, had lasted all of two months, one of which she was away for. He said they'd broken up because she wasn't his type, but I figured the real reason they split was because she was a cold, heartless bitch who looked down her nose at everyone and loved to stir up trouble.

"Good night, Peyton," I said to her now, darting away from her and into the living room, to where Stuart waited.

She'd said they were in love just to unnerve me. But the part about his mother felt like a dire warning.

"You okay?" he asked me as I reached the front door. Brandon had followed Stuart to the door—always the good host—and was trying to find our coats. He looked as though he was losing a fight against a stuffed closet. Eventually, with Stuart's help, Brandon extricated our coats from the mess. Stuart raised an eybrow just before he held open my coat and I turned around to put my arms in the sleeves.

Bundled up, Brandon hugged me and wished me a happy new year.

"Hey, don't worry about her," he whispered, as we separated. "I saw her come out of the bathroom. She's drunk. I'm not sure why, because it's been ages, but she still likes Stuart. But when we were away, he actually told her that you were his girl. Yes, *his girl*. I died laughing. That sounds so 1960s. So don't let her ruin your night."

"I won't," I promised, hugging him one more time. "Happy New Year. And thanks for also inviting Grace and Tristan, wherever they are now. I'm sorry if you have to wash the sheets."

Brandon rolled his eyes and laughed as Stuart gave him some sort of man-hug, and we headed out into the frigid night. I huddled close to Stuart as we walked back to his car, my legs freezing in my tights, the midnight black sky freckled with stars.

When we arrived at his house, a soft glow from the Christmas lights Stuart had hung on the eavestrough felt warm and inviting. I released a sigh of relief that we were the only ones there. I'd worried that we'd pull in only to discover his mother and Nicole waiting to wish Stuart a happy new year. In that instance, he would have needed to do a lot of explaining. I'd once overheard Caroline say to him, when she thought I couldn't hear, that I'd better not end up pregnant, before he shushed her with a firm, "Mother, enough!"

He unlocked the door, turned on a lamp on the side table and then closed and locked the door. I reached for him and it was as though neither of us could wait any longer. He nudged me up against the wall and began taking off my coat. He kissed me, smiling, teasing. He stripped off his coat, letting it fall to the floor. He took my hand, walking backwards to the living room. I followed. I helped him delicately pull my dress over my head and we lay down on the carpet. He took his time as he removed my tights, kissing my stomach, then near my collarbone, as his fingers traced my cheek. I wanted to be with Stuart this way but was nervous and tense. He must have sensed it because he asked, "What's the matter? Are you okay with this?"

"Stuart, why do you like me?"

Shit, I thought. I couldn't believe that had slipped out. I was mortified to be speaking. Every movie I'd ever watched where characters were getting ready for sex, the scene involved some hot and heavy panting. They didn't carry on conversations and I wasn't sure if I should either.

He stopped and propped himself up on his elbow, his eyes hooded by the dim light. He kissed me before saying, "I don't just like you, Caitlin, I love you."

A warm feeling glowed in my stomach. He'd said it. All the times I imagined how he would sound, saying those three words, was nothing compared to the complete rapture I now felt. Goosebumps travelled up my arms and I held my breath.

"I've never met anyone like you. You're confident, you're

ambitious, you work so hard at school." The look he gave me was full of pride. "And at tennis? Holy crap, you should see how you concentrate, how you try to hit the ball harder than anyone else. You just care about stuff. You're beautiful. I love your brown eyes, your little nose, and your cowlick, here," he said, touching my forehead. "Caitie, I love you. If you're ready and want to move forward, we will. If not, we'll wait. But I'm ready because I know I love you more than I've ever loved anyone else."

I was speechless. There were so many things I wanted to say but couldn't. I felt tears prick my eyes. I had once asked my former boyfriend, Mark, what he liked about me and he shrugged and said, "I don't know. You're kinda smart." Stuart *knew* me. And he loved *me*.

His words broke my vacillation. I pulled his sweater over his head and unbuckled his belt so he could shimmy out of his pants. He reached up to the couch and grabbed a blanket that we'd snuggled under many times to hide what our hands would now do to each other out in the open. I helped him spread out the blanket, and I lay down on top of it. He lay beside me, and I took time to survey him. I'd seen him naked before but he looked different tonight—the way his hipbones angled, his flat stomach, the way the hair curled around his penis. As I touched him, he watched me, with patience, allowing me to explore. I was suddenly grateful this first experience would be with Stuart, who had my entire heart. I'd heard so many stories—I wasn't sure how many were true—about first times. Most of them sounded like nightmares. Stuart took time to explore my breasts with his mouth, his fingers running up the inside of my thigh. He was backlit by the soft white light of the Christmas tree. The house was silent and I heard him sigh.

"I love you, Caitlin," he whispered.

"I love you, too, Stuart," I said.

A few moments later, I heard him tear open a package and felt him getting ready. He propped himself up on his elbows. Then he looked deep into my eyes. I nodded, staring back at him, wordlessly giving him permission, and I felt him push himself inside me. It was uncomfortable, painful almost, but right. I was overwhelmed. Not only was I filled up with his words—they said everything I felt—but the sense of him inside me was incredible—so intimate, so perfect. He kissed me tenderly at first, and then more passionately, his rhythm quickening. After he came, he caressed my face with his hands.

"I love you," he whispered, nudging my lips with his, remaining like that for a moment. "I am so in love with you."

"I love you, too," I whispered as I looked into his eyes, knowing he had captured a piece of my soul and I felt closer to him at that moment than I could have ever thought possible.

After that night, Stuart and I lived in a haze of bliss, a cocoon of our own making, where nothing existed outside the thin membrane. Every weekend was highlighted by a romantic dinner, going to the movies or hanging out with our friends. We spent hours hiding away, having sex, exploring a wild and passionate side of our relationship. When Stuart said he loved me for who I was, I knew he was telling the truth. That is an all-encompassing and engrossing feeling when you're almost eighteen, a vast departure from the usual feeling that everyone is judging you—because they are.

People at school made comments about my relationship with Stuart—about its intensity, about how devoted I seemed to be. In my eyes, these people were just opinionated, mean-spirited or just downright jealous. Stuart didn't demand my time. I gave it of my own accord. I wanted to spend so much time with him because he was one of the few people who *got* me.

When Valentine's Day rolled around, we joined Grace and Tristan, as well as Heather and Peter, her new boyfriend, at my school's annual Hearts Dance. We also joined them for a pre-dance dinner and then went to Terry's for the after-party. When Terry welcomed us into his house, I couldn't help but notice Stuart look sideways at him. Terry gave Stuart a lopsided smile before giving him a complicated kind of hand slap. We stayed for a couple of drinks and then Stuart and I left for his house—his mother was away again—and we spent the night and the next morning in bed.

A few weeks later, Grace hopped on the city bus alone when it stopped at Central, en route to tennis.

"Where's Stuart?" I asked her when she reached our usual seats at the back of the bus.

"Don't know. He was at school today. Maybe he went home sick?" she said, leaning down to hug me.

Since we were Stuart-less, we sat side by side, talking about the upcoming school break. Grace and Tristan, along with some of his friends, were going skiing in Quebec, near Brandon's parents' chalet. Grace was so excited she kept interrupting herself. Tristan would also celebrate his eighteenth birthday there, and she kept reminding me that he would now be able to buy booze without a fake ID. I listened, a tad envious that I wasn't going away with Stuart.

We hadn't made any March Break plans and he was vague when I asked him if he wanted to do something that week. Now, we couldn't join our friends skiing because the chalet was booked up. I hoped Stuart had something else in mind.

After we changed and got out on the court, I saw Stuart for the first time. He came over to me, kissed my cheek and said, "Call your mother and tell her I'll drive you home."

"Everything okay?"

"Yes, I just need to talk to you," he said, not looking at me.

Stuart avoided me for most of our lesson, which was odd. Even Coach Adrian got the impression something was amiss.

"Morissette, your lover boy okay?" he yelled to me when Stuart missed an easy smash during one of his rallies.

After the lesson, I got changed, said a quick goodbye to Grace and then hurried outside to meet up with Stuart. I knew it couldn't be me he was upset with, but doubts started creeping in. We walked to his car, the gravel crunching underfoot. Stuart held my hand but remained silent. He looked ahead and it felt like he was a million miles away. When we reached his car, he opened my door, but I touched his chest and looked into his eyes. He looked at me, his eyes slate grey.

"Tell me what's going on," I said.

"I will. Just get in and we'll go to The Castle. It's warm enough," he said.

I had christened the stone gazebo at the university "The Castle," and Stuart was right, we were enjoying unusual, balmy March temperatures. I felt panic rise in my throat as we drove to the university, and I tried to swallow it down, but it was almost impossible. I twisted my hands together and stared out the window, not seeing the scenery pass by. I couldn't figure out what was so wrong—because something was very wrong. Every time I talked myself out of a scenario, a nastier one popped into my head. *He's going to dump me*, I thought at first, which morphed into, *He's cheated*, which meandered down the path of, *He's been seeing Grace*. At that point, I knew I was being ridiculous, but I couldn't torture myself any longer, waiting for him to speak.

"God, Stuart, if you're dumping me, just tell me now," I blurted.

"What? Jesus, Cait, is that what you've been thinking since we left tennis? I'm not breaking up with you. We need to talk but it's not because of you." When Stuart drove, his hands were always at ten and two, and he never took his eyes off the road. Now, he looked sideways at me, and the car moved to the right side of the lane before he returned his gaze straight ahead. "I love you. I don't want to be apart from you. Please just wait until we get there. I don't think I can drive and talk about it."

Stuart didn't park the car at his house, which is what he had done before. He drove to the university and we meandered our way in on foot, in silence. When we got to The Castle, it was warm. The sun was still up, casting shadows on the walls. As soon as we knew we were the only ones in the area, Stuart grabbed me and we started kissing, as though he needed reassurance. When we broke apart, he looked at me and I felt a chill move through my body. The look on his face was one of absolute distress, as though he was on a sinking ship and just realized there were no more life jackets or spots available in the lifeboat.

"Caitie," he whispered. "I'm moving to Boston."

eight

MARCH 2017

UNLIKE SUMMER, when warmth escapes too soon like a cranky old man from a child's birthday party, that winter felt like it would stay longer than an unwanted houseguest. Part of my malaise was the turn of the calendar. I took stock of the past year. What confounded me most was that more than twelve months had passed since I'd lost my job at Legandcy—an entire year. And most days, I felt similar to how I'd felt back then: unsure, anxious and somewhat disappointed. My relationship with Rob mirrored that, too, and most days I blamed it on my restlessness and the demands of running a household with young children whose parents worked full time.

But there was something else. In early January, Rob came up behind me in the kitchen as I chopped potatoes. He nuzzled my neck, his hand slipping under my sweater.

"Rob," I said, my voice a warning. There was no way we could have sex then. My mind ran through everything I needed to do in the next couple of hours to prepare for the upcoming week.

"C'mon, Caitie, the boys just started watching a movie, we've got at least twenty minutes before they ask for a snack," he murmured into my neck, as his fingers stilled my potato skin-covered hands.

"Rob! Do you have any idea how much stuff I still have to do?" I snapped, regretting how nasty I sounded but knowing I just didn't have the time. I pulled my hands back.

"Caitie, you seem to always have too many things to do. You certainly seem to have many things that don't include me."

"What does that mean?"

"Well, your work, for one."

But before he could list another item, I cut him off. "Do you want to come to work with me? Do you want to spend some time making out in our storeroom behind the stacks of shoes?" I asked, knowing I sounded mean.

"Of course not." His eyes steeled; his mouth set in a firm line. Rob didn't get upset very often, but for some reason, I wanted him to get mad at me. I wanted to unleash some of the emotions I carried around with me on someone, even if they didn't deserve my ire. "But for Christ's sake, Caitie, you come in here frustrated and upset after work. When you've got a day off, you mope around, snapping at the boys and me. You don't want to do anything, saying you're always tired. And—" He lowered his voice as he delivered his next line. "We don't have sex anymore. It's like you don't even want to."

"Of course I want to, Rob," I said, not sure I was telling the truth. "But I'm overwhelmed most days. I'm trying to be a good mom, run the household, deal with Trevor and the store and somewhere in there, you've moved to the bottom of the priority list."

"Well, gee, thanks, Caitie," he said, backing away from me.

"Rob..." I said, as he started the leave the room.

"Let me know when dinner's ready, okay?" he called over his shoulder.

I was being unfair to Rob. I knew it, but part of me didn't mind that. Since the night of the Christmas party, Stuart was always on my mind. I was confused that I didn't feel guilty about going to the restaurant with him, and that also concerned me. We kissed only once when he walked me to my car. And because it was just one kiss, I thought I was on the right side of things. If Rob found out, he would be mad. There was no question. But would it end my marriage? Not a chance. Where, though, was the line? Could I continue to hang out with Stuart and flirt with him? What if there was more kissing? I knew that more than kissing would definitely cross a line because Stuart and I were former lovers. I remembered reading an article about spouses who had been cheated on in a magazine at the boys' doctor's office. The article quoted experts as saying an affair with a former lover was *worse* than a random one-night stand with a stranger or acquaintance. To justify what I was doing, as I drove home after that holiday kiss, I had talked myself into believing it had only been a Christmas embrace between two old friends. When I explained my logic to Siobhan, she saw through it, telling me I was kidding myself.

"Right, Cait," she said. "A grown man who took your virginity and is now divorced only wants to be friends as adults."

"It's not like we talk on the phone all the time and go on dates," I whined.

"Caitie-cat, listen to me. Figure this shit out with him. I don't give a fuck if you sleep with him. Do. Don't. Doesn't matter to me. I'm not going to judge you. But figure it out. Rob doesn't deserve this."

It was because of Siobhan that I met Rob. After Stuart and I broke up, I refused to go anywhere that might be fun. Six months post-Stuart, she managed to drag me to a Halloween party being hosted by the guy she was dating at the time.

"C'mon, Caitie-cat, I won't know anyone else there," she said.

"Since when do you need someone to go with you somewhere?" I asked, lying on the couch channel-surfing through a lot of nothing. "Anyway, don't you just want to be with Sam?"

Siobhan sat down on the couch, forcing me to look at her. She gave me one of her direct stares. "Caitie, I wish Stuart was coming back, but I don't think he is. I don't know why. Please come to the party. I'm not saying you need to date someone. Fool around a bit if you want. Maybe a one-night stand would help you move on."

"Okay," I said, sighing, surprising both of us. I gave her the remote before forcing myself to roll off the couch and onto the floor. I stood up and dragged my feet to my bedroom to get ready. "But I'm not wearing a costume and you can't make me talk to anyone!"

"Whatever," she said to my retreating back.

The house Sam shared with four other guys was in our Sandy Hill neighbourhood so we walked, which meant we saved on cab fare. Like most students, I was stingy when it came to money. I worried I'd run out and not have enough for groceries the next week. The walk there also helped dull the slight buzz from the wine we'd drunk before leaving. For Siobhan, the drinks were fun. But I needed the liquid courage. Since Stuart had left, my confidence had escaped, my trust in people shaken and I was suspicious of others' motives. Siobhan insisted I couldn't hide from people forever, and if it took getting me half-drunk to get me out of the apartment, so be it.

An hour after arriving, I sat on an uncomfortable wooden chair with a rounded back, away from the majority of partygoers, who were huddled around a small television screen watching a hockey game. My shoulder blades ached and my brain was whipping up excuses to give Siobhan so I could leave when a tall man with neatly trimmed, dark brown hair and warm brown eyes sat down in an identical chair next to me. He wore a red plaid shirt and jeans.

"You look like you're having a good time," he said, smirking before breaking into a smile. He had nice teeth and a trustworthy face.

"Yeah," I answered, trying to return his smile. "What are you dressed as? A lumberjack?"

"No," he said, laughing. "I forgot it was Halloween because I've been so busy at work. What about you? Edith Piaf?"

"Good one," I said. I chuckled, not feeling at all insulted as I peered down at my black NIN t-shirt and black tights. "No, sorry. Just not feeling that great."

"I get it," he said. "I hate being dragged to parties, too."

The rest of the night sped by as Rob and I chatted, until Siobhan and Sam had a fight and she wanted to go home. I enjoyed talking to Rob but was glad for the excuse to leave.

In the time we'd spoke, I learned he had graduated with a degree in advertising and worked successive contract jobs, trying to create some semblance of a resumé. He was four years older than me and had ended a long-term relationship a few months before. He was a little shy and introverted, which I found appealing because it was the opposite of Stuart. Rob was also thoughtful, interesting and sincere. I believed him when he said meeting me was the night's highlight.

From there, our relationship moved at a glacial pace. We dated on and off for about a year. He dated other women and I remained focused on school. I dated occasionally, but I didn't feel as comfortable with anyone the way I felt with Rob. When I was with Stuart, our love was all-consuming and passionate. With Rob, it percolated. Once I graduated, I realized I wanted to only be with Rob and to start planning a future together. He had already made the same decision and the following year, we got engaged. We married the following May and then moved to St. Catharines in 2006 when I was hired at The Leg.

Now, eleven years later, I was juggling both my past and present. In my skewed logic, I felt as though I had erected some barriers. Stuart and I texted a lot, but I refused to chat on the phone, except when I was at the store and for work-related issues only. What a moral compass I kept. Every time his voice tumbled through the receiver, my pulse quickened.

"Caitie, we've got some opportunities coming up in the corporate offices," he said the last time we'd spoken. During our five-minute conversation, Stuart also said, "Please Cait, just see me." But I pretended I didn't hear that part, telling him about the store's bestsellers, instead. But I was glowing. A few minutes after I hung up, the warm feeling remained until Trevor snapped me out of my reverie.

"What's the matter with you?" he asked. "Did your husband surprise you with tickets to Paris? You've got a stupid look on your face. Wipe it off and get to work."

The temptation of Stuart added needed excitement to my life. Rob was a good husband. If he walked past the farmers' market on his way home from his office, he'd bring me flowers—bunches of tulips, dahlias and sunflowers for the kitchen table. He surprised me with nights out to our favourite restaurant, Chili & Agave, arranging a babysitter, usually Julie, all on his own. Sometimes, when he saw I was at a peak frustration level, he would have me stop whatever I was doing—dishes, bathing the kids—and he'd take over. "Go read," he soothed. "I'll take care of this."

Rob was an excellent father. He was patient with the boys, long after I would have resorted to yelling, and when they asked him to play hockey in the driveway or help them build towers from blocks, he almost never said no.

But there were times when being married to Rob—or maybe just being married—was routine and boring. To be fair, I hadn't really thought about my marriage and its excitement level or my satisfaction in it until Stuart resurfaced. But now it was as though I looked for problems and ways in which Rob didn't measure up, as though this could justify my indulgences into my fantasies. Just a week before, I'd asked Rob to go see a movie I'd waited months to see.

"It's not one of those chick flicks, is it?" he joked.

I wasn't amused. It irked me that if books or movies were written for a female audience, people assumed they weren't serious in nature.

"I've been waiting ages for the movie to come out. I read

the book two years ago and loved it. I'll let you get double butter on the popcorn," I said, upping the ante.

"Caitie, you know how stressful my week was," he said. "Can't we just stay in and watch something on TV?"

It was a reasonable request. Rob worked hard. And most of the time, staying in was what I wanted as well. But when he said that, a little voice told me Stuart would have taken me out if I'd asked him. Stuart was anything but run-of-the-mill. It had been a long time since a man—Rob included—looked at me the way Stuart did. The idea of fooling around—even just once—with Stuart was thrilling but unrealistic. I knew if I crossed any lines, I'd be asking myself to make some tough choices, and I certainly wasn't looking to alter anything at home.

The years Stuart and I had been together were some of the best of my youth. We dated during that remarkable time in one's life when everything was exciting. We went through milestones together—the first time I had sex, prom, moving away from home—and I grew into the Caitie I was today. He'd been there for that. Those years were also the only time in my life when it seemed not only that everything was possible but that my life *should* turn out the way I imagined simply because it was what I wanted. Everyone I knew was moving in the same direction. Now, the more time I spent at Heusten, the more I became convinced that I wasn't moving toward any of my goals.

The new year forced me to consider where I wanted to be in three and five years—I couldn't at this stage think past that. And, during those sleepless nights, as I listened to Rob's rhythmic breathing, I felt there was something deep down inside me fighting to get out. Was I supposed to be a corporate woman? Should we move to Toronto, as Siobhan suggested? Was retail the field I was meant to be a part of? Or was there another version of myself yearning to break free, if only I dared to free her?

In early March, I was working with Caleb. I enjoyed the rare silence as we arranged sandals on shelves for the optimists as well as those lucky enough to be travelling somewhere warm. The doorbell rang, announcing a customer. I looked up and froze. Standing in our store was Cyril. I hadn't seen him—or anyone else from Legandcy—since losing my job. I ignored the texts and emails sent to me by former colleagues who still worked there. Cyril's twenty-eight-year-old niece was still there because they were related. I couldn't get past it. Even if she was talented.

When Cyril saw me, his eyes narrowed and then flung open. His eyebrows shot up.

"Caitie?"

"Hi Cyril. How are you?"

"You work here?" He stood just inside the door, blocking the path for anyone else.

"Looks like it," I said, trying to be witty but knowing I sounded bitter. I moved closer to where Cyril stood but wished I could go hide in the backroom. Out of the corner of my eye, I saw Caleb walk to the far wall and start rearranging the socks, pretending he couldn't hear this painful exchange. "Um, are you looking for something for yourself?"

"Shit, Cait. You're working here. Do you *like* working here? I'm sorry we had to let you go." He wore a dark suit with a red power tie—impeccable, successful, professional. He looked around the store, as though trying to remember what he'd come for.

At Legandcy, I had gotten along well with both Meredeth and Cyril. While Meredeth had been the one to take me out for birthday lunches or join co-workers and me at the occasional after-work winery event, Cyril had always been kind to me when I worked at their agency. He knew my boys' names and made sure to spend time catching up with Rob at the annual holiday drinks and nibbles fête we would hold the Thursday night before we shut down for the Christmas break.

"I know, Cyril. Now, are you here for yourself?"

He said he and Meredeth were going to the Bahamas for a vacation. I guess with fewer salaries to pay, there was money for vacations now. At first, Cyril brushed off my attempts to help but then realized I needed to know what he wanted. He apologized for sending me to the backroom for sizes. But I appreciated the distraction. Once in the back, I leaned my head on my hand, taking a couple of deep breaths. *Easy*, I told myself.

He said he should buy both pairs he tried on. He could always use another pair for the summer. "I'm sure these will be ruined by the sand," he said, his cheeks flushed.

I asked about Meredeth as we walked to the till and I rang up his purchases. My right hand tapped at buttons on the computer screen; my left rested on the counter. He put his hand over mine and I stopped tapping to look at him.

"If you love this job, Cait, I'm happy for you. But if you're not, please follow your dreams. I know I sound like an asshole because I'm partially the reason you're here, but I think you could do better." He removed his hand to pull out his wallet and hand me his credit card. I popped it into the pin pad and turned the device around for him to use.

I handed Cyril his receipt. He put it in his wallet and then stuffed the wallet into his back pocket. He looked like he wanted to say something else, but I cut him off.

"Have a great trip," I said.

Cyril closed his mouth and nodded. He looked at me once more and then I turned away, my shoulders slumped. I swallowed. Hard. "Caleb, just going to the bathroom."

"Take your time," he said, not looking at me. "I'll hold down the fort."

I raced to the back and managed to close the door before the tears began streaming down my face. I sat on the toilet seat and let them pour out, balling my hands into fists and pushing them against my forehead. My omnipresent feelings of inadequacy and failure descended upon me, enemies that first appeared when I left Legandcy. Until today, though, I thought I'd swept them under my emotional carpet. However, like with most specks of dirt, I couldn't rid my house of them entirely. Even though my dismissal from The Leg had been the result of classic downsizing, I still felt disgraced, all these months later.

It wasn't just that I'd lost my job—my career, in fact, my calling. It was that now I was camped out in the forest of mediocrity, just biding my time, trying to accept that I needed to stay here so my children could have skating lessons. I'd fantasize about quitting in a dramatic cloud of expletives hurled at Trevor. But then the reality of the situation—the steady paycheque—shocked me back into real life, shaming me at the same time.

It seemed I had started doing a lot of crying about (and at) work. In mid-February, Trevor had called me a couple of hours before my morning shift, asking me to come to the store early for a meeting. His tone was cryptic, and for a moment, I was seized with panic, possible reasons for his call setting off warning bells. The major one, of course, was that he was going to fire me. And that triggered two main thoughts. After putting up with his bullshit for more than a year, I would need to start all over and find another job. The second soon followed, though: I'd be okay, I'd figure it out.

I told Trevor I'd be in and hung up the phone. Regardless of what he wanted to discuss with me, sitting around imagining all kinds of possible endings, as I'd done with Choose Your Own Adventure books I'd adored as a kid, wouldn't help. I got my sons off to school and then showered, dressed and drove to work.

As soon as I walked into the store, I saw Stuart and knew I wasn't getting fired.

"Thanks for coming in early," he said. He walked over to me and embraced me, holding on just a beat too long for the hug to be strictly professional. "It's so good to see you," he whispered in my ear.

"You, too," I said, smiling. "It's been a while."

"Ah, good, you're here," Trevor said, as he walked into the showroom from the back, his shoes clicking on the floor tiles. "Let's sit so we can get this over with and you can start getting ready to open up."

Stuart and I sat on a bench at the end of a long row of shoes, while Trevor perched himself on a wheeled stool that staff used to measure feet. I felt Stuart's heat, and my stomach tingled when his arm brushed mine.

"Now, Caitlin, you've been a great team leader the past year," Trevor began. "I'm impressed, actually. You came here with no retail experience except for a brief stint at an ice cream store, was it? In high school? Mr. Taylor is here because he's reviewed the financials and, well, he was the one who suggested it, really, but we want to promote you."

"Really?" I said, coughing.

"Well, Mr. Taylor has okayed the promotion. You'll now

be the senior assistant manager and you'll get a pay increase of five thousand dollars." Trevor looked over a document as he spoke. "We have the details here, and, if you accept, things will remain pretty much the same, but you'll now be able to act independently if I'm not here for some reason, such as vacation. It's a lot more responsibility. I hope you recognize the significance of our gesture."

"That works out to what? Less than a hundred dollars a week?" I said, looking at Stuart, who had the good grace to at least blush. "Whatever will I do with all the extra money?"

"You're at the top of the allowable pay grid for store management," Stuart replied, cutting off Trevor, who looked like he was about to yell, affronted that I would consider his offer anything but generous. "I'm sorry we can't offer you more. You certainly deserve it."

I should have been grateful. Everything I'd read pointed to a tough job market in Niagara. Canada's unemployment rate kept rising and the millennial generation would be the first in a century to be worse off than its parents. But I *wasn't* grateful. My cheeks felt warm and words bubbled up inside me, threatening to spew out of my mouth. I knew this wouldn't end well.

"Is it okay if I just take a walk for a minute?" I asked the men, springing up, ignoring Stuart. I could sense him studying me. I didn't want him to comfort me because he'd been in on this.

"Of course, Cait, take whatever time you need," Stuart said, just as Trevor said, "Well, make it snappy, we open in a few minutes."

I had walked outside the store, huddled into my coat, pulling my scarf tight around my neck. Tears stung my eyes, and I wiped them away. I wanted to call Rob to have him commiserate with me, but he was working on an important project and I forbade myself to bother him. Siobhan would instruct me to tell Trevor to shove the raise up his ass and walk out.

 I popped inside the food court, grabbed a coffee and sat down at the edge of the sea of tables. I watched some of the fast food workers opening up their stores, wondering if, back in high school, they'd thought they would work here as adults. I remembered relaxing with my closest friends at that time, talking about our futures, our amazing careers, who we would marry and the exciting lives we would live. I sighed. I didn't think everyone in the food court aspired to be here.

 I accepted the new position and in mid-February, I was told I needed to return to Toronto for a three-day training seminar. Trevor should have been the one representing our store, but he'd gotten a promotion several weeks earlier, too, and was now a district manager, overseeing the Burlington store as well as our Niagara outlet. The change meant I was again promoted—to acting store manager—but our location remained Trevor's base so I still saw him every day. While insufferable before, Trevor now strutted around in his new Armani suits and was the most egotistical and self-aggrandizing person I knew—and that was saying something after working in an industry that created pretty things. Caleb and I, laughing so hard tears leaked down our faces, suspected he'd begun hair replacement therapy, too.

 Trevor's new vocabulary included words like "corporate says" and "on the corporate side of things, you see," phrases he used to point out how someone did something wrong. I argued with Trevor about going to the training seminar, which would be at the Radisson Blu hotel in downtown Toronto, telling him how disruptive it was to our family. What I didn't say was that I didn't care about the conference. I worried I was becoming too entrenched with Heusten Shoes, and the long-term plans I'd begun to concoct didn't include the company.

"We—and by *we* I mean Mr. Taylor and I—can replace you if you feel it's too much work," Trevor said, his condescension at an all-time high.

"Stuart wouldn't fire me," I blurted. It didn't seem possible, but Trevor hadn't yet figured out our history. And I wasn't about to tip my hand because he'd use it against me at every opportunity, so I backpedalled. "You've said yourself that I'm doing a great job. Listen, do you know if he'll be at the training?"

"I don't think so," he replied, raising an eyebrow. "Mr. Taylor, I believe, is in Eastern Ontario, working with some of the newer managers as our corporate expansion is about to begin in the Kingston–Ottawa area. You know, it's a very exciting time for the company. You would do well to keep applying yourself. You might find yourself on the corporate side of things one day, just as I am now."

When I told Rob I needed to go to Toronto, he gave me a quizzical look.

"Is this absolutely necessary?" he asked. I couldn't read his face. I didn't know why he seemed so perplexed. "Is Trevor going?"

"If he was going, I wouldn't have to. See? That's the whole problem."

"You're the only one going from your store?"

"Yes! But I wish Caleb was going, too. He'd make it bearable. Listen, I know it's a hassle for you. Believe me, I don't want to go."

"Then don't," he said.

"If I refuse to go, Trevor's made it clear that I could be replaced," I said. "I have to go."

Rob didn't say anything. He was sitting in his favourite chair, reading the newspaper, his socked feet resting on the coffee table. He put the paper down and looked at me as though he had something else to say but then he just sighed and began reading again.

"Rob, you okay?"

"Just fine, Caitie," he said, his voice muffled behind the broadsheet.

The night before I left, I double-checked the complex pick-up and drop-off schedule I'd hammered out with Birdie and Sue for the boys' after-school activities. I had also arranged play dates with three mothers, bought two birthday presents for parties on Saturday morning, which Sue was dropping the boys round to. Rob would pick up Aidan, and Birdie would grab Jacob. I marvelled at how much coordination was needed so I could disappear for three days. I was underutilized—I could run a small country.

After I got off the phone with Birdie and Sue, I tucked the boys into bed, promising I'd see them the next morning before I left, and then went into my bedroom to start packing. I selected the essentials, along with business outfits and sweaters. I knew from experience that most hotels kept their air conditioning high in conference rooms to ward off sleeping, and I didn't want to find myself distracted by severe shivering. I also packed an out-on-the-town top and one dress. I hoped there would be other women I could befriend.

I had visions of us getting together for dinner and drinks. I prayed I wouldn't be stuck in meeting rooms watching PowerPoint presentations the entire time.

In a way, I was relieved Stuart wouldn't be there. We continued to text, and many of our exchanges were flirty—some were downright over the line—but he'd stopped asking if he could see me. The only times I saw him were the occasional visits he made to our store to check on Trevor. Every time I saw him, though, I felt a thrill ripple through my body. In one quick glance, I could tell what he was thinking, his every gaze fraught with meaning. And I liked it.

As I put the finishing touches on my packing, placing my favourite spring pyjamas on top of my swimsuit (in case there was a hot tub), Rob came into our room. One of his oft-repeated complaints about my leaving was the timing. He'd become a Cre8tive partner in January, and we celebrated his achievement with a big catered meal with our entire family. I was thrilled and proud of Rob for making partner, but the evil part in me, the piece I tamped down most days, was jealous. Would I ever feel as satisfied about my work as he did? Could I ever reach a level where I felt I'd achieved something again? From where I stood now, that didn't seem possible, and it made me resent Rob's success.

"Hey, you know what I was just thinking about?" I asked him as he sat on our bed.

"No, what?"

"The last time I packed to go away was for our five-year anniversary when we went to Jamaica," I said, refolding a sweater to make everything fit. I stopped what I was doing and smiled at him.

"We need to do that again, Cait," he said. "Or maybe we can all go away next winter."

"Uh-oh. What?" I said, hearing the catch in his voice, realizing he hadn't come in the room for a pleasant chat.

"Listen to me. It's not like you even really like your job and you're spending so much time at it. And now this? You're going to be gone for three days. I just made partner, and there's a lot of work to do at the office. I don't think it looks good if I need to make sure I'm home because you're off gallivanting in Toronto. The boys will miss you and I know you'll miss them. And it's going to be so much rushing around here, trying to get everybody to everything on time."

I tried to be objective as I listened to Rob's litany of complaints, his reasons why my leaving was too disruptive. While he spoke, a little voice in my head got louder, convincing me that he meant what he was saying. When he started on his most recent favourite topic—why didn't I consider working at Cre8tive?—I snapped.

"Rob, if this was a design convention, you wouldn't be badgering me about it. For Christ's sake, I'm going to be gone for seventy-two hours," I spat. "I'm quite confident you can manage the home front for three days so your wife can feel productive, that she's making a contribution to the family dynamic. Surely it's not too much to ask of you, is it?"

After our fight on the phone the night of Cre8tive's holiday party, Rob had changed his tone and become fervent in his support of my work. He took me out to dinner when I was named the store's new manager. Stuart also sent flowers to the store to congratulate me. Now, Rob looked shocked, as though I had slapped him. But he stopped complaining; morose and silent, he left the room. I finished packing, got ready for bed and slipped underneath the covers, fidgeting with rage. When he came to bed an hour later, he said, "Caitie? I'm sorry," but I pretended to be asleep.

The next morning, Rob got up early and cooked eggs and bacon and made the boys' lunches. I was still angry from our fight the night before, but seeing him make an extra effort reminded me of how lucky I was.

"Have fun," he said to me, as he grabbed his leather carryall. He refused to carry a briefcase and I loved that about him. He kissed the boys and gave each of them a hug before coming over to me and kissing me for so long that the boys started giggling and then one of them said "Eew, gross." He smiled, kissed me once more, collected his keys and scampered out of the house.

"C'mon, you guys. Eat up," I said to the boys, as the pair of them continued to stare at me as though snakes were crawling out of my head.

I dropped them at the bus stop, hugging them harder than usual and giving them extra kisses, until Aidan had had enough and said, "Geez, Mom, everyone's looking." Jacob turned around on the bus steps to wave and then blew me kisses from the window as I waved goodbye. I watched them find a seat together and remained where I was as the bus took off down the street.

At home, I finished packing, draining the last dregs of tea in my mug. I washed my cup out and placed it in the dishwasher, along with a few other stragglers from breakfast, and brought my suitcase and handbag out to the car. As I closed the trunk, I heard my phone ping for an incoming text.

STUART

Can't wait to see you today.

My heart skipped a beat.

> Thought you were in Kingston? T said you were training new people there?

> I switched with someone else.

Realizing I was holding my breath, I exhaled. My heart was thumping in my chest. I would be in Toronto with Stuart. Alone. Unsure what to type, I signed off with a happy face and a noncommittal response. But I was nervous. I didn't know if I should continue to Toronto. I knew I'd have some serious explaining to do to Rob if I backed out, though he'd be relieved. He understood—to a point—how I felt about my career, but as someone who hadn't been fired from his life's work, he couldn't sympathize with everything. It would also mean jeopardizing my position at the store, and Stuart wouldn't be able to come to my rescue. I called Siobhan using my Bluetooth as I backed out of my driveway.

"Siobhan, I just found out Stuart's going to be there this week," I said as soon as she picked up. My voice sounded frantic, even to me.

"Cait! This is fucking perfect. You now have the opportunity for a full-on affair, if you want one. I think it would be fun, but I do adore Rob, so really, it's your choice. But what you need to do is find out why he left. I think there's been enough of this getting to know each other again crap for you to just ask. I don't think, for one second, that he doesn't remember what happened. And I think he owes it—hang on." I heard her cover her phone and say, "For fuck's sake, I'm on the phone!" before rejoining our conversation. "I think he owes it to you to let you know that none of it was your fault. If there's a little fooling around in the hallways between sessions or late at night in your room, you must tell me about it but I already forgive you."

"Siobhan!" I cried. I laughed because she was speaking so quickly, but inside I felt uneasy. I paused before continuing. "Think about what you're saying. Okay, seeing him has stirred up a lot of my old feelings. And I sent you that last exchange we had through texts. I love the flirting. I hate to admit it but I do. But here's the thing—I love Rob, he's the father of my children and I'm not looking for an affair. I don't even think I'm unhappy in my marriage. Let's say I did give into the temptation. Then what? We run away together? We have an affair behind Rob's back? That's crazy."

"Nobody's saying you don't love Rob, Caitie. I know you do. But you loved Stuart, too. And I think you still do. None of my relationships were ever open-ended. They all finished, and usually with a bang. Stuart never ended for you. He's in front of you now and I think you should do what you need to do. Now, I've got to run off because my pathetic boss will be back here any minute, telling me I'm late for the meeting. When, I ask you, have I ever been on time for the weekly meeting? Never, is the answer, but this guy seems to think he can mould me into someone who's prompt."

I hung up, laughing. As I joined the other motorists travelling along this busy stretch of highway, I thought about what Siobhan had said. She'd touched a nerve. When Stuart and I were together, I loved him with abandon—fully, completely and without any reservations. At twenty, I hadn't yet joined the cluster of relationship cynics, people who believed all unions would end and lifelong loves were only the stuff of fairy tales. I had trusted everything Stuart said and, when he left, I felt ripped apart because it was as though everything I'd believed in and had staked my future on had been wrong.

But since I first saw him again almost a year ago, I knew I still loved him. And if I allowed myself to get carried away, I knew it would be mean so much more to me than a casual fling. But I wasn't sure I wanted that to happen. I fantasized sometimes about calling him, telling him I wanted him and playing out what would happen next. But when the sun came up and I turned over in bed and saw Rob's outline and heard his gentle breathing, I knew I was happy right where I was. But being happy and doing stupid things aren't mutually exclusive.

nine

MARCH 1997

"CAIT, STOP!" Stuart exclaimed, as I bolted from The Castle.

When we'd entered the stone sanctuary, it was warm, but the air now felt cold and menacing. Tears stung my eyes and I didn't bother to wipe them away. I heard Stuart running behind me, getting closer. I was a fool to think I could outrun him. He was nearly six inches taller than me, his stride much longer. I shivered. I wanted to stop and loop my arms around my body, not only to keep myself warm, but also to remind myself that I was still there, that I was still whole. I felt as though I was coming undone as I ran, little parts of my heart scattering behind me like birdseed. Stuart caught up to me and grabbed my arm to stop me from running.

"Cait," he said, out of breath. "Caitie, please wait."

Fully engulfed in tears, I made horrible gasping sounds. He kept hold of my arm and directed me to a large oak tree. I turned to look at him, tears streaming down my face. I knew my nose was red from crying and I didn't care. Stuart took my other hand in his as we stood under the tree, sheltered from the view of students walking between buildings or hanging out on the lawn. He pulled me toward him, kissing my forehead and face as I wept. I felt his tears mix with mine.

"It's my mother," he said, sniffling.

Out of my sorrow came a bolt of rage and I wanted to run to his house and confront her. But I looked up at him, willing myself to gain control. His eyes, normally bright and alive, were glassy and sad, and I knew I was being selfish—this was harder on him than me. I touched his cheeks with my fingertips, moving them toward his chin as he cried.

"I can't live with her anymore. You've seen what she's like. She watches me all the time. She begs me to stay home with her and watch movies or to go shopping with her or just to spend time with her. It drives me crazy. I can't do it anymore. I can't be her stand-in husband. My father left her ten years ago and she's never gotten over it. She wants me to be the 'man of the house.' I've been speaking more to my father—you knew that—and he suggested I go live with him."

"For how long?" I interjected, hoping he meant only a few months.

"A year?" he said. "I don't want to go, but I have to. I'm going to miss so much—prom, graduation, my friends. Caitie, it's killing me to leave you."

"Take me with you," I said, knowing he couldn't. Boston was out of the question. My parents would forbid it, I had nowhere to live, and I hadn't taken my SATs so I couldn't pretend I wanted to go to college there.

"I would love it if you could come with me. Oh, could you just see it? We could live in the same room together in my dad's house—in the same bed," he said, giving me a look that made me melt. "I'm going to think about you like that all the time."

"But what does this mean for us, Stuart?" I asked, holding my breath. "Do you want to break up?"

"No, Cait, I don't want to break up! It's only a year, right? Look at Mackenzie and Quinn. They've managed long distance for over a year and they're happy. I'll be home for a few weeks in the summer, Canadian Thanksgiving, Christmas. I don't want to be without you, and I can't let you go." As he spoke, my breathing returned to normal. Of course, we could get through this. "But, Caitie, look at me. If things get too tough for you, I won't blame you for wanting someone else. I only want you to be happy. You have my heart. I am yours. Don't think there could ever be anyone else but you."

"When do you leave?"

"Next Friday." He paused when he saw the shock register on my face. "I'm sorry. My dad thought it'd be best to get into school as soon as possible. It's already not ideal, starting a new school six weeks into the semester. Maybe things at home will be better by the end of the school year, but my dad is really pushing me to stay for at least a year, maybe come back to London next February. Or, if things don't get better at all, finish high school in Boston and then figure out where to go from there."

"Stuart, no, not more than a year," I pleaded, fresh tears threatening the equilibrium I had restored. "Please. Can you live at my house? I'm sure my mom would be okay with it. My parents love you. They wouldn't want to see you go. It's not like you're going to be two hours away. This is a huge change."

"I love your parents—your whole family, really—but I know they're not going to want me living in their house. 'Excuse me, Mr. Morissette, your daughter and I are just going to go upstairs and, um, study,'" he said, a grin breaking across his face. I mirrored it, imagining him skulking out of my bedroom in his boxers. "We're going to make this work, Caitie. I love you and I promise we'll make this work."

The next few days passed in a blur. Stuart and I spoke on the phone all the time if we weren't together. I didn't care if his mother eavesdropped on our conversations. The Saturday before he was set to leave, Brandon threw a going-away party. His parents were never home on weekends anymore, figuring their eighteen-year-old son hadn't done anything too drastic yet, so why bother pretending to chaperone him now.

Brandon called me before announcing he would host the gathering.

"Caitie, I'll understand if you just want to be with Stuart this last weekend before he goes," he said, sounding morose and as though he would cry.

"It's okay, Brandon. Stuart would want a huge party to say goodbye to everyone. Thanks for doing that."

Since Stuart had told me he was moving to Boston, my soul felt as though it had been hollowed out. I kept hoping Stuart would announce he was playing a big joke on us, a pathetic attempt to gauge our true feelings. But I knew this was real. This was happening. He was leaving.

My parents tiptoed around me, not wanting to broach the subject because they couldn't comfort me. Stuart called back after we hung up one night to tell them himself that he was moving and I heard my mother cry as she told my father. She knocked on my bedroom door, but I didn't answer. Instead, I cried silent tears into my pillow, my body shaking with grief.

The day of the party, Stuart showed up to my house just before noon, spending time with my mom, who fretted over him, asking him what he needed to take with him. The more Stuart refused her offers to get him a going-away present or "something he really needed to bring to Boston," the more fervent she became. After what felt like an eternity, Stuart told her he could use a couple of new towels, and my mother beamed. She had something new to focus on instead of his impending departure.

"Well, Stuart, I'll make sure we get you some then," she said.

I told my parents I was staying at Brandon's house that night, along with everyone else going to the party, and they didn't argue. The night before, we'd returned to his house after dinner and a movie—I no longer had a curfew, it seemed. We sat at the kitchen table, dutifully speaking to his mother for a few minutes. His foot rubbed my leg and his hand rested on my thigh. I ached to get away and be alone with him.

"It's good for him to go," Caroline said, refilling my glass with water. Her tone inferred she had nothing to do with the decision, as though he was a troublesome teen being sent to his father to be straightened out. "It will make him grow up and be more responsible."

I opened my mouth just as Stuart said, "Quite right, Mom, moving one thousand kilometres away to a place where I don't know anyone will certainly make me grow up.

Let's go, Cait." He saw the look in my eye, my absolute fury at her selfishness, and wanted to keep the peace.

Earlier that week, Stuart had promised we would steal away some alone time on Saturday despite everyone demanding to see him. After he had hugged my mother and thanked her again for the towels, he carried my bags to the car—"Really, Cait, all this for one night?"—as I scrambled to figure out where we could be going. I knew his mother was home, as were my parents. And I would feel awkward if we fooled around at Brandon's house as he sat in the living room or—even worse—if he left to give us privacy, only to interrupt us when he returned.

"You're never going to guess, so just enjoy the fact that I'm surprising you," he said, smirking.

We drove to a wealthier area of London, a neighbourhood I didn't spend much time in. We meandered along a golf course and I ogled the large, stone homes that would be manicured by professionals in the summer. They were twice the size of my house and the air smelled rich.

As we drove, I kept stealing glances at Stuart, trying to imprint his profile in my memory. I couldn't believe that, in just a few days, he'd be gone. Until now, I'd been able to see him whenever I wanted. I carried his latest school picture in my wallet, as well as a few photos of us, including my favourite, one of us kissing, which we'd snapped in a photo booth at the mall.

When we'd lie together on his bed when his mom was out or snuggle together while watching movies at my house, I'd spend hours examining him. I memorized his face, the way his hair fell on his forehead, the way his eyes seemed to lighten when he smiled, the three small freckles to the right of his mouth. In an instant, I could call up the way he looked as he hovered above me when we made love, his eyebrows knitted in complete concentration, or his delight when I was on top, which sometimes seemed to border on pride.

"Caitlin, why are you staring at me?" he said, giving me a quick glance before returning his gaze to the road.

"I want to memorize every angle of you," I said. "Plus, you're so hot, I can't stop looking at you, even when you're driving." He laughed, and my heart broke just a bit.

Stuart signalled and pulled into the driveway of a large, two-storey, brown, stone house with wrought iron detail on the doors and frosted glass. A few Christmas decorations lingered in the yard, including a browned wreath. I wasn't sure if we were picking someone up or going inside, so I sat still. Stuart turned off the car and swivelled toward me, putting his hand on top of mine, which rested in my lap.

"Brandon's uncle's house," Stuart said, by way of an explanation. "He and Brandon's aunt spend their winters in the Dominican. They're not home. You want to go in?"

"Lead the way," I said, grinning.

Stuart grabbed a small backpack from the trunk of his car, along with my bags, and retrieved a key from under the mat. That surprised me. We were in a really rich area. Wouldn't that be the first place a burglar would look? We entered the house and Stuart expertly disarmed the alarm. The house was immaculate, and not just because no one had been there in a while. To the left of the foyer was a living room that featured white leather couches, a large television in one corner and a fireplace. A red rug was the centrepiece of the room. A glass table with pewter legs rested on it.

Stuart moved me to one side because I stood still, mesmerized. The house was incredible, like something you'd see out of a *Martha Stewart Living* magazine. A large, curved, wooden stairway led to the second floor. Past the staircase, I could see a hall, which opened into the kitchen. I peered to my right and, just off the foyer, was another large sitting room, painted hunter green, with a majestic grand piano near the full windows. A soft, beige chaise longue was the only other piece of furniture in the room.

"Well?" Stuart said, breaking into my thoughts. "What would you like to do first? We have the house to ourselves."

"Wow, Stuart," I said. "This is amazing. But do you think we could get into trouble? I mean, what if Brandon got caught? I'm sure his uncle doesn't want his nephew handing out the keys to everyone he knows."

"Brandon told me about this place and said his uncle pays him to keep an eye on it. He trusts that we won't have a raging party or break anything," he said, laughing.

I walked into the living room and sank down on one of the couches. The leather was soft, buttery. All of a sudden, I felt a fluttering of nerves and my palms became sweaty. I rubbed them on my thighs. Our intimacy was passionate, but sex was often rushed because we didn't want to get found out. Once, my mom came home early and almost caught us. But Stuart was wearing his socks and had a blanket wrapped around his entire body as he lay on the couch in my basement. When I heard her footfall on the staircase, I pushed him off me, threw my dress on and pretended to be walking back from the washroom. Fortunately, Stuart's underwear was behind him and I threw his jeans underneath the pillow on the chair across from the couch. Aside from those socks, Stuart was naked under the blanket.

But here, we were alone. No one could interrupt us because no one knew where we were—except Brandon, and he was busy getting ready for a party. And then a calm overcame me and I almost burst with pride and a sense of overwhelming appreciation. I'd heard too many girls at school talk about how their boyfriends treated them. Some guys ogled other girls in front of them or made crass remarks about them or other girls behind their backs. Some guys stood up their dates, letting them wait outside a movie theatre alone. And, most despicable, some guys spent an entire night making out with a girl at a party, only to act as though she didn't exist at school. Grace called me a few nights before to complain about Tristan, who'd forgotten it was an anniversary of sorts and went out with some friends to watch a hockey game.

Stuart had thought of all of this—for us. For me. For him. He wanted to be with me as much as I wanted to be with him.

Stuart watched me, not saying anything. I wasn't sure I could tell him what I thought. "I love you" is what I settled on.

He walked toward me and sat down on the couch beside me, tucking a stray hair behind my ear. "I love you, too, Caitie," he said. "I can't believe we won't be together next week at this time."

"Please don't talk about it," I begged. "I'm having a hard enough time keeping it together most days."

Stuart looked at me for a minute and then kissed me the way he had that night when I stood against his car.

"What's upstairs?" I asked, nearly breathless with longing.

"The bedrooms."

"Take me there."

He stood, took my hand and pulled me up. He lifted me

and then carried me, the way grooms carry their brides, all the way up the stairs and into the master bedroom. He laid me down on a canopy bed, its covering a stylish grey-black, pushing my hair out of my face and kissing my cheek. My heart melted. I reached to unbuckle his jeans but he stopped me.

"Hold on. I have something for you," he said, starting to walk toward a dresser.

"I love that you took the time to think of all this, Stuart. Really, I don't deserve someone as good as you."

"Oh, yes, you do. You deserve better, actually. You deserve someone who could stay with you," he whispered as he returned the bed I was sitting on. "I want to give you something to remember me by so you won't look for anyone else while I'm gone. This is totally a selfish move. Really, it's all about me at this point."

I laughed and turned to face him and stroke his cheek. I couldn't believe we had grown so close. Sometimes, when I thought about what my life would be like when he was in Boston, it was as though I couldn't breathe. A part of my soul would be missing.

He kissed my mouth, then my cheek and my neck. I closed my eyes, savouring all of it.

"Caitlin," he said. "I love you more than I can even express and if we were five, ten years older, I'd want to marry you. I can't possibly ask for such a commitment and I can't give you one now. But I did want you to have something special."

He handed me a delicate, pink-wrapped rectangular box. "Open it."

I bit my lip as I smiled at him, curious to see what was inside. I ripped off the paper, opened the box, and gasped. It was a silver necklace with intricate links, holding a diamond-encrusted circle. It was stunning and must have cost Stuart a fortune. He worked, doing odd jobs for several neighbours, and he taught ski lessons from time to time at the local ski hill. He never lacked cash, but we never talked about money. I remembered what Grace had said about his family being wealthy. I looked at the gorgeous piece in my hands and began to cry.

"No, don't," he said, taking it from my hands and opening the clasp. He draped it around my neck and then closed the clasp. I touched the circle of diamonds, which fell perfectly between my collarbones.

"Thank you," I breathed, tears falling down my cheeks. "Please stay. There's got to be another solution."

Stuart leaned toward me and we began kissing. *Remember this*, I told myself. I closed my eyes, my fingers trailing over his back, his shoulders, his curly hair, everywhere, trying to etch the feel of him into my memory. Afterwards, we fell asleep, our arms wrapped around each other.

A few hours later, we showered and got ready for the party. When we had first arrived at Brandon's uncle's house, I'd felt uncomfortable with the idea of being there, especially having sex in their bed. But after that moment, I never gave it another thought. It wasn't until I tried to make the bed after dressing that I felt a little sheepish.

"We're going to need it later," Stuart said, as he came out of the ensuite bathroom, a towel around his waist, his hair wet from his shower. "Just leave it. And I know what you're thinking. Don't worry about it. I'm sure when we're older, our kids will do crazy things when we're away on vacation."

On the way to Brandon's party, we grabbed a quick sandwich. We were ravenous—both for food and each other. I knew most people at the party would guess what we'd been doing, which made me blush. In my embarrassment, my face was nearing purple. I always developed a slight reddish colour on my cheeks and neck after sex that took a while to dissipate. Stuart teased me about it, which made me more self-conscious.

"Don't be," he said. "It makes you cuter than you already are. And besides, we're the only ones who know where it comes from."

Grace watched for our arrival, and as soon as we stepped inside Brandon's entryway, she yelled, "Jesus, Cait, how many hours have you guys been doing it?" I flushed a deeper red and didn't say anything.

Stuart laughed. "Hi, Grace!" he yelled back, before hugging Brandon and some others who rushed over to welcome him. I spotted Peyton hanging around in the kitchen, her gaze transfixed on Stuart.

Stuart and I were inseparable as the night progressed, our hands intertwined, me parked in his lap. Every spare moment was an opportunity to kiss. It wasn't until I excused myself and went to the bathroom that we were apart. I spent time talking to our friends on the way there, while in line, and on the way back. As I came down the hallway, back toward the living room where most of our friends were congregated, talking with Stuart and reminiscing, I was surprised to see Peyton sitting in his lap.

I touched the circle pendant around my neck with absolute confidence in our relationship, knowing everything I felt for Stuart was reciprocated for me. I stopped to talk to

Grace. She began to bitch about Tristan, who was now watching a hockey game.

Out of the corner of my eye, I saw Peyton lunge at Stuart, kissing him on the mouth.

"What a bitch," Grace said, as I stared, unsure what to do. "She's such a tart. Always pushing up against him, trying to get him to notice her. She's so fucking clueless. He only sees you, and he only wants you. You know this, right?"

I did know it. But it wasn't something I needed to know—I felt it. Grace started to move toward the room where they were, but I held her arm. She looked at me, surprised.

"It's Stuart's battle to fight," I said, watching him push her away from him. His eyes knitted in a frown and he looked mad. Peyton burst into tears, but Stuart just walked away from her. I watched her wipe her nose on her sleeve and then rush out of the room. "But what am I going to do without him?"

"I don't know," she said, her eyes also sad. "I don't know, Caitie."

As we drove to Brandon's uncle's house from the going-away party, Stuart tried to bring up Peyton and apologize, but I didn't care.

"Stuart, please don't talk about it. I know it's not you. She's never really gotten over you guys breaking up or whatever you'd call it. We have so little time left; I can't stand to think we're going to spend any of it talking about her."

What bothered me most about the incident was witnessing someone else kiss him. When Stuart told me he was moving away, I'd considered the possibility of that happening, but the image of him and Peyton meant there really could be someone else he might fall for in Boston. He had every intention of keeping our relationship going, as did

I. But I had just turned eighteen—he was nearly nineteen—and as much as we loved each other, even I realized we were young. If people got tired of each other when they were married, how were Stuart and I going to maintain a relationship across a thousand kilometres, when neither of us could hop on a plane at a moment's notice to visit for the weekend?

When it came down to it, most of our options revolved around being granted permission by our parents, no matter how liberal they were or how much freedom we experienced. I still had one year left in high school before university and now—best case scenario—Stuart would need to repeat some courses or—worst case scenario—go to school in Boston for the next year and a half, followed by college in the States. And we had no idea what he was going to choose. For that matter, I didn't know where I was heading. I worried I wouldn't—and really, I couldn't—be a factor in his decisions about his future.

My stomach turned when I thought about Stuart touching another girl the way he touched me, and I was nauseated at the idea he might have sex with someone else. For myself, the thought of touching someone else, even looking at another guy across a bed, a sheet draped over his torso but not his feet, which was how Stuart slept, repulsed me. I couldn't imagine being with anyone other than Stuart, which was, perhaps, ridiculous, as I was certain few people married—and stayed married—to the first person they slept with. But I couldn't see my life with anyone but Stuart. His imminent move forced me to consider that his future, which had included me, might change, even if we wouldn't admit it.

Five days later, he was gone.

For the next couple of weeks, I walked around in a haze. I spent many hours reflecting on our time at Brandon's uncle's house. We'd stayed up all night, and I'd paid for it by falling asleep in science class on Monday, earning jeers from my friends. I relived those final hours often, remembering how his head had rested against the pillow as we lay side by side, or how he felt as we moved together.

Though he asked me to, I didn't go to the airport. "I can't handle saying goodbye to you in front of her," I said. "She's why you're leaving. I can't ride in a car with her, listening to her cry or—God forbid—say something about how you weren't a great son or whatever bullshit she might come up with. I wouldn't be able to handle that."

"I understand."

Stuart called the day he arrived at his dad's and we spoke every few days on the phone. When I called, I got to know his stepmother, Gloria, though, at first, I had trouble understanding what she said due to her Bostonian accent. Edward, Stuart's father, and Gloria had heard about our relationship from his mother and Nicole, but it was obvious to both of us that we'd been maligned. We pieced together that they made me out to be a troublesome and desperate girl, infatuated with Stuart, and that Stuart was taken with me but our relationship wasn't too serious.

"He really misses you and his friends," Gloria said. "I feel bad for him, actually. He's heartbroken, and I wish I could do something to help him."

"Take him skiing," I suggested. "He loves to ski and he didn't get to do too much of it here. We didn't have a lot of snow this past winter. The irony is that now the runs are fully open, after the dumping we had the other day."

A few days later, Gloria took Stuart and the twins to the

slopes. "It was the first time he laughed and seemed happy since he got here," she said to me that night when I called. "Thanks, Caitie."

Our first fight came a month later, when Stuart asked me about the upcoming spring dance at my school. I was going but hadn't thought about bringing anyone.

"Why not?"

"What do you mean, why not? Why should I bring anyone? I thought the whole point about having a long-distance relationship meant we didn't see other people because we intended to be together once we were living near each other again. No? Was I wrong?" I'd had a long day. I felt tired, my patience sapped.

"Of course, you're not wrong," he said, laughing. "I just thought you might want to take someone, even just as friends. We've got what they call the Spring Fling here, too. I guess it's a big deal and I'm planning to go with a couple of people."

I felt sick at once and couldn't speak. I was jolted with the image of Peyton kissing Stuart the night of his going-away party, and then I saw his arms above a bed sheet, reaching for a woman who wasn't me. I must have made a choking sound of some sort, a tone of pain from my subconscious.

"Caitie? Are you okay? Are you still there?"

I couldn't answer. I tried to swallow but my mouth felt like it was full of sawdust. I tried to fight these thoughts, but I'd known this day would come. Stuart was so magnetic. He drew people to him, whether it was in London, Ontario, or Boston, Massachusetts. I knew girls would love him there, and I felt, at once, abandoned.

He muffled the receiver and called to Gloria, saying he

thought the phone wasn't working, that it had cut out, because he couldn't hear me but I didn't wait to hear any more. I hung up the phone and placed the receiver on my desk and then inched my way to my bed and crawled under the sheets. I covered my head when the phone rang again. A few seconds later, I heard a knock on my door.

"Honey, it's Stuart. Are you okay? He said you guys got disconnected," my mom said through the door. When I didn't answer, she told him she'd have me call him back. I pretended to go to sleep and, eventually, my tears must have run out because that's what I did.

When I told Grace what had happened the next day, she became angry.

"Caitie, where in that conversation did you get that he wanted to take someone to his school dance and that he's now with someone else?" We sat in my school cafeteria. She came to our school during lunch hours to spend time with Tristan. I picked at my pita as she stuffed bits of her Cobb salad into her mouth. Tristan, who had put away two hamburgers and was contemplating going back to the hot food line for some fries, sat beside her but was yelling across the cafeteria to someone else. "Tristan, do you think she's being an idiot?"

"Well, I wouldn't say she's being an idiot. He might be going to that dance with someone else." Tristan waved goodbye to the guy he'd been yelling to as Grace shot daggers at him. Then he looked at me. "But, honestly, Cait? Knowing Stuart, if he was, it'd be a group thing, not a date thing. He's been gone like, what? A month? Do you honestly think he's replaced you? C'mon, give the guy a little credit. You chicks are always so quick to jump down a guy's throat." And then, sensing an invective about to flow from

Grace, he scooted from the bench we were sitting on and joined some other guys at the hot food line.

"Caitie, please call him back," Grace said, taking my hand. "And why not consider going with someone to the June dance? You know a lot of people at your school. Tons of guys would want to go with you. Not as a date, just with a group of people, like me and Tristan and Heather and Noah, and maybe a few other people. We won't go for dinner before. We'll just hang out, go to the dance and then go to an after-party."

That night, I called Stuart back. Gloria answered, saying Stuart was worried when he couldn't reach me.

"Caitie, what's the matter?" he said, as soon as he got on the phone. "I'm talking to you one minute and the next you're not saying anything. Did you hang up? Why? When I called you back, your mom said you were asleep. What's going on?"

"Stuart, are you seeing someone?" Before I got on the phone, I'd rehearsed what I was going to say. It wasn't that. I'd planned to be supportive, but when I heard his voice, I morphed into paranoid girlfriend instead. As soon as the words were out of my mouth, I wished I could take them back. He didn't deserve my distrust.

"For real? You've got to be kidding. Of course I'm not seeing someone. You're my girlfriend," he said, sounding a bit miffed, and then angry. "Oh! I see. You think because I was talking about going to this school dance that that must mean I've got a new girlfriend? I'm a little surprised and a lot disappointed, Cait. I've finally got some friends and was thinking it would be fun to go out with them, and I thought maybe you should go to your upcoming dance with someone, too. I wasn't asking for permission to date someone else. Fuck. I don't even want to date anyone else. And the thought of you being with someone else...well, I don't want to dwell on that, okay? I thought, well... I don't know what I thought. I miss you."

He was livid. Stuart didn't swear very often. He thought it was common and made people sound unintelligent. He saved up these words for important times, like the conversation we were having. I liked to drop the F-bomb pretty often, so it wasn't as shocking when he heard me say it, but after he said it, I felt ashamed.

"I'm sorry," I said, lamely. "Tell me about your new friends. I'm so glad you're finally fitting in."

"I wouldn't say I'm exactly fitting in. I still hate it here. You should see my school. What a nightmare," he said, sighing. "They have metal detectors at the entrance doors to make sure nobody brings in any guns. And the drugs! It's too bad I'm not into that because I could be really enjoying myself. And, I got in a fight."

"What?" I said, my voice rising.

"I went out to the movies with the one decent friend I have here and when we came out of the movie, this guy, who also goes to our school, started saying things to us about being gay. The two of them start fighting and I tried to intervene and got clocked on my left eye, but to the side, so I didn't have a black eye. Instead, I got cut from the guy's ring," he said, sounding morose.

"I don't know if I'm more concerned about you getting punched in the face or that you're hanging around with a homophobe," I said as my mind raced, trying to come up with a plan to bring him back home.

"Appalling, isn't it? But given the choices I have for friends, he's better than the drug dealers. You should see that bunch. So, anyway, this guy and a couple of his friends and then a couple of their female friends are going to the dance. I guess it's just a big drunk fest, but I've got to get out and meet people. I love my dad, and Gloria is pretty great. I love the twins, but they're seven so we can't exactly hang out. I took them to see a kids' movie, but I got a look from one lady when I was buying the tickets. I think she thought I was their father."

"I don't know, Stuart, this guy sounds like a nasty piece of work. I'd stick with the kids and come home as soon as things get better with your mom." When we spoke, we usually avoided any mention of him coming home. It was too difficult to think about him being here when we both knew he couldn't be.

"Caitie, you know I would if I could. I think about you all the time, and I can't wait to see you. I'll be home soon."

ten

MARCH 2017

I WAS FLIRTING WITH INFIDELITY. And I liked it.

My first day of meetings dragged on and, at times, I felt myself nodding off. I tried to pay attention to how Heusten Shoes was on track to hit its expansion plans. The company's sales pitch for new managers like me was that this was a great time to be with Heusten Shoes. The chain offered opportunities unlike most retail companies. There was talk of company-wide benefits, even a pension. But I didn't get my hopes up. I'd read too many stories about people who worked for myriad companies, from manufacturing plants to small mom-and-pop outfits, who lost every penny of their retirement savings when those companies went under. It was heartbreaking. Rob had some sort of profit-sharing program at Cre8tive, so I wasn't worried about what he'd get out of his career, barring the company going bankrupt. We were also diligent about saving on our own. Right after we'd married, my father talked to us about investing and other long-term wealth strategies. Matt now took care of our investments and financial planning, and Ken and Sue saved for Aidan and Jacob's college funds.

When I listened to the speakers, I longed to toe the company line. I liked everything I heard and desperately wanted to believe they would achieve their main goal, which was employing thousands of Canadians. But then we hit a budget meeting, and any sense of altruism I thought was a pillar of the company's foundation crumbled. Talk of projections, sales targets and savings through layoffs if necessary all amounted to the bottom line, and I felt myself float back to being jaded. I needed to get my head on straight and figure out my long-term career plan.

After the budget meeting, we had no further sessions that day, though a company-sponsored buffet was slated for seven. I wasn't about to turn down a free meal and decided to stay close to the hotel. I hadn't made any inroads into the old boys' club and, though there were only a handful of female store managers, I was wrong in assuming we would hit it off.

When the conference began, I recognized Tom, the brown-noser from Sault Ste. Marie, as well as Brittany, who I'd overheard gushing about Stuart in the bathroom during the Toronto training meeting. I didn't want to hang around with either of them, and I guess they felt the same way about me.

I emerged from the budget meeting room and heard Tom talking about his store's sales, which exceeded corporate expectations. I paused. I knew to whom he was speaking and felt a thrill when I saw I was right.

"You know, I think it has to do with my managerial

prowess," Tom said. "My staff are on their toes at all times, working as hard as possible because they don't want to be responsible for a downturn on our monthly balance sheets. Ha ha ha."

"You know, Tom, maybe you should reverse psychologize yourself," Stuart said as I came into view and he spotted me. He smiled. "Try praising them and creating an atmosphere of positivity. See how that motivates your staff. I'd bet your sales would triple."

"You were waiting for me," I said, as I walked up to him. He leaned against the wall. Tom, after being rebuked, scurried off to catch up with some of the other male managers. I'd overheard them talking earlier about a sports bar a few blocks away.

"You know me," he said, dressed in a dark navy suit, with a white dress shirt and aqua blue paisley tie. He looked incredible. "We've got an hour before dinner. Care for a drink?"

At the hotel restaurant, I tried to relax. I played with my hair and kept tapping my fingers against the wood table, which had been gouged from years of utensils. I texted Siobhan to make sure I wasn't breaking any rules, and she told me to cool it and stop texting until I did. I convinced myself that her advice was a harbinger of me sleeping with Stuart—and that she approved. During many conversations about fidelity, Siobhan had always backed the argument that people were bound to cheat. She believed that didn't mean cheaters loved their partners any less, a theory that had wrecked at least three of her relationships.

But I wasn't Siobhan.

While seeing Stuart thrilled me, I was horrified that cheating had become a serious option. When I'd said my vows to Rob, the idea of being with another man had never entered my mind. Up until I got married, I'd had four partners in total—Stuart was my first and I'd slept with two others during that time Rob and I casually dated in our relationship's infancy. I was curious about what it would be like to be with another man at this point in my life, even though Rob didn't seem to mind the cellulite that had arrived on my thighs and the baby fat that refused to leave my middle.

On the few occasions I'd picked up the boys at school, I'd eyed some of the other fathers—I'd even found myself blushing while speaking to a particularly nice-looking man with a neat, close-shaven beard, something, until then, I hadn't considered to be attractive. I needed to decide what I wanted from Stuart—not what I wished I could have in a consequence-free daydream. If I wanted to have a relationship with him, what would it look like? Was I willing to potentially sacrifice my marriage? One thing I knew I wanted was the truth about why he left. I felt I deserved at least that. But if I slept with him, I'd dishonour Rob, and the idea of doing so filled me with shame.

However, being with Stuart was complicated. I loved his quick wit, his ability to laugh at himself and his stories of his daughter Paisley. And the more we reconnected, the more I realized I still loved him in my core. When he'd left for Boston, I'd felt as though a portion of my soul had been ripped out, and when we were reunited in London, it was like finding the final puzzle piece that had gone missing under the couch.

Stuart and I had time for just one drink, before we were ushered into a meeting room, which was filled with round tables. Stuart sat at a table for corporate employees, so I found some colleagues to dine with. Once the buffet dinner finished by nine, I called home and Rob said he had everything under control. I tried not to ask him details. I wanted him to know I trusted him and believed he could handle it. But I knew part of his success was because of Birdie, who was staying over that night. She'd made a tuna casserole, the boys' favourite, and helped Rob bathe the boys, read them stories and tuck them into bed.

Just as I finished my call, I noticed Stuart waiting off to the side, clicking on his cell phone. He came over and invited me to his room—"Just to catch up, Caitie," he promised—and we shared a bottle of wine. To be accurate, I drank three-quarters of the bottle, while Stuart had one glass before switching to water. Then, we started talking about the past.

"I was inconsolable for weeks after you left for Boston," I said, pouring the wine, watching as the last droplets splashed in my glass. I sat on his bed, my feet bare, my hair in a messy ponytail. Stuart sat on a chair across the room.

"I know. In my teenage boy way, I was, too. It wasn't just you I left, though being away from you was the hardest thing I'd ever gone through. But I knew we'd still be together. What we had was different, special. It was my mother who was the biggest issue, and then I was trying to re-establish myself with my dad's family. I hadn't lived with my dad for ten years at that point and was trying to assimilate myself in his family, in a new city—in a new country, for crying out loud—and you were a thousand kilometres away, along with my other closest friends." He shook his head. "It was, without question, the worst time of my life. When Erin and I divorced, that wasn't as bad."

I looked at him, head cocked to the side. My lips were pinched and my brows furrowed.

"No, really, Cait. Like I told you, it was sad, but it wasn't devastating the way moving to Boston had been. Caitie, I know I told you this when I came back to visit, but really, knowing I could see you, that you'd be the one constant in my life—that's what kept me going. Sometimes, when I think about how we were and what I felt about you, I can't believe we're not together now."

I was stunned. For months after Stuart left, I couldn't believe we weren't together either. To hear him say this tonight, I was transported back to that confusing and devastating time. During our relationship, when Stuart spoke about his feelings, I knew he was being genuine. He didn't waste words. Sometimes, he couldn't even find the words for how he felt. I knew he was conflicted about this mother. While he loved her, he also resented her and couldn't understand why she didn't trust him and demanded so much of him. No matter what he did, it never seemed to be enough for her. He was always enough for me.

I put all thoughts of how attractive I found Stuart to the side. What I needed now was to know *why* he had left. Before I could make any decisions about my future, I needed my past resolved. And while just speaking about our time together was causing me to feel such joy, there was always an undercurrent of unease because I knew, intimately, the hurt that lurked around the corner.

eleven

JUNE 1997

THE SPRING DANCE ended up being a lot of fun. I went (as friends) with Terry. He'd gotten dumped two weeks before by a Grade 9 girl, who turned out not to be as naive as he'd thought and refused to go to third base with him. I kept expecting him to try to kiss or grope me while we danced, but he kept his hands and mouth to himself and I was relieved. At one point while we danced, he leaned toward me and said, "Caitie, Stuart is one lucky guy," which made me flush and smile.

I was beyond busy as the school year wound down, with track and field, student council work, planning for my final year in high school, and my ice cream store shifts. Tennis lessons were over for the spring season, and I toyed with the decision of whether to continue summer lessons with Grace.

Stuart's exams were finished and he bought a plane ticket for London for June 20th, just days before school let out for the summer. Counting down the hours until he arrived became my most important activity. He would be home for two entire weeks before returning to Boston, where he'd been hired as a landscaper for the summer. Edward told him he should get a job and I agreed. I thought it would give him something to focus on other than his loser friends or missing home. Plus, he would have money for when I came to visit. I saved every cent from my extra shifts to buy a plane ticket to Boston for the end of August. We planned for me to stay with his father's family for one whole week.

It was Friday, the end of the second-to-last week of school. With only a few minutes to spare, I rushed to my locker to grab everything I needed for the weekend. I had a scant six seconds to reach my bus or I'd be begging a ride home from my dad—if I could reach him at his office in time—or taking the city bus. Neither option was appealing. I grabbed my bag and ran down the hallway out toward the bus, calling goodbyes over my shoulder as I went. Outside, I couldn't believe how warm it was. June could be a hit or miss. Most days, it was beautiful, but sometimes we got tricked into thinking we'd survived winter, only to be surprised with a brisk morning. Today, there was no doubt summer was just ahead.

I kept my head down and began running for my bus, which was straight ahead of me, when I heard his voice. I stopped and whipped around. Stuart was leaning against his car across the street.

"Wanna ride?" he called, his face lit up by his smile.

I couldn't believe he was here—my Stuart—standing in front of me. I hadn't seen him in three months. His hair seemed lighter, but I couldn't be sure. He jogged across the street toward me and he grabbed me in a hug. I started crying, my tears dampening his shirt. Then he kissed me. When we broke apart, I couldn't stop touching him, afraid he would disappear. I sensed he felt the same.

"I thought you were coming home next Friday. I had a huge surprise planned," I said, grabbing his hands with mine and interlacing our fingers.

"I did that on purpose!" he said, laughing. "I had to surprise you. You, by the way, are stunning. Absolutely gorgeous."

I reddened, thrilled. Determined to look like a strong, lean and muscular woman instead of a little girl, I'd revamped my wardrobe. Today, I wore a red dress with white polka dots and black sandals, and my hair was pulled back into a ponytail. In my transformation, I'd moved from plain looking to somewhat pretty, and lately, I'd noticed the way guys looked at me when I was at the mall or at the movies with Grace and Heather. When we were at Joe Kool's on weekends, sometimes university guys approached our table, asking to buy me a drink. I would never be drop-dead gorgeous, but I felt comfortable in my own skin, which was quite a feat for an eighteen-year-old. Part of that was because of Stuart—that I'd captured his affections and his entire devotion meant I deserved to be loved.

Stuart stayed for two-and-a-half weeks and the time seemed to rush away just as the final days of a Christmas break always did. Before he arrived, I had called Caroline to let her know we would be away for a weekend camping. I expected her to argue, to plead for just a one-day trip instead of the two I'd planned.

"Oh, Caitie, he'll love that," she said. "I can't wait until he's back. I miss him so much."

"I know, Mrs. Taylor, I do, too," I said, hurrying to get off the phone in case she changed her mind, though I was prepared to fight her for his time. I felt I could lay claim to it.

While the other campers got drunk at night, Stuart and I holed up in our tent, making out, talking and sometimes just looking at each other in the darkness. Things were much better in Boston—he had friends, he was excited about starting the landscaping job, his grades, shockingly, were excellent and he got along very well with his dad's family.

"It's ideal, really, except you're not there," he said one day as we ate a quick lunch at a burger joint.

"How long will you be away?" I asked, not wanting to talk about the future but knowing we had to broach the subject. It was becoming obvious that things were looking less clear and more convoluted. Stuart, who should have graduated in June along with his friends, was now a few courses short to graduate in Ontario. If he wanted to graduate from his high school in Boston, he needed to complete an entire additional year there. "Please don't tell me you're going to stay for the whole year."

"Right now, Caitie, that's the plan. But I've decided I'm going to university where you're going."

"Are you sure?" I said, relieved to hear him say so as I licked salt from my fingers. "What are you going to take? What if my university doesn't offer it?"

"Here's the thing. I'm not quite sure what I want to do, but if I came back here and went to Western, it'd be a disaster. I could stay in Boston, but the tuition is a killer. I can't live at home with my mom, likely not ever again for any long period of time. So, you figure out where you're going, and I'm going to go with you. I can't stand to be away from you. It's like a piece of me is missing."

"I know. I feel the same way."

Aside from yearning for Stuart, that summer was idyllic. I worked full-time, scooping so much ice cream into cones, containers and shakes that I got a small bout of tendinitis in my wrist and I hated the taste of ice cream by the time mid-July rolled around. Grace and I returned to the courts, taking lessons three times a week.

Grace had dumped Tristan at the end of June, before he took off for a two-month camp counsellor job in northern Ontario.

"Why?" I asked her, shocked and a bit angry because she could, if she wanted to, take the bus up to visit him on weekends.

"Caitie, we're not you and Stuart. I want someone here."

Soon after, she started dating Scott from her school. They'd known of each beforehand but didn't run in the same circles. Scott knew Stuart, too, and from time to time, he asked me how Stuart was. Scott's best friend, Walter, also knew Stuart, and the four of us spent a lot of time together. It was a relief that not only did Walter know about Stuart and me, but he'd ended a year-long relationship not long before. I felt no awkwardness or pressure that he thought we could become a couple.

After Stuart left, schoolmates wanted to introduce me to their boyfriends' best friends or hook me up with someone who'd just became single. When someone approached me, I felt on guard. My instinct was to turn away before they reached me. Sometimes, I forced myself to breathe, to unclench my fists. People were only trying to help, I told myself. At first, I set the record straight, but after a few weeks, I no longer cared what anyone thought. I spent most of my time staying busy, trying to forget how much I missed him.

Brandon and I spent time together as well, going to movies and just hanging out. It was as though he was the only one who understood my feelings because their bromance was nearly as strong as our romantic relationship. A couple of weeks after Stuart returned to Boston, Brandon picked me up and we sat together in a coffee house, not saying much, just feeling comforted by the fact that the other person also knew and loved Stuart.

The calendar flipped to August and the days melted away. I drew a black "x" through each day, excitement growing for the day I could leave. I got busier, trying to pass the days as fast as possible. On top of tennis and my job, I ramped up the number of kilometres I was running each week so I'd be in top shape for the fall cross-country season. My body was tanned and toned, my hair soaked in natural highlights from the sun.

My vision now spanned past my final year of high school. The idea of leaving London and venturing out on my own was both daunting and exciting. I researched universities in Ottawa, Montreal and Kingston and, though I was nervous about moving away from my family, knowing Stuart and I would be together relaxed me. I would soon strike out on my own, developing into who I would become —famous writer, perhaps—and that kept me focused on what needed to be done next.

The day before my flight left for Boston, I spent most of my free time repacking my suitcase, making sure to take my birth control pills. Stuart and I were both adamant about using protection. Neither of us wanted to be teenaged parents. I knew if I got pregnant, Stuart wouldn't abandon me, but I didn't want to see a look of disappointment permanently etched on my parents' faces.

Sarah drove me to Toronto's Pearson International Airport as she and two of her bridesmaids headed to an appointment at a fancy downtown Toronto wedding boutique. I had already been on a few dress-finding expeditions with her, looking for a bridesmaid's dress for me. Though I tried to bow out, she insisted I be one of her attendants.

Stuart had said he would meet me just outside the baggage carousel of Terminal B at Logan International in Boston. After disembarking, I speed-walked down the ramp and into the terminal, and I followed the signs to the baggage claim area. I scanned the suitcases as they clanged onto the metal carousel, the annoying buzzing sound only making me more antsy. My suitcase appeared. I grabbed it and sped toward the street exit. There, waiting with a brown sign that read "Caitie" in children's printing was Stuart. I ran and jumped in his arms.

"You look better every time I see you," he said, scanning me from head to toe. I wore a pink seersucker dress with spaghetti straps and espadrilles. "I can't wait to get you alone."

"Me neither," I said, grabbing for his hand as he slung my duffle bag over his shoulder and wheeled my suitcase behind him. I wore just my cross-body purse.

I kept stealing glances at him, feeling just as I had when he'd been in London in June—unsure I was really in Boston and afraid he would disappear and I'd be alone again. But there was something else. This was where he now lived. A few misgivings started to creep in, niggling thoughts I'd banished from my mind until this point. What if his life here didn't include me or have space for me? It was fine when he was in London. I lived there. Our relationship lived there. But Boston? Part of his play was an entire cast of characters I didn't know.

"What's the matter?" he said, looking at me as we walked through the parking lot. "You've gone pretty quiet. Don't like Boston? We're parked over here."

"It's not that. I've just all of a sudden realized you have an entire life that doesn't include me. What if no one here likes me, or you decide to stay here?"

"Caitie, c'mon. My dad and Gloria will love you, as will the twins—they like anyone who'll play Game of Life with them. And my friends? They'll like you, but it doesn't really matter to me. They're not like Brandon and the others at home. Those are my real friends. These people are substitutes—and sometimes, they're not very good ones." We reached his car—Gloria's new silver Mercedes. He opened the trunk, lifted my bags into it, slammed it shut and then grabbed me, pinning me against the car. He nuzzled my neck and kissed me. "I've missed you so much. Don't go making up problems." He gave me another kiss before letting me climb into the passenger's side.

We drove out of Logan International and across Interstate 90 into Boston. Edward and Gloria lived in Brookline, about thirty minutes from the airport. Stuart said their house was nice, but as we drove along the Mass Turnpike, I wondered what constituted nice. Stuart's dad was a lawyer, a partner in a prestigious law firm, to be exact. Gloria owned a small, yet successful, boutique that sold high-end women's fashions in downtown Boston and was thinking about expanding to include a second location.

As we drove, I couldn't help but notice how comfortable

Stuart was driving on these strange streets. He exited the Turnpike and drove along another highway until we found ourselves on Walnut Street, which featured a full tree canopy. Stuart played tour bus operator, letting me know Brookline was home to Boston University and Fisher College, the oldest country club in the United States, as well as several world-renowned hospitals, and it was the birthplace of President Kennedy.

"Damn, Stuart, you never told me your father was rich," I said, pulling on the hem of my dress and wondering if I would show up to a mansion with a cook, gardener, and butler on staff. I felt ill at ease in my clothes. Television shows were the only reference points I had for rich people. My parents did well, and we were comfortable, but we weren't wealthy. On TV, rich people looked down their noses at anyone less well-off than them. Stuart never made disparaging remarks about anyone's financial status. His mother looked at you as though you weren't good enough but she did that to everyone Stuart was friends with (except Brandon), so I didn't let it bother me.

"Relax," he said, smiling. He touched my hand before returning his to the steering wheel. "You look great, and they're going to love you."

We passed a majestic, old stone church, with three adorable arches perched on mini columns and a traditional flower-like stained glass window in the apex. Then we hung a left onto another street, which was even lovelier and quainter than the road before. Behind wrought iron gates lay manicured lawns, stone driveways and beautiful Colonial homes. A little way down the street, Stuart slowed and I got my first glimpse at the paradise he'd been calling home for the past six months. A short, white picket fence curved along the perimeter of the property. The white steel gates, anchored to stone pillars, opened to welcome us. We drove up a long, interlocking brick driveway, which intersected a freshly mown lawn. The house, which featured grey siding, boasted four white-painted chimneys and black shutters. There was a dormer on an addition at the back of the house, overlooking the original building, which featured four widow's peaks. It was stunning.

"Stuart, you live at Greystone Manor!" I grabbed his arm as he pulled into a parking spot beside a deep burgundy Jaguar. When we drove around the most exclusive parts of London, we came up with charming names for the mansions. We called a brownstone with a beautiful full-lawn garden Garden Estate and christened another the White House, which boasted a flag pole and a circular interlocking brick driveway.

We got out of the car and the front door opened. Two kids, who looked nothing like Stuart, raced out, stopping just in front of me. Meghan's fiery red, curly hair was tamed into a ponytail. She had blue eyes and freckles and wore a yellow dress with a chocolate stain. Her brother, Parker, was skinny with straight brown hair and brown eyes and was about six inches taller than Meghan. His two top teeth were also missing and when he said "s," he had a sweet lisp.

"I'm Caitie," I told them.

"We know. Stuart talks about you all the time," Parker said as Meghan smiled without saying a word.

"C'mon, you two, let's go inside," Stuart said, opening the trunk and grabbing my suitcase and bag.

The kids raced back into the house and I could hear them shouting to someone inside, "She's here! She's here!" I smiled. We walked alongside impeccable, landscaped gardens as we meandered to the front of the house. Stunning greenery accented with deep purple and red flowers wove a welcome pathway for visitors. The front door was still open. We entered and I was surprised that the living room was less grandiose than I'd expected. A white leather couch contrasted with the Cape Cod-blue walls, which were adorned with picture frames showcasing family members.

I looked at the faces and found a few of a young Stuart, as well as Emma and Nicole, though the majority featured the twins. There was one of Stuart's father with a beautiful woman on their wedding day, and I was amazed at how much the two Taylor men looked alike. I was looking at Stuart a couple of decades into the future. He would still be extremely handsome. A short, fit woman who looked a few years older than the one in the photo came into the room from the kitchen, which was all gleaming stainless steel and dark wood cabinets. She grinned.

"Caitlin, welcome to our home," she said. She hugged me and then kissed me on the cheek. "I'm Gloria. You must be tired from your flight. Sit down. Stuart, get Caitlin a glass of tonic." I gasped.

"Oh, Caitie, don't be alarmed, it's a soda. Look at you. You're as pretty as a flower," she said, holding my hands in hers and appraising me.

I liked her and knew I wouldn't tire of her Boston accent. At the airport, I wanted to stop everyone I saw and ask them to say "car park."

"Stuart's father will be home soon. He was leaving the office early so he could meet you. I know Stuart wanted to take you downtown tonight."

We chatted with Gloria as I ate the ham sandwich Stuart

had whipped up for me. When I finished, he carried my luggage to one of the guest rooms, which was next door to his room. The cream-coloured space featured huge windows overlooking the swimming pool and gardens, with an antique desk and black wrought iron bedframe, decorated with a cream, Pottery Barn quilt accented with shades of green. It was like staying at a country club. Stuart wheeled my suitcase to the bed and, in two strides, walked back to the door. He shut it without making a noise and then grabbed me, his mouth finding mine, his hands in my hair, then moving down my back, lifting up my shirt.

"Stuart," I said, giggling. "Here? What if the kids come back? What about Gloria?"

"We've got at least ten minutes," he panted, and before I knew it, we were naked, lying on the floor, which was carpeted in the most exquisite fibres, fitting perfectly together once again.

My week with Stuart was exhilarating. We explored Boston, walking Freedom Trail, catching a Red Sox game at Fenway Park, strolling around Harvard, even checking out the famous Cheers, though neither of us had watched the show when it was on television, and exploring the fancy-schmancy Beacon Hill area. The rest of the time, we found places we could be alone, making out as much as we could before someone caught us, which was thrilling all on its own. Gloria, I was sure, knew what we were up to. A couple of times, she asked me if I was hot or if I needed anything to drink because my cheeks were red, which made Stuart snicker.

On the day before I left, Stuart and I revisited the most unsettling aspect of our long-distance relationship. I met some of Stuart's high school friends, and, like him, wasn't fond of most of them, especially a girl named Jennifer, who had short brown hair, large breasts and a gap-tooth smile. She was pretty but not at all what I thought of as Stuart's type. She was nothing like me. She reminded me of Peyton because it was obvious she liked Stuart. I was more than a little shocked when I found out from her, while we were at a Beacon Hill coffeehouse, that they "went together" to the school's spring dance. I tried to show I neither cared nor found this to be new information, but Stuart knew I was angry. I felt his eyes on my face, which I kept frozen in a smile, as she spoke about how much fun they'd had as they danced together. When I looked at him, he stared back without flinching. She also watched us, trying to gauge whether she had stirred the pot.

"I hope you had a good time," I said, before leaning over to kiss Stuart on the mouth.

On the T ride home that night, I stayed silent, trying to figure out what to say, how not to be jealous, how to not lash out at him, which was my first instinct. He pre-empted any fight by saying he was going to tell me.

"We had discussed going to school dances and, after you got upset, I figured I wouldn't talk about it again," he said, sitting beside me, holding my hand. "It's just so hard without you. I'm not looking for anyone else, Caitie, but sometimes I wonder if maybe we should date other people. I don't know how long it's going to be before we're back together."

I spun around to look at him, my mouth snapped open, my eyes wide. A chill seeped through me. He backpedalled. "That's not what I mean. I don't want anyone else. I only want you. Only. You. But I can't have you now. And what if we don't end up going to the same university? I'm never going to hold you back, Cait. I love you too much for that. But should we stay together if the next time we'll be living in the same city is when we're twenty-five?"

"Are you kidding me, Stuart?" I said, my voice rising, relieved the subway car was nearly deserted. The only other people near us were a couple of passed-out teenagers. I hoped they wouldn't miss their stop. "You're going to have this conversation now? Tomorrow I'm going home and you spring this on me now?" I felt tears prick my eyes and I tried to brush them away by blinking as rapidly as I could. I wiped my eyes on my sleeve.

"Hey, hey, Caitie," he said, handing me a tissue. Stuart was the only guy I knew who often carried a tissue around in his pocket. "I'm not breaking up. I don't want that. I. Only. Want. You. I don't think you're hearing me."

"But you're saying we should date other people," I said, as I hiccupped. I was crying hard now, trying to keep breathing, wondering if I should get off the train but having no idea where we were. In the next second, I thought, I should leave his house tonight and get an earlier flight out. Sometimes, I made myself laugh when I thought about how calm Stuart always was compared to my more impulsive and, I was ashamed to admit, dramatic personality. Tonight I didn't find it so amusing.

"I'm not saying that. I'm telling you if you don't want to keep working so hard at this relationship—because, sometimes, it's really hard, Cait—that if that's something you want, I would give it to you."

I understood. Sometimes, Grace suggested I meet someone new, that I try going out with someone else, to see if they might be able to fill the void that Stuart's absence created.

When we both lived in London, our relationship was uncomplicated. His move was a challenge we needed to overcome. It was too easy to take your partner for granted when the person was with you all the time. Now that Stuart was in Boston, and we were still together, I knew my love for him was complete and unconditional. I knew he loved me as well, and that brought me comfort—most of the time. Though I still missed him, I had come to terms with our situation. When he left after visiting in June, the ache wasn't as severe as it had been when he'd first moved to Boston. I felt whole most of the time. It was only in moments like this that I began to fear and doubt. What he said was like a dagger being plowed into my chest and twisted.

"You don't think I know it's hard work?" I asked him, dabbing at my eyes. "But, for me, it's worth it. I thought for you it was, too."

"It is. Do you know how happy I am that you're here? It's like I can finally breathe again. But now we both have to go through the leaving—again—and that sucks. I don't know when we'll next see each other. Christmas, I guess? I'm not coming home now for Thanksgiving, and I know you can't come here in a month. My next break is American Thanksgiving, but it's so close to Christmas, I'll just wait and come home for two weeks," he said, sighing. "Listen, I'm sorry. This is stupid. It's only three months. It's just that after seeing you practically every day for a year, I see you a few days every few months. Shit. At Christmas, we'll have a better idea about university. We'll know more then about where we're headed."

Though Stuart seemed to have talked himself off the ledge, I remained unnerved. Before tonight, I'd thought our long-distance challenges were resolved. Yes, for the next year, we were looking at long gaps between our times together. But come next September, we'd be at the same university, maybe even living in the same house. Our future would be clearer then—our future together. But it was obvious to me now that Stuart didn't see that as vividly as I did.

My tears let up and, because I didn't want to start again, I kept quiet. Sensing I was out of sorts, Stuart held my hand but said nothing. Just before our stop, he touched my chin with his finger.

"Hey, look at me. I love you." I blinked away tears.

He pulled me up to stand and, when the train had stopped, we exited the car. He reached for my hand and we began walking toward the parked Mercedes. I felt beat up, as though someone had taken a rolled up wet towel and hit me with it several times. I was stinging but my welts were invisible.

The drive back to Edward's house was silent, the radio turned off. There were no lights on when we got to the house, except the small one above the stove in the kitchen. Gloria had left out a plate of freshly baked cookies with a note urging us to eat as many as we wanted, signed with a heart and smiley face. I breathed in, trying to intercept a sob, as I realized that I was in love not only with Stuart, but also with his American family.

"I'm just going to go to bed," I said to Stuart, pecking him on the cheek. He didn't stop me.

I moved through the beautiful, silent house, leaving him in the kitchen. I vowed not to cry, hurrying to the bathroom, where I brushed my hair and teeth and washed my face. Back in my room, I undressed in haste and lay down in my luxurious bed. A few minutes later, I heard Stuart moving around next door, and my heart ached. Stuart had told me the first night I arrived that Edward had asked him not to leave his room at night. Though he knew we were "sexually active," which made us chuckle, and that we were practically adults, he didn't want his son going into his girlfriend's room at night in his house. And, as Stuart respected his father, he adhered to his rules. This didn't mean, of course, that we didn't have sex in the bathroom after swimming—running the shower as though I was in it, while Stuart pretended to be napping in his room—or in the family's large entertainment room in the basement, which had a lock.

I felt ridiculous about our fight. No one could know what would happen in the future, I told myself. Ever since that first night, when Stuart told me he would never lie to me, he hadn't. He was faithful and devoted, and I needed to give him some slack. He was doing the best he could. Marriages broke up. Stuart never talked much about what it was like when Edward and Caroline were married, though I knew there had been a lot of fighting, which was why Stuart hated conflict and arguing.

I swung my legs out of bed and tiptoed to my door. I opened it, slid out into the hall and waited, listening to make sure no one moved about the house. When I was convinced no one could hear me, I put my hand on the doorknob to Stuart's room and turned it. The room was dark and he was in bed. At first, he didn't hear me, but then he saw me enter his room. He watched me close the door without making a sound behind me, tiptoe to his bed and climb in beside him.

"Your dad didn't say anything about me coming to your room at night," I whispered before kissing him. He sat up, tenting his legs, the sheet falling to reveal he was shirtless, wearing only lounge pants, his nighttime attire. I touched his chest with a bit of pressure. He leaned back until he was lying down once again. I nuzzled his face and neck, running my hands through his hair, stopping to pull on a curl, which always made me smile. I kissed his arms, tracing my tongue down his stomach to the top of his pants. I pulled them down, and he was already hard. I pulled my pyjama tank top over my head, revealing my breasts, which he reached for, attempting to sit up before I nudged him, indicating I wanted him to lie back down. I pushed up on my arms, using my legs to free my lower body from my short pyjama bottoms. He watched me as I lowered myself onto him.

"Cait," he moaned, his eyes closed. He whispered my name again a few minutes later as he stared into my eyes and said, "Stay forever."

twelve

MARCH 2017

"THAT WAS a fun time when you came to see me, Cait. I had really missed you," Stuart said to me in his hotel room, glossing over our time in Boston. We stayed up past midnight, reminiscing about some of our best times together. We kept things PG, skirting over any intimate occasions.

The second night of the conference, my sessions stretched past dinner. Stuart texted me at eight o'clock to say he had finished, but it was another hour before I could say the same. I felt exhausted and had created a fantasy of going to bed and curling up in the quiet and the luxurious sheets. But then I thought, if we picked up the conversation from where we left it the night before, I might get some answers about why our relationship imploded. I continued to struggle with why Stuart wanted to spend so much time with me now because it was his decision to end our relationship seventeen years ago.

After saying goodnight to a few colleagues as we left the meeting room, I found Stuart in the lobby having a drink with other store managers. The first one, a woman dressed in a tank top and Daisy Dukes, rested her hand on his forearm and laughed throatily at everything he said, while giving him a good glimpse of her cleavage, which was pushed up for his viewing pleasure. The other woman wore a sweater over her turtleneck, even though it was a mild evening, and a permanent scowl.

"Caitlin," Stuart called as I walked into the lobby. "I was just talking with these ladies as I waited for you." After introducing us, Stuart popped out of his seat, eliciting a "no-o-o," from the breasty woman. Her friend's disapproval vanished for a second and she looked relieved.

"I'm off to bed," said Frumpy, without giving us another look. The chesty woman looked at Stuart, then me and back to Stuart, waiting for one of us to ask her to join us.

"Well, I think I'll head over to the bar across the street. I know a few of the guys were heading there tonight. See you tomorrow, Stuart," she said, ignoring me.

"Ah, brings back wonderful memories of watching you interact with Peyton," I said, as soon as the women were out of earshot.

"Really? Are you jealous?" he said, already steering me toward the lobby.

"I was never really jealous of Peyton—she was an interloper. Where are we going?"

"Where would you like to go?"

"I don't know, but out. I was pretty tired when that last meeting finally wrapped up, but now I feel like I want to go out somewhere." Then I glanced at myself in the lobby mirror and started second-guessing my decision. "Actually,

Stuart, I'm not dressed for anything special and my makeup has probably worn off. I think I'll just head upstairs and go to bed."

"Stop," Stuart said, facing me. "You look fantastic, Caitie. Let's grab a cab and head to the Distillery District."

I looked out at the huge expanse that was Lake Ontario as our cab drove along Queens Quay, the clear night making it possible to see lights on the other shore. *My family is there, sleeping in their beds,* I thought, but didn't say anything. The cab went north on Parliament Street and then right onto Mill Street, stopping outside The Maldives. At one glance, I knew my clothes were inappropriate and I began to sweat and rub my hands on my pants. Beside me, Stuart's outfit screamed urban hip—dark blue jeans, a blue gingham shirt that was open at the neck and a black jacket. He also had a five o'clock shadow, and I watched some of the women on the patio appreciate his appearance when we emerged from the vehicle. He reached for my hand and I saw their faces flicker with disappointment. I felt triumphant until I saw them look me up and down and felt my cheeks prickle. My hair was limp, my eyes tired and my black pants were a tad too big. My flowing red shirt was out of date. Thank God, I had at least thought to bring my COACH clutch with me.

"Stuart, I'm not so sure about this place," I said. "It's uber-trendy. Look at me."

"I am," he said, with a wolfish grin.

We entered the upscale bar and I noticed how much thought had gone into restoring the building. The Distillery District had got its name from a bygone era, and the way these buildings had been repurposed amazed me. We walked into a low-lit room with exposed brick, large wood beams, plank flooring and archways. Its opulent décor featured rich leather banquettes, acid-rusted chandeliers and grand lounge furniture boasting illuminated onyx bars. The speakeasy chic room was also filled with beautiful, trendy people. We perched on the last two available bar stools and I gave the bartender my order for a Tom Collins. Stuart ordered tonic water with lime. The bar was a safe place and I was a wallflower nobody would notice—a mother of two young boys, thrilled to be out in the big city, sitting next to my gorgeous former lover. After my second drink, I remembered I'd forgotten to eat dinner—a bag of chips didn't count—so we left and headed to a restaurant. I knew Stuart earned a multi-six-figure income, so I didn't worry about him picking up the cab fares and the Maldives tab.

We walked toward Yonge and Wellington and popped into a bistro. I was tipsy by the time we arrived and felt my inhibitions relaxing. A battle waged in my brain—should versus want—and morality had begun to lose by increments. We looked at the menu posted in the plastic box outside of Keith's Bistro and I couldn't help but link my arm with his, as though caught in the gravitational pull he always emitted. He was the sun and I was a little planet orbiting around him. Stuart accepted my subtle touches without comment. The hostess showed us to our table, but I didn't register what she was wearing; I looked only at Stuart. He pulled out my chair and then sat beside me, which was how we'd always sat when we dined together. Rob and I cuddled together in banquettes when we'd dated, too. But whenever we went out now, we sat across from each other, especially if we were with the boys, as no reasonable parent would allow two young brothers to sit beside each other.

We ordered more drinks and nibbled off each other's plates, just as we always had. I was heady with alcohol and infatuation. Bolstered by the liquid courage, the question I was dying to ask him, seeking the answer I'd desperately wanted to know for seventeen years, poured out of my mouth.

"Stuart, why did you leave?"

thirteen

AUGUST 1997

ON THE FLIGHT from Boston to London, I decided I would try dating others—only to see if I could. When I explained the verdict to Grace and Heather, they looked at me with puzzled expressions.

"Did you guys have a fight?" Grace asked.

"Did you break up?" Heather wondered.

"No, we're definitely still a couple."

We'd buried our subway conversation. But on our last day together in Boston, we were morose. I knew he was as upset as I was at the prospect of waiting months to see each other again. When he carried my bags out to the car to take me to the airport, Gloria hugged me, saying, "It was so good of you to come, Caitlin. Stuart is a different man since you've been here."

Edward, too, shook my hand, and then embraced me. "I hope we see you again soon, young lady. You're always welcome here."

I'd brought the twins stuffed animals from London, and their faces lit up when I pulled them out as going-away presents. Stuart parked the car so he could wait with me at the terminal instead of just dropping me off. I checked my larger suitcase and grasped his hand so hard my fingers ached. But I didn't let go. I stared at him, wanting to say so many things but overwhelmed by the impending separation.

"I love you," I said when they called my flight. Then I crushed my lips to his. "I can't say anymore because it breaks my heart. But you know how I feel."

"Caitie," he said, drawing me into a bear hug, "I'll see you soon. I love you."

I brushed away a few tears, grabbed my carry-on and slipped through the gate. On the other side, I headed straight for the restroom. I pulled open a stall and sat down on the toilet seat, my shoulders heaving as tears streamed through my closed fingers. When I heard my flight called again, I flushed the toilet and dabbed my nose and eyes with toilet paper. I exited the stall and moved to the row of stainless steel sinks, where I washed my face. My eyes were red and puffy, and I looked like I was going to a funeral.

"I love him so much," I told Heather and Grace. "We're perfect together, but this can't last forever. I've decided to see other people—just to try it. I don't want anyone else, but what if he decides to stay in Boston and we don't go to university together? Then what? I get over him then...? Or we do another four years apart and then live...where? Having seen him in Boston—and you should see it, he has an entire life there—woke me up to the fact that he's got a life away from me. He's not just on a vacation."

"Are you going to tell him?" Heather asked, wide-eyed.

"I haven't figured that out. I'm thinking it won't go far with anyone else."

When school started up again, I was so busy I didn't have time to think about other guys. Stuart and I could manage to speak on the phone only a couple of times a week. On top of my school work and part-time job, I was running cross-country and again on student council. I could hear the frustration in Stuart's voice late one evening. I was a couple of hours late getting home because I was spearheading a fundraiser for the following day. I was at Heather's house making posters with her and a few other people. I mentioned to Stuart that Anthony had been a great help—he at least had some artistic skills and was funny, which kept us going long past the point when most of us had wanted to quit.

Stuart's voice was glacial. "I'm glad you had him to keep you company."

"Stuart, you can't be serious," I said, yawning. "I'm tired, you're tired. Why don't we just go to bed and we'll reconnect tomorrow?"

"Caitie, I've waited all day to talk to you. Do you have a few minutes?" His tone was uncharacteristically clipped.

"Of course. It's thrilling just to hear your voice. Tell me something," I said, lying back on my bed and closing my eyes, listening to the inflection of his voice, seeing his face in my mind. He told me he was going to a dance with a bunch of people, and that Jennifer would be there. I knew there was nothing going on between them, but it bugged me that he didn't see how much she wanted something to happen.

As September became October, I found myself checking out Anthony, who was the same age as me and a starter on the school's senior basketball team. When the team took the city championship, Heather and I went to the party at his house. As soon as we entered the foyer, Anthony lifted me up in a bear hug and kissed my cheek. He was about Stuart's height, with dark wavy hair and brown eyes, and his sense of humour was his best attribute. He was also single, and Heather said he'd asked our mutual friends about me. I shivered when she told me, my mind starting to race with possibilities, and then my heart sank as I thought of doing anything that would hurt Stuart. But despite that news, Anthony gave me no indication he might want to get involved. His flirting was just part of his personality, I told myself.

He put me down, beaming, the adrenaline from winning still coursing through him and infecting everyone around him. His teammates and other partygoers were in the kitchen doing shots. Anthony took my coat and asked if he could get me anything. I opted for the safe choice of a light beer, and when he returned, we sat down on his couch to hear him replay the game's highlights. Anthony gestured wildly with his hands. He stood up and acted out how he shot a three-pointer to pull our school into the lead with less than twenty seconds left in the game. On the very next play, one of his teammates forced a turnover, dribbled down the court and sent a bounce pass to Anthony, whose nice lay-up sealed the deal. It had been a great game, and I felt relaxed for the first time in a while. In Boston, I adored and treasured my time with Stuart, but it was tinged with sadness because each new day had brought us closer to being apart once again. Anthony could be elated tonight and happy tomorrow because he wasn't going anywhere.

After a while, the talk turned to the upcoming semi-formal dance, which had been postponed to November this year, and Anthony turned to me and asked whom I was going with. I squirmed a bit in my seat. I'd planned to help with the set-up crew and ticket collection at the door.

"I know you were dating that guy in Boston, but I'd love to go with you," he said.

My breath caught in my throat. A thousand thoughts flitted through my mind. Should I correct him? Stuart and I were still together. And what did it mean for us if I didn't? Did I want to set things straight? What should I say?

"That'd be great," I said, settling for the easy way out. He beamed at me and then took my hand in his.

It took me a week to work up the courage to tell Stuart. I spilled my news the day before the dance. The only thing I could think of was how much difference a year made. Last fall, I'd gone to the same dance with Terry. Stuart and I had kissed for the first time that night.

"Well, I'm not going to stop you from going, but I'm not thrilled about this," Stuart said, his voice even.

"Well, I wasn't so thrilled you were going with gap-toothed Jennifer," I retorted.

Stuart called the day after he went to that dance, and though I didn't admit it to him, I was thrilled his night had been a complete disaster. Jennifer had gotten shitfaced before the dance and then vomited on Stuart's shoes as they left their school. As he called her a cab, she kept blubbering about how she wanted to be naked with him. I felt sick as he told me what she'd said.

"Why would you want to hang out with someone like that?" I asked him, nauseated and thinking I might gag if he told me she kissed him.

"Oh, Caitie, she didn't know what she was saying. She's just silly and immature," he said, laughing. "Everyone told me she just thinks she likes me. She knows about you—she's met you, for crying out loud. They all think she just loves the challenge of getting someone who's already taken. She's done it before."

I didn't agree but didn't want to fight. I didn't doubt that Stuart loved me, but the distance between us and our uncertain future was beginning to drag on him, too. We didn't spend much time talking about our relationship. We just were. But some nights it felt like we ran out of things to say, and I was seized with the fear that our lives were moving in different directions. I always asked about Gloria, Edward and the twins, as well as what was going on at his school. He always inquired about school and my family, and we never failed to laugh about Grace's latest relationship mishap. But that night, I offered him a chance to see other people.

"That's not what I want, Caitie. We're going to be together again, I promise. If you want to go to this dance with this Anthony, go ahead, but I'm not looking for anyone else. I'm glad you're telling me about him ahead of time. I couldn't stand to think you'd go behind my back. Now, I don't want to hear another word about this dance unless you're going to send me pictures in the mail afterwards of only you. Just know that I love and miss you."

I told Anthony I'd meet him at school the night of the dance, which was the first time our school was hosting a MuchMusic Video Dance Party. It seemed like everyone—myself included—preferred the more relaxed aura than a traditional formal. Meeting Anthony there discouraged the date-like feel of the night, but I also needed to help set up the gym and collect tickets at the door. No one except freshmen came to the dance when the doors opened at eight, so I didn't expect to see any of my friends until about nine-thirty or ten. I was surprised, then, when Anthony appeared with a bouquet of flowers and an offer to help me collect tickets at eight-thirty. When I finished my shift, I joined my friends on the dance floor. Heather was half in the bag, moshing without a care to "Tubthumping" and doing some wild sort of booty shaking during "Wannabe."

I threw my head back and laughed. I felt free. It felt good to let go, to just be in the moment. For one night, I could *not* worry about who I missed, where I wanted to be and what the future held. In the bathroom, Heather talked a steady stream, giving me the details from the pre-party and sharing her hidden flask of vodka and orange juice. When she arrived with Noah, speaking a little too loud and with great excitement, I pushed them through the gym doors into the dance so the teacher chaperones wouldn't confiscate it.

"You know, Caitie, you're not going to want to hear this, but Anthony really likes you. You should have heard him talking about you." She looked at her reflection in the mirror as she reapplied lipstick and tried to tame her hair. "I didn't tell him about Stuart. I wasn't sure if you wanted me to. But I thought you should know about the way he feels, in case you...well, you know you've been talking about a lot of different things lately."

"Thanks, Heather," I said, meeting her gaze in the mirror. I smiled. "He seems like a really good guy."

I danced with Anthony, his big arms holding me in the school-approved hands-on-waist pose. I laced my hands around his neck. He looked good. He wore a black jacket with a white shirt and red tie. He'd borrowed his dress shoes from his older brother, and I appreciated his effort. I hadn't spent much time worrying about my ensemble. The night before, I'd scanned my closet, looking for anything that would do. I settled on a black dress that had hung in my closet for about a year with the tags still on.

Despite my stern instructions to myself, I compared Anthony and Stuart. I always knew where I stood with Stuart. Though we suffered misunderstandings from time to time, I never had any misconceptions about his intentions, and I didn't spend time analyzing what he said to me for hidden meanings and half-truths. Anthony was different from Stuart, but I could also see him as a solid and dependable kind of guy, whose actions and words meant what he intended them to. There would be no second-guessing with him, either.

If I dated Anthony, I could do everything couples did: go to his house—he lived with his parents and two older brothers, who both played football for Western; go on dates; see each other at school; and, even if we didn't look past the summer, we had nine months in front of us. With Stuart, I had three upcoming days. During our phone call the night before, as I'd searched my closet for something to wear, Stuart had let it drop that he'd be in London only from Christmas Eve to Boxing Day before flying back to Boston to go skiing in Vermont with Edward, Gloria and the twins. When he said "home to Boston," my stomach knotted and I told him I needed to go, ignoring how baffled he sounded when he asked what he'd said wrong.

Many times, when he called, he sounded pained and almost depressed. But as he described his family's plans to ski at Jay Peak and the villa Edward and Gloria had rented, his voice came alive, animated for the first time in ages. I glowed inside when he sounded like that, disappointed as I was.

At the after-party, I sat beside Anthony, enjoying his

stories and getting to know him better. I let him hold my hand. I also tried, unsuccessfully, to ignore the whispers from other partygoers who wanted to know if Anthony and I were now an item. I didn't want to lead him on, but I enjoyed his attention. I also liked him. If there had been no Stuart, being Anthony's girlfriend wouldn't have been a consideration—it would have been a certainty. But there *was* a Stuart—a Stuart I loved with every fibre of my being. A Stuart who would be crushed to see me touch another guy.

Heather's brother agreed to pick us up from the party, and when it was time to go, we climbed the stairs from the basement to wait in the living room.

"Be back in a sec," she said, giggling as she disappeared with Noah down the hallway toward the bedroom where all the coats were piled on a bed.

Anthony and I stood alone, looking uncomfortable. I gave him a half smile and then turned my head to look out the door. I heard laughter, the occasional yell and a constant thumping bass. When I turned my head back toward him, he leaned down and kissed me. I kissed him back. Our lips parted and I felt his tongue, searching. He kissed me tentatively, as though asking permission. Stuart was passionate in his affections, almost always putting his hands at my neck to tilt my head to the side or running his hands through my hair. Anthony placed his hand on my arm, as though to still me. Heather interrupted us when she returned with my coat but no Noah.

"Bye, Anthony," she said, passing me with her eyebrows raised.

"Bye, Anthony. Thanks for everything. I had a great time," I said, before following her out the door. Butterflies flew around my stomach, my head buzzed from the drinks and my heart ached that it wasn't Stuart's lips I'd touched.

When Anthony called the next day to ask me to see a movie the following weekend, I agreed. Stuart also called, but before I got on the phone, I heard my mother laughing with him, telling him I looked very pretty and that our family looked forward to seeing him over the holidays. She even asked him to join us for Christmas dinner. I felt a little sick, unsure if I'd cheated. I chastised myself, telling my inner voice the kiss was just a thank you for a great night. Anthony and I weren't a couple. I knew several girls who dated multiple guys, and going to see a movie with someone didn't mean we were in a full-blown relationship.

"Babe," I said, when I picked up the phone in my bedroom.

"Hey," he said, his smile coming down the line. "Your mom said you looked great last night. I bet you did. I can't wait to see a picture, as long as I don't have to see the guy you went with. Did you get your university application form? Did you fill it out? What universities did you pick besides Ottawa U? I was thinking Western—I could figure something out if we went there. And also Queen's."

"Same, Stuart," I said, not able to say anything else.

Stuart was sticking to our plan. In a moment of weakness, I'd folded like a lawn chair, catching an unsuspecting victim in its painful clutch. Me. We chatted for the next hour, and he entertained me with stories of school from the past week. The entire time, my guilt bubbled inside me.

"Stuart, I miss you," I blurted out, starting to cry.

"Hey. We agreed not to cry on the phone," he whispered. "What's the matter?"

"Nothing." I sniffled, wiping my nose with the back of

my hand, scanning my room for anything else I could use, even a dirty sock. "I just ache for you sometimes, you know?"

"I do," he said, softly. "I'll be home in just over a month. We'll figure this out, Caitie. I promise."

Over the next few weeks, I continued dating Anthony. My duplicity amazed me. When I was with Anthony, I missed Stuart, but I felt flattered by Anthony's attention and enjoyed his company, which allowed me to sweep aside the overriding ache and love I felt for Stuart. We laughed and went to restaurants with Heather and Noah and Grace and Tristan, who were back together again. It was Grace who found the courage to challenge me as we rode the bus to tennis one day. When she remained quiet after boarding the bus, that was the first red flag. The next was when I told her Anthony wanted us to all go out the following weekend. She gave a noncommittal "hmm."

I knew she had something to say, and I figured it had to do with Anthony. I waited for the moment and, really, I wanted it. I needed someone to fight for Stuart.

"Out with it, Grace," I said.

"Look, I know you're lonely. Anthony is a great guy. But I know you're in love with Stuart and, aside from the fact that he's going to be pissed when he finds out you've been out with Anthony, don't you kind of feel as though you're cheating? On Stuart, of all people," she said, her eyes flitting from side to side as she avoided my stunned expression. "Seriously, Cait. I don't know why you're fucking around with this. Does he know about Anthony?"

"Jesus Christ, Grace, there's nothing to know about," I practically shouted, before lowering my voice. But I heard the edge in my tone. "I hang out with Anthony. We hold hands once in a while. Yes, we've kissed, but I'm not sleeping with him and I'm not going to. To be honest, I try to forget about Stuart when I'm with Anthony, and he doesn't ask about him. In fact, he's never asked me if Stuart and I are still together. I think he just wants to ignore him and hope for the best.

"I'm so confused most of the time. And I'm afraid. Stuart says he'll go to university wherever I go, but I know he's taking his SATs next week. What if he decides to stay in Boston? What if he meets someone else? What if he doesn't love me anymore or enough to fight for me?"

"Caitie, don't think like that. You thought he was just playing you a year ago. You're still together. Don't fuck this up because you're lonely." She took my hand and I looked out the bus window, willing myself not to cry. My nostrils flared as I got myself under control. We sat like that, in silence, immobile, until the bus slowed to a stop outside the tennis centre. Then Grace reached down and grabbed my bag, adding it to the one she carried on her back.

I wanted to end things with Anthony before Stuart came home for Christmas. If I kept seeing Anthony, I would have to come clean to Stuart, and that was a conversation I wanted to avoid at all costs. He would be at Caroline's house for three days, and I vowed not to spend one minute of our time together talking about anything other than us. Anthony also made things complicated because he started talking about doing things an actual couple would do together. Every time I wanted to tell Anthony about Stuart, I chickened out. I told myself the timing wasn't right, that he'd be crushed. I convinced myself I had to let him down easy and, I thought it would be just plain mean to do it before Christmas.

IN REPAIR

When Anthony invited me to his family's Christmas Eve open house, he looked at me with a smirk on his face and suggested the party would be a good time to escape notice and find some quiet time alone together. I knew he wanted a more physical relationship, but I couldn't move past kissing. He placed his hands up the back of my shirt, but I batted them away. Once, in the student council office—we had replaced the table with a couch—I got carried away for a few minutes. But the second his hand brushed the button on my pants, I bolted up.

"Caitie, I really like you and I think I could go all the way with you," he said in the next breath.

I felt sick and knew I had to get out of the office. "I'm going to be late for class," I said, grabbing my top and throwing it over my head. I jumped off the couch and stuffed my feet into my shoes. I didn't stop to tie them and ran out of the room and down the stairs to the cafeteria, where I found Heather. I needed her to help me brainstorm how I could let Anthony down without hurting him too much.

Stuart was arriving Christmas Eve. In the end, I didn't say anything to Anthony, just begged off the party, telling Anthony my entire family went to church on Christmas Eve and I would catch up with him a few days later. His family headed to Toronto to visit his grandparents on Christmas and Boxing Day, so there was no chance we'd bump into each other with Stuart in town.

On Christmas Eve, I tried on one set of clothes, changed my mind and then spent another twenty minutes in my closet, scrounging for the perfect outfit to reunite with Stuart. After an hour of fruitlessness, I discovered a tight, black, V-neck sweater and red tartan skirt with black tights that showed off my legs, my best feature, thanks to the endless kilometres I still ran even though it was cold outdoors. I brushed my hair and put on eyeliner, mascara and lipstick. Stuart called the minute he arrived at Caroline's and told me he'd see me later. His mother had invited over a few friends and family members, and he needed to spend time at home, but after dinner, his mother, Nicole and Emma, who was home for the holidays, were leaving to visit some family friends. Stuart stayed home to be alone with me.

As I drove to his mother's house, I remembered the last time Stuart and I had been together. I ignored my activities over the past month and a half and, instead, focused on the way he'd looked at the airport and the fun we'd had in Boston. I debated whether I should be honest and tell Stuart about Anthony. Though I hadn't yet told Anthony I only wanted to be friends, from my perspective we weren't together. That decision was so clear to me. Stuart was the only person who mattered to me. He was the only one I wanted.

I pulled into the driveway and swung open the car door. I scurried up to the front door, being careful not to slip on any ice. London had been blanketed in snow a few days before and it was knee-deep on his lawn. The walkway was clear. I knew Stuart must have shovelled it, as well as the pathway that ran along the garden. I lifted my hand to knock and the door opened. Stuart grabbed me, wrapped his arms around me and nuzzled his face into my neck. His ravenous kisses stopped me. He pulled me inside, shutting the door with his foot and we remained locked together.

"We're alone," he said, lifting me up. I linked my legs around his waist and he walked us down the hall, toward his bedroom. Once inside, he set me down and took a minute to study me before pulling my sweater over my head, unhooking my bra and laying me down on the bed. He yanked off my kilt, tights and underwear and then tossed his own clothes onto a pile beside his bed.

"I've missed you," he said, as I let go, my heart whole again.

Afterwards, we lay together in bed, my head resting on his chest, and I listened to his heart beat. We got dressed, in case his mother came home early. He played with my hair as we talked about his 1600 SAT score, a good mark, as well as my school grades and life in Boston. I asked about his family there, and he chatted about their upcoming ski trip. But when he asked, "What've you been up to?" he heard the catch in my voice. I had barred all thoughts of Anthony after the car ride over to Stuart's house and now I felt ashamed to bring him into our bed.

"Don't be mad," I said, moving my head off his chest so I could look into his eyes, unsure how to proceed.

"Okay, I know I'm going to be mad now," he said, looking bemused. "What did you do?"

"You're not going to like it," I said, trying not to be defensive but realizing I was edgy because I was guilty. I hadn't been fair to Stuart or to Anthony, for that matter. "You know that guy, the one I went to the dance with last month?"

"Yes..." Stuart said, propping himself up on his elbow. His hand, which played with mine, stilled. He pulled his hand back, resting it in front of his stomach. His eyes were glued to mine, and I couldn't look away. I knew I must confess everything with a fixed gaze.

"Well, we've been out a few times," I said. Stuart didn't

say anything but looked at me expectantly. Instead of answering, I looked at Stuart for a few beats and then raised an eyebrow. I waited, expecting him to tell me he had been out with Jennifer or a different girl in Boston. He remained silent.

"Cait?" he asked. "Go on. What do you mean you've been out?"

"We've gone to the movies and a restaurant in a group, that sort of thing," I held my breath. Stuart held my gaze but said nothing. The moments ticked by and I felt panic sweep over me. It was in moments such as this that I wished Stuart didn't hate fighting as much as he did. I wanted him to get mad or swear. I couldn't figure out how to defend myself while he remained so calm.

"Has he touched you?" he asked, finally, his voice measured.

"It's not like that, Stuart," I said, my cheeks aflame, my skin prickling. "Well, we hold hands sometimes."

"Does he kiss you?"

"Oh, Stuart, please," I said, starting to cry. Stuart's calmness was worse than anything I'd imagined in the hundred times I'd run this scenario through my head before tonight. When he refused to say anything else, I wiped my tears away and made my admission. "Yes."

"Do you love him?"

"What!" I exclaimed, feeling a coldness come over me. This was the first time I thought I might lose Stuart. "No, I don't love him."

"Do you love me?" he said, his eyes drilling into mine.

"Of course I love you," I said, flabbergasted. For the first time in over a year, I couldn't read Stuart. I wanted to touch him but didn't know if he wanted me to. I berated myself for being so selfish, for not staying strong for both of us. "How could you think otherwise? I have nothing with him. I don't want to be with him. Stuart, I miss you so much and we just went to the dance and yes, I let things get a little out of hand, but I promise you, my heart belongs to you. I'm so sorry. Can you forgive me?"

And then, I reached for him. Instead of pulling back, Stuart dropped his body down, lying level with mine. He took hold of my wrists and held my hands above my head. We kissed for what felt like an eternity. It was as though he reclaimed me. He hadn't said anything, but I knew he forgave me. Relief flooded my body. He released my hands and then stared at me. I was breathless, panting, wanting more, but I knew we wouldn't be alone much longer.

"Caitie," he whispered. "I want to be with you forever."

The day after Stuart returned to Boston, I called Anthony, telling him I had to come over. His voice told me he was happy; mine was a warning he missed. His mother answered the door, giving me a few minutes to prepare to deliver what I came to say. Anthony bounded to the door and pecked me on the cheek. He wasn't as daring as Stuart, who now kissed me on the mouth in front of my family. Nobody batted an eyelash because they were so used to him at this point, though it still made me blush, which was the reason why he did it. I looked around as I entered the foyer. I noticed the green porcelain tiles, the glass-topped wrought iron side table, where Anthony's family dumped mail and car keys, as well as Survivor, a large tropical plant that had got its nickname from its refusal to die. The more I observed these things, the worse I felt. I just wanted to say what I had to say and go home. I felt bad, but the secret I'd carried around nearly choked me and I needed to release it. Anthony asked to take my coat, but I suggested we go for a walk instead. He left me at the front door and hurried off again, returning with his coat, hat and mitts. Once outside, he reached for my hand, but I pulled it back.

"You okay?" he asked, reaching for my hand again. I gave it to him and we walked down his street in silence. He knew something was off and I could see him trying to figure out what was going on from the corner of my eye. I searched for the words to explain. I'd rehearsed my speech the night before, but now, I felt nervous, and the words "Stuart and I" wouldn't come out.

"Cait, what's going on?" he asked after we passed the sixth house. He turned and stood in front of me. And when he saw my face, my eyebrows knitted in concentration, my mouth set in a moue, he knew. "This is about your guy in Boston, isn't it? I don't want the details. I really don't want to hear anything... No, wait, actually, I want to know how long this has been going on."

"More than a year," I said, wringing my hands, just as Grace did that day when she'd fought for Stuart on my behalf.

"You were seeing him the entire time we were together?"

"Well, it's complicated," I managed. He rolled his eyes. "I didn't think we, you and I, were together, as you put it. And Stuart and I have never really been apart, though he's in Boston."

"You let me think I was your boyfriend," he said, his voice raising. "What is wrong with you?"

"I don't know. I'm sorry. I can't explain Stuart and me. We're illogical. I want to be with him, but I have no idea what's going to happen with us. We want to be at the same university." I stopped when I saw his face, which was part shock and part budding anger. I realized how this all sounded. But not only did he need to hear it, I needed to say it. "But we just don't know. And, Anthony, you're a good guy. You're a great guy. I really like you. And I enjoy spending time with you. You make me happy. When I'm with you, I can forget about him, at least for a while. I'm so confused most days. But when Stuart and I are together . . ."

"He was here at Christmas, wasn't he?" he interrupted. "Did you sleep with him?"

"He is my whole heart," I said, feeling bereft. I felt bad about what Anthony must feel—I'd been dumped before—but my grief was for Stuart and the thought that I could have lost him. "He is my everything. I love him and I always will. I feel bad, not because of what Stuart and I have together, but because I hurt you. I never wanted to hurt you."

"You led me on and you made me look like a fool. Your friends knew the whole time, didn't they? And you didn't care. You just used me while whatever his name is was away," he said, his icy words sounding louder on the quiet street. He wouldn't look at me. "Just go. You've said what you wanted to say and I want you to go now."

I turned and started walking back toward his house. When I was halfway there, I looked back to see him still standing in the place I'd left him, one hand on his forehead, the other on his hip, trying to figure out what had just happened. I turned back around and shuffled toward my car, taking care to drive home in the opposite direction.

The day after New Year's, Stuart called from Boston.

"Caitie," he blurted out as soon as I answered. He sounded ecstatic. "I'm moving back home at the end of the month. I'll be back at Central for the final semester."

I held my breath. I couldn't believe what I was hearing. Just like that. After ten months of being apart, we'd be together again. Emotions swirled in my chest, making me lightheaded.

"Caitie?" I heard Stuart say. "Did you hear me?"

"I heard you," I whispered, excitement bubbling up inside me. And then I exhaled.

Brandon and I picked him up at the airport in London. When he came through the terminal, I started crying. So did Brandon. So did Stuart. After they hugged, he looked at me and I leaped into his arms. He kissed me as I wrapped my legs around him, holding tight. His luggage came through the carousel, and we walked toward Brandon's mom's car. I climbed in the back, despite Stuart's most chivalrous efforts —"No, really, Cait, I'm going to feel bad that you're back there" —because I knew Brandon needed Stuart almost as much as I did.

After graduating the previous spring, Brandon had chosen to go to Western and was dating a really nice girl named Cassandra. I hung out with them a few times, never feeling like a third wheel. Sometimes, by the end of these nights, Brandon and I reverted to telling our "best of Stuart" stories, and Cassandra would be sad for us, telling us he sounded like a great guy. That she let us talk about him so often made my respect for her immense. Most girls our age lacked self-confidence and needed to talk about themselves all the time. She never complained about hearing about Stuart. But when she once asked if the sex was good, my cheeks flamed and I was shocked into silence. Then Brandon and I laughed.

"Don't wanna hear about it," he said.

"Then don't tell me what he says about me, please. I'll die of embarrassment," I said, laughing.

"He's just says you're insatiable and that when you're together it's like you guys never stop." I must have looked aghast because Cassandra playfully hit Brandon on the arm, telling him to cut it out. "Just fooling, Cait. He doesn't talk about you like that."

But when I was alone with Cassandra, I let my guard down and dished because it gave me a chance to relive some of those moments—though not in too much detail. I tried to be more open when I spoke to Grace about our private life, and though she begged for details so she could compare our intimacy to hers, I just couldn't talk about it. I wasn't trying to be coy or prudish; I just couldn't explain what it was like to sleep with Stuart. It was too emotional and exhilarating. *Awesome* just didn't cut it.

Brandon dropped us off at Stuart's mom's house. As we stood at the car, waiting for Brandon to unload Stuart's luggage from his trunk, we released huge plumes from our lungs into the icy air. We hurried into his house, and Caroline stood there, her arms open, waiting to greet him. They hugged and I felt a sense of calm permeate my every pore. I broke into a wide grin. I was elated that they'd been able to work things out enough for him to come home and finish high school so he could go to Ottawa U in the fall, the university we'd decided on together. As they broke apart, Caroline looked over at me and smiled. I would study English Lit, and Stuart hadn't yet made up his mind. But at that moment, it didn't matter. He was home.

fourteen

MARCH 2017

WE ALL HAVE moments in our pasts that we wish we could go back to. If we could, we'd change the outcome or better understand what happened—you would take back what you said in a heated argument; you wouldn't go to that guy's apartment; you would ask out the cute guy in gym class, regardless of his answer. And for me, that moment was the day I came home to the apartment we shared in Ottawa and found Stuart's note.

"First of all, you have to know how incredibly much I loved you," Stuart said, looking at me. I sat beside him in the noisy restaurant, holding my breath.

Stuart sighed, unsure what to say next. He held my gaze and then looked around the restaurant. Even at midnight, it was packed with people out having a good time, not rehashing painful memories. He ran his fingers through his hair, and the gesture reminded me of how I used to do the same, back when he had more of it and it was more corkscrew curly than its current wavy. We sat thigh to thigh. He was so close that his hand brushed my knee when he gestured while talking. Right now, though, he was still, his hands resting on the table. I mirrored his stance, afraid to move even my eyes, hoping he would finally explain what had happened between us, what had caused him to abandon me.

I didn't remember much that happened after I'd read the note, which was brief and to the point—"I have to leave. I love you, S." I called Siobhan, who hadn't been able to understand anything I'd said but had the good sense to come over. She found me, lying on the floor, bawling, the note clasped in my hand. After my initial shock, I tried to call his cell phone, the first one he had bought a few weeks earlier, but was sent straight to voicemail. I tried again and again, but was always sent to voicemail. After a couple of weeks, it was clear he wasn't coming home. Siobhan stayed with me at first but then moved back in with her roommates. She'd been my lifeline, but she couldn't be my nursemaid forever. And, unless I started showing up at my summer job, they'd replace me and I needed the money.

He finally called. At that point, I was furious. I felt betrayed, duped, stupid. I wasn't sure if Stuart remembered that call, the vile action he admitted to that I couldn't make sense of and how I told him I hated him. It was the only time I ever said that. At the time, I thought I meant it. What I really meant was I didn't think I could live without him.

"Cait," he said, looking at me again. "I left because I loved you too much and I didn't know what to do."

"Explain, please," I whispered. It was as though all the

background noise had faded away, enclosing us in a vacuum-like bubble. "Stuart, please? I've always thought it was me, that I had done something. I worried about the pregnancy. I know I wasn't easy to live with at the time, and I thought maybe I was too demanding. Then I thought you left because you couldn't trust me anymore. I understood that. Maybe I wasn't good enough. Or maybe we got to that point where we were talking about life after graduation and you realized you didn't want it to include me."

He looked pained, shifting incrementally in his seat. If I hadn't been so in tune with him, I would've thought he was a statue. But I felt his discomfort. I realized that for years, I'd been wrong. Stuart hadn't left because of me, though my actions toward the end were almost unforgivable. But I still needed to hear him explain how he'd come to the decision that shattered my confidence and my heart.

"It wasn't any of those things," he said, after a long pause. I heard the reverberation of the restaurant increase, as though someone had gently returned the volume to its previous level. I picked out an animated discussion between the woman and man sitting at the table next to us. Behind us, a couple of guys debated the merits of the Argonauts' newest quarterback and whether he could help the team to a Grey Cup win this season.

"Cait, we were young. I never thought of it at the time, but we were thirty-year-olds in twenty-year-olds' bodies. I wanted everything with you—the wedding, the kids, the happily ever after—but I was twenty-one and you were twenty. And I panicked. I knew I'd be ready for those things —with you—and I wanted those things—with you—just not then. After you waited for me through Boston, I couldn't possibly ask you to wait for me longer..."

"You thought leaving was a better idea?"

"It wasn't one of my best, obviously," he said, giving me a lopsided smile. "Christ, Caitie, do you know what it's like to see you sitting here now, at thirty-eight, knowing I should be the man you're going home to? At the time, I thought you deserved better. I assumed you wanted to get married, and I still wanted to travel. I managed to get to Australia. Back then, I couldn't see how I could marry you and still do that. And I felt that if you wanted to get married, you deserved that. Fuck, you deserved so much more than I ever gave you, Caitie. So much more.

"But please don't think it was you," he said, linking my hand with his on the table. "I wanted to give you everything but knew I would fall short."

"You should have asked me," I said, pulling my hand away. I rubbed my neck, feeling the tears well up inside me. "You should have asked. How could you leave like that?"

"I'm sorry. I am so sorry," he said. "It was the worst thing I ever did."

"Do you have any idea what it was like to come home to that note? A *note*, Stuart? After three years? A note?" I started crying. "I'm sorry." As I got up to leave, he stopped me.

"No, let's do this. I owe it to you. Just not here. You can come up to my room."

"Oh, God, I have to get up tomorrow morning for those meetings," I said, regretting my drinking. I'd have a hangover the next morning, not just from the alcohol but the emotional scabs we'd just opened.

"I can fix that," he said, smirking.

Stuart and I stayed silent during our cab ride back to the Radisson Blu, the only noise an occasional squawk from the scanner. We held hands, giving each other strength like kids in trouble with the principal, sitting in uncomfortable wooden chairs, waiting to be yelled at and reminded of our faults. At the hotel, we strode through the lobby and I exhaled a sigh of relief at its emptiness. I didn't want anyone seeing me head to Stuart's room past midnight.

In the elevator, we remained quiet and apart. I looked at his reflection in the mirrored walls as the bell announced each passing floor. He caught me and raised an eyebrow. I blushed and looked away, pretending to study the ascending numbers in the little box above the doors. When we hit the top floor, we got out. Stuart's room was a suite and he used his key card to open the door. Once inside, I marvelled at the breathtaking view of the city's skyline. My room overlooked Lake Ontario, which was a vast expanse of inky blackness at night.

The room's décor resembled mine, but its square footage was much larger. Though I'd been in this room the night before, I now took stock of my surroundings. My favourite piece of furniture was a glass-topped wooden desk, piled high with papers. Stuart was neat, and there was a definite order to his stacks, just as he'd always kept his papers and books tidy and organized in our apartment. Stuart walked over to turn on the fireplace. He shrugged off his jacket and laid it over a circular leather chair, which looked uncomfortable, yet chic.

"Drink?" he asked, walking to the mini fridge, which was stocked with diet pop and vitamin water. I selected water. Unsure at first where to sit, I decided on the bed because it looked comfy and it was far away from Stuart, who had chosen a twin to the round leather chair, turned it around and sat in it. He took a long drink of his water, his eyes fixed on me. He looked weary, as though preparing himself for what was coming.

"So, how much do you want to know?" he asked, finally.

"Everything."

fifteen

JUNE 1998

THE REST of the school year passed in a whirlwind. I spent most of my free time with Stuart. At times, I feared he wasn't really staying, that someone was playing a cruel trick on me and he'd be taken from me again with just a few days' notice. After a few weeks, those thoughts abated and I felt grateful he was home. On rare occasions, he mentioned his mother. Things weren't perfect, but there'd been a definite improvement. And we were—finally—just two normal young adults on the verge of independence, writing exams, hanging out with friends and looking forward to university. We'd both been accepted to the University of Ottawa. I enrolled in the school's English Lit program; Stuart, still unsure of his major, registered for a general arts program. We went to both of our proms, spending those nights wrapped in each other's arms. My parents were accustomed to me coming and going and seldom asked where I spent my time. Part of this non-interest was due to Matt and Sarah's upcoming July wedding, but I think they also realized they wouldn't be able to keep tabs on me six hours away, come September. And, when it really came down to it, they loved Stuart.

Grace and Tristan called it quits for good on the night of Central's prom. After the dinner and dance, we went to a hotel party and then back to Grace's house because her parents were in Vancouver at her brother's soccer tournament. Stuart and I had just settled into the guest room bed when we heard her shrill voice through the wall.

"What do you mean?" she yelled. Next, we heard her voice, loud and angry, though we couldn't make out what she was saying. We heard Tristan's deep voice and then a door slam. A few minutes later I heard the door reopen.

"I've got to go see her," I said, slinking out of bed to put my pyjamas back on.

"Of course," Stuart said, lying back down.

I found her in the kitchen, pouring a glass of wine from a box. She didn't look up when I entered the room, though I knew she'd heard me.

"He cheated."

"Oh, Grace," I started, as I moved toward her, but she cut me off.

"You know what the worst of it is? I wish I'd done it," she said, keeping her back to me, as she sipped her wine. "He told me tonight. He wanted to wait until after prom so he wouldn't spoil the night for me. Fat chance of that. It happened last week, when he and Terry went to the University of Toronto to check out their dorms. They got invited to a party, and he just met this random girl and slept with her. I guess he felt like the big man on campus, screwing a girl older than him. But, really, Caitie, I should have dumped him a long time ago."

I didn't say anything. Compared to how Stuart treated me, Tristan acted like an immature idiot. I knew boys could do stupid things, but it seemed as though Tristan couldn't do anything but. He forgot things that were important to her, like their anniversary, and then made fun of her because she was hurt instead of apologizing and making it up to her. He cancelled on her a few times to go out with his buddies. If Stuart and I hadn't made each other a priority, our relationship wouldn't have survived Boston. And because it had, it felt ironclad. But that was our choice. I didn't have to talk him into it. We willingly made it work. I was glad Grace had dumped Tristan. She deserved her own Stuart.

The summer was hectic. I worked a lot, stockpiling as much money as possible before heading to Ottawa. My parents surprised me by telling me they'd pay for my room and board. I was only responsible for tuition. I'd saved enough for my entire first year, and their gift, along with a scholarship I earned, meant I wouldn't have to work four days a week as first planned. Stuart didn't have to worry about money. When he got his acceptance, Gloria told him that she and Edward would pay for his entire schooling, though Caroline was put out by Edward's generous offer. When she called with the news, Gloria next asked to speak to me.

"I'm so glad he's going to be with you," she said. "Just make sure he studies. His father won't be happy if he just coasts through the first year."

Suddenly, it was September. I was nineteen—I would turn twenty in January, and Stuart was already twenty. Being in Ottawa was much better than living in London. I fell in love with the city—the Canal, the vibrant Byward Market, the exciting seriousness of the parliament buildings and the architectural jewels dotting the downtown. I met Siobhan the first week of school and we became fast friends. I became her *Caitie-cat*, she my person. She was in a couple of my classes and lived in the same residence building as me, just on a different floor. Stuart and his roommate, a guy who also hailed from Central, lived about a fifteen-minute walk away, on Goulburn Avenue. There were several embassies near his home, so he nicknamed it the Embassy District. My parents gave me a resolute no when I brought up the idea of living with Stuart, so I lived in the school dorms. My roommate, Linda, an anthropology major, was a total bore. Right after meeting Stuart, she told me she wouldn't put up with finding us *in flagrante delicto*. She planned to get a PhD and become a professor, so studying topped her list of priorities.

"No problem, we'll just fuck at his apartment," I retorted, trying to shock her.

Siobhan, however, was the one Linda needed to worry about. We came home after a night of partying in the Market, singing and laughing, waking up Linda as well as Siobhan's roommate, a quiet, studious girl named Matilda. After a few run-ins, we had to face the floor mother, who was really just an older student, and promise to stop. We didn't, and a month later, Linda moved in with Matilda, while Siobhan and I bunked up. In November, just before we got ready to hunker down for our first round of exams, Grace and Heather took the train from London to visit me. I told Stuart he would be on his own that weekend, but at their insistence, we met up with him and his roommate, as well as a couple of Stuart's new friends. It was the most fun we'd had all semester. I remember looking at their faces, laughing from the latest shot we'd downed, and thinking, *I'm so happy. I have everything I could ever want.* At that exact moment, Stuart looked at me, and I swelled with love. He leaned over and kissed me to a chorus of, "Guys, geesh." But they were only teasing. I saw Grace and Heather trade smiles with Siobhan.

My marks slipped a bit in my first year, but not enough for my parents to withdraw their financial assistance or insist I return to London and go to Western. That summer, I got a job with the City of Ottawa as a day camp counsellor. Stuart went home to London and then to Boston, but returned in August to help look for a new apartment—with me. Matt and Sarah had moved into a ranch-style house that was a five-minute drive from my parents' and were expecting their first child, so when I dropped the news that I was moving in with Stuart—not Siobhan, who'd found three other roommates to party with—nobody argued.

"We know you'll probably marry him, Caitie, and you're an adult," my mom said. "Let us know if you need any help moving."

Caroline put up more of a fight. She worried I would end up pregnant, derailing Stuart's academic plans. His marks had been high enough to earn him a scholarship for the next year and he switched his focus to business.

"Now?" I asked when he told me. "She's worried about that now?"

He just shrugged and went back to scanning the newspaper, looking for two-bedroom apartments. There was no need for two beds, but we agreed to have a second room to give us extra space to study or just be alone. We found something close to the university in Sandy Hill, which was where Siobhan had also found a place with a few girlfriends. I loved our apartment, not only because of its high ceilings, wide, dark wood baseboards, hardwood floors and radiators, but because it was our first space together. We had a physical manifestation of Stuart-and-Caitie. Stuart's bike found a spot in the living room. And we loved the worn-out IKEA couch his roommate had given us. The roommate couldn't tolerate Ottawa's bitter winters and had left for the University of Windsor. We'd picked up a bookshelf at the Great Glebe Garage Sale earlier that spring. It held all of my books—they filled nine boxes—and Stuart carried them up the stairs and into the apartment without complaint.

And I loved our bed. We decided to purchase a new bed as well as linens. I had my eye on a hot pink set that Stuart, usually agreeable and easy-going, turned down with a resolute, "My penis will vanish if I have to sleep in those sheets." We compromised on a white duvet with green paisley accents and dark green sheets. Our decision felt grown-up and it was the first time I let slip, "It's good to buy the bed now because we won't need to do that when we're married."

I saw Stuart pause when I said it, but it was such a quick hesitation, I thought I'd imagined it. After all, Stuart mentioned marriage every so often. On the night of Matt and Sarah's wedding, we danced like old people, with Stuart holding one of my hands in the air, his other arm around my waist. At one point, he whispered in my ear, "Will you become Mrs. Taylor when we're married?" which sent a ripple through my body.

Starting our second year of university meant we had two additional years left in our respective programs. We hadn't made any concrete plans about what we'd do after graduation. It just felt like whatever it was, we'd do it together. I wanted to stay in Ottawa and had started looking at a career in graphic design, afraid to stake my future on being a starving writer, though Stuart said I didn't have to worry because he would get a swanky job.

In December, we finished writing our first-semester exams and rented a car to drive home. As we clipped along Highway 401, I started thinking again about what life would be like when we graduated. Some people I'd gone to high school with had already gotten engaged, and Matt and Sarah seemed to be going to a wedding at least once a month. Grace had started dating someone she had met at Western and they were thinking about finishing three-year degrees and then going to build homes with Habitat for Humanity. Heather gushed to me over the phone a few days before that her boyfriend, a teacher's college student at Western, might ask her to marry him at Christmas. I was surprised because they'd only known each other a few months. When I told Stuart, he didn't say much.

Brandon called Stuart a couple of days before we left for home, asking if he'd be his best man if Cassandra said yes on New Year's Eve. Both planned to hit the workforce right after graduation, so they didn't see the need to wait. I never listened in on Stuart's conversations but happened to walk into our bedroom while they were on the phone. Stuart faced our back window and his shoulders slumped a bit as I heard him say, "Marriage? I don't know, Brandon." I didn't want to hear anything else, so I slid the papers I was carrying onto our second-hand dresser and slipped out of the room. I asked Siobhan if I should ask Stuart if he thought we would get married.

"Why? It's obvious to everyone that you're headed down

that road. Why do you need a pre-commitment guarantee? Please don't tell me you're hoping he's gotten you a God-awful promise ring for Christmas."

"No! He's just been acting a little strangely with all this wedding talk. And I'm not doing any of the actual talking. I'm afraid to bring it up in case he thinks I'm expecting something."

"Well, if you're worried about it, maybe you should bring it up so he knows there's no pressure. I don't know what it is with people and fucking weddings, especially at our age. I just want to have fun. We're only going to be in our twenties, carefree and with few responsibilities, once. Why jeopardize all that potential fun—and sex, Caitie!—with a contractual bullshit relationship, a mortgage and, God forbid, kids?"

She was right, of course. Unmarried, Stuart and I could live apart if we needed to. The only place Stuart said he wouldn't move to was the Northwest Territories. Since I didn't want to go there either—the idea of going back to the ice cream shop appealed to me more than working through all-day darkness in the dead of winter—we didn't have to worry. Stuart didn't fret much about the future. It was part of what I loved about him. I was a wreck about upcoming deadlines, rewrites, essays, exams and other self-imposed, high-achiever goals, like running a half-marathon. He looked at his school calendar and figured out how much time he still had before he needed to "get serious," as he called it, at which point he'd slouch off to the office, shut the door and emerge a few hours later with a completed paper.

But in the car, with hours of travel ahead of us, I brought it up.

"Stuart, I know there's been a lot of talk about weddings

and getting engaged, but I'm happy, you know? I love us, just the way we are." I glimpsed his hands clench the steering wheel a little harder, his eyes staying focused on the road ahead.

"It's just a little ahead of us, don't you think?" He glanced over at me and smiled. "I'm relieved to hear you say that. Honestly, I've been worrying that you're looking for a proposal this holiday or on Valentine's Day or whatever day women hope for these things. We're in second year, we're broke and we have no idea what we're doing past graduation. I mean, I don't see us not being together. But we're just twenty. I'm not saying I don't want to get married, but not now."

"But to me?" I blurted out. "Would you eventually want to marry me?"

I fretted sometimes that we would hit a plateau, but so far, that hadn't happened. Since Stuart returned from Boston nearly two years earlier, our relationship had moved along what I assumed was a normal track. We just were. We spent a lot of time together. We enjoyed the same movies, we went to concerts together or with groups of friends, with whom we also played trivia at the neighbourhood pub. We lost all the time. We made love five or six times a week, sometimes several times a day. We stayed up all night talking. I still got that fluttery feeling in my stomach when I saw him waiting for me after class, or coming to walk me home after a shift at the Royal Oak pub, where I worked as a server on weekends. I kept expecting the bottom to fall out. No one could have a relationship like ours nearly three years in, right?

"I wouldn't want to marry anyone else," he said,

cautiously. "Caitie, my parents got married right out of university. My mom was pregnant four months later with Emma. She had Nicole fourteen months after Emma was born and then I came along two years after that. I'm convinced my mother resented being a housewife. As a kid, I never felt like she hated being home with us, but as I got older, I wondered if she felt trapped. Then, when we were in school and she was ready to go back to work, nothing was available. She just took whatever work she could. She started volunteering more and became good at fighting with my dad, and then, later, me. I'm not going to do that to you—or to me. I want to go to Australia. You know that. We've talked about it. I like what I'm studying. I know you have to write. I'm just saying we've got time."

"I agree," I said, though I felt a little confused. I expected him to sound a little surer. I didn't know what else to say, so I looked out the window, watching the scenery whip by. More cars joined us on the road, and the highway expanded from two lanes to three on each side, which meant we were nearing Toronto. In my mind, I replayed our highlight reel—our reunion in Boston, our proms, assembling our bed in our apartment where we spent the next four hours inside a cocoon of sheets.

"Caitie," Stuart said. "Hello? Caitie? Did I say something wrong? Do you want to get married? Now? I guess we could do all that stuff married."

"I was just thinking about when we got the bed and, after trying to put it together for like eighteen hours, we finally got to use it," I said, forcing my mind back into the small, two-door Toyota.

"Oh, yes, I like to think about that, too." I flushed, which made him laugh. "Seriously, Cait. If you need me to, I'll marry you tomorrow, just as long as I'm able to go to Australia with Brandon."

"You would do that?"

"You are my everything."

The next day, I woke up in my old bed at my parents' house. I listened to them clinking spoons and dishes in the kitchen down the hall. I thought about what day it was and then quickly counted backwards. I was late.

I didn't tell Stuart.

I figured not only was the timing bad with all the wedding news still fresh, but I'd also read articles outlining a thousand reasons why women could be late besides the obvious. The Christmas break ended up being the rest we'd needed. We celebrated with Brandon and Cassandra, who said yes, of course, and Heather, who got a ring from her schoolteacher. Nicole had also gotten engaged, surprising us all, but which meant Caroline was in a great mood, and that spared Stuart from any cross words. We saw Grace, who was moving to London, England, for a semester, having broken up with Mr. Habitat, and Matt and Sarah, as well as my nephew, Daniel, who was an adorable mix of Matt's dark hair and Sarah's blue eyes. Stuart and I had shopped at Mrs. Tiggy Winkle's before we left Ottawa, and the saleswoman did a great job of helping us buy him gifts. Daniel loved the chewable book, big blocks and stuffed elephant we showered him with.

We returned to Ottawa and resumed our normal routine, though I found excuses—a headache, the flu, my period, a lie which made me flinch—to avoid having sex, a particularly difficult feat. Two weeks later, blood flowed. There was so much. I worried I'd have to tell Stuart and go to the hospital, but called Siobhan instead. She came to our apartment, cooing over me in the bathroom. Stuart, completely at a loss outside, rapped his knuckles on the door, asking if everything was okay. I sent Siobhan outside the bathroom, telling her to make something up.

"Caitie-cat, listen to me, you need to tell him the truth," she hissed at me as I sat on the toilet, my stomach cramping.

"I can't tell him. I don't even know what this is," I said, trying to convince myself I was ignorant.

"C'mon. He's not stupid. He's going to figure it out. And besides, he loves you."

"Why are you always on his side?" I spat at her, knowing she was right but, in my grief, lashing out at her anyway.

"Fine, but you're wrong here," she said, getting up and moving to the door. "Stuart, I'm coming out."

I heard her mumble through the door, lying about how sometimes a period was extensive and heavy and my cramps were excruciating this month. She suggested he get a heating pad to help with the pain. I took Tylenol and she told him she'd help me get into bed. Two of her sisters had had miscarriages and she had called them to ask what we needed to do and what to watch for.

"She's never had this before, Siobhan," I heard him say, the worry evident in his cadence. "Shouldn't she go to the hospital?"

"She's okay, Stuart, but if it's still heavy at this time tomorrow night, then take her." She banged on the door. "You hear me?" I mumbled my assent. Stuart went out to get a heating pad and that night, lying in bed, he stroked my hair, his chest against my back, spooning me. I waited until he was asleep, his breath slow and steady, and then I unleashed silent tears.

I was irritable and upset, burdened by my own oath of

silence and deception. I found myself snapping at Stuart, punishing him for not understanding, even though he had no way of knowing about my dishonesty. Stuart was kind and attentive, but he also suspected there was something I wasn't telling him. The bleeding let up, and I went to my female, on-campus doctor, who gave me the all-clear to resume our sex life, which thrilled Stuart. The first time I felt sore and was consumed with thoughts that it could happen again. I took the pill religiously but suggested Stuart go back to using condoms until I had my next period.

"The doctor suggested it, just because that time was so wonky," I fibbed. That I introduced lies and deceit into our relationship weighed heavily on me. I feared telling so many tales I'd get trapped, but, after a few weeks, Stuart and I resumed our pattern—school, studying, nights out for trivia, date nights, my shifts at the Royal Oak and making love. But a new element found its way into our daily lives—arguing. I hated it and I could tell he did, too, but I didn't know how to fix it.

"Go away for a couple of days to Montreal," Siobhan suggested. "And maybe tell him about what happened."

It was now the end of March. We had celebrated Stuart's 21st birthday the week before with a big surprise party at Siobhan's house. I had spent weeks planning it, inviting almost everyone he knew, including Brandon and Cassandra and some of his other friends from high school (but not Peyton). Even Emma flew in from Calgary for the occasion. Nicole had declined, saying she was too busy planning her wedding, but Matt and Sarah were there, though they had to leave early to put Daniel to bed at the hotel. I ordered a huge cake and had made a photo album containing highlights from the past few years. Stuart cried when he walked into

Siobhan's large living room and saw all the smiling faces turned toward him. I did too. He was elated. I had wanted to make sure he knew how loved he was, how much he meant to all of us.

We finished up final papers and prepared for our second-year exams. But Siobhan was right. I needed to come clean to Stuart, and I primed myself for his response. My greatest fear was that he wouldn't love me. When Stuart was mad, such as when I had told him about Anthony, a sort of stillness came over him. His words became measured and he spoke deliberately. I had never, in the three years we were together, heard him yell, either at me or anyone else, his easy-going nature taking over even when he wanted to call someone an asshole. And while I imagined sitting him down after exams finished and having a heart-to-heart, telling him exactly what had happened and asking him to forgive me, that's not quite how he found out.

After fighting about who'd forgotten to pick up the toilet paper earlier that day, the same day I had two final exams, I blurted it out.

"Well, thank God I'm not having another miscarriage or we'd have real trouble."

Stuart froze. His eyes went wide. He stared at me, blinking, trying to process what I'd said. I didn't move, afraid to breathe, mentally kicking myself for being so crass and disrespectful, yet standing on edge, waiting for him to say something else so I could tear into him. At that instant, I realized all the months of hiding this secret—from Stuart, of all people—had made me bitter, resentful and angry, which was spectacularly unfair to him.

"What did you say?" he said, breaking the deadlock.

"Stuart, I'm so sorry. I couldn't tell you," I managed. The

words, now released, came pouring out of my mouth. "I discovered I was late at Christmas. I didn't want to say anything. I didn't think I was pregnant. I thought I was late because of the holidays and school and exams—you know, the stress of it..."

"That night, when Siobhan came over—that was what happened, right?" he interrupted. "I called Brandon. I was so worried. He asked Cassandra and she said you might have been pregnant and that was what was happening. But I thought you would have told me. You were pregnant?"

"I think so," I said, gulping, trying to calm myself. "I'm not sure. I never did a test. But the doctor said I was clear when I got a checkup."

"We could have had a baby?"

"No, Stuart, we wouldn't have had a baby. Something was obviously wrong. When it happened, I did all kinds of research, and they say a lot of women have miscarriages before they even realize they're pregnant. I was only a few days late and, by the time it happened, it was just a couple of weeks. But regardless, neither of us wants a baby. You've made it clear that we might not even get married, never mind have children. You've made that point over and over. I would have figured something out. I..." I sniffled, willing myself not to cry. I looked at Stuart, who continued to process my words. "We're too young. We're not ready. You get bent out of shape anytime someone talks about lifelong commitments, and a baby would be a lifelong tie to each other."

"I can't believe you kept that from me," he said, softly.

"I'm not proud of it," I said, my shoulders slumping. I unclenched my fists. "I'm deeply and utterly sorry. I should have told you."

"You're damn right you should have," he said, punctuating his words. "I don't think I'm going out a limb here when I say when you're in a relationship like ours, where we live together and are planning a life together, that you omit telling the other one that you might have been pregnant. I know I've been flipping out a bit with all this talk of weddings, but Christ, Caitie, I love you. I'm committed to you. And a baby? Our baby?

"Is there anything else you're keeping from me?" he continued, his voice loud. "Oh, what about that guy you were seeing when I was in Boston? Anything you need to fess up about?"

"Don't," I said, unsettled by how angry Stuart was. I'd never seen him lose his cool. I didn't know how I should react, whether I should remain calm or try to match the level of his rising voice. "You know everything there is to know about that. I'm so sorry, Stuart, I can see you're gutted. I'm not really sure what to say for myself. I thought it would be better if I didn't tell you, but then I was planning to tell you. I promise. I was going to sit you down and tell you all about it as soon as exams were over. I'll leave and go to Siobhan's tonight. Just promise you'll speak to me when I come back. Please?"

And then all of a sudden, he fell silent. He didn't answer me. He walked into the office and closed the door. If he'd slammed it, I would have felt better. But he shut the door with care, not looking at me. He stayed in there until my bag was packed and I was rifling around in the kitchen, looking for a bottle of wine to bring to Siobhan's. When Stuart had gone into the office, I called her and, in a few words, told her what had happened.

"You're doing the right thing, giving him his space," she said, softly. "Love you."

I had my head in the fridge so I didn't hear Stuart come up behind me. When I turned around, I nearly dropped the bottle. His face was blotchy, his nose red from crying. I felt hollow inside, seeing him so hurt. I realized how wrong I'd been. He took the bottle from me, placing it on our tiny, two-chair dining table. He lifted me up and sat me on the table, my legs dangling at its side. I vowed to give him whatever he needed at that moment. He sat on the chair and placed his head in my lap. Tentatively, I ran my fingers through his curls. We stayed like that for a few minutes, but then he stood up so we were face-to-face. I kept silent.

"I forgive you, but I want you to leave tonight," he said, his gaze intense and heartbreaking. My face crumpled. "I'm going out with the guys. We'll talk tomorrow."

"I love you," I said, my nostrils flaring, trying to regain control of my emotions. I swallowed. He just looked at me.

After my admission, we seemed to enjoy a couple weeks of relative peace. I was extra vigilant. I didn't pick fights, I let things go and I gave him space when I sensed he needed it. Aside from being distant in the days following our blowout, Stuart appeared to have forgiven me. But that didn't mean he wasn't grieving. Once, when I sneaked into the bathroom to surprise him in the shower, I heard him crying. I crept back out of the room, feeling ashamed. We never spoke about the miscarriage again. A few days later, he left.

sixteen

MARCH 2017

"IT WAS ALL the wedding talk, wasn't it?" I said, not waiting for him to start explaining. I had so many questions. From years of watching *Oprah*, I knew it was best to let people tell their own stories. You find out so much more if you just shut up. But right now, I felt as a prospector might, being inches away from striking gold. I was impatient. I wanted to know what had caused him to walk out on me. Even now, seventeen years later, I couldn't believe he'd left the way he had. "The note, Stuart, it was..."

"I know, Cait. I replayed that for years, knowing I should have handled it better, that I owed you so much more. After I left the apartment, I couldn't believe I'd written it. I almost went back that night to apologize and to try and explain, but I knew you would have found it by then—I saw the missed calls on my phone—and I couldn't handle knowing I had caused whatever you were going through at that moment."

"Where did you go?"

"I rented a car, one-way, and drove to Brandon's in London. He told me to go back to you, that I was being ridiculous. I had decided the week before to head to Boston for the summer."

Gloria had called me a few days after he arrived. She didn't know he'd planned to visit, though she and Edward were delighted to see him. She was concerned and thought we'd broken up, because he wouldn't leave his room except to eat dinner. And then, he only ate and went back to sleep.

"I don't know what to say, Gloria, he just left. He said he had to leave," I told her, hardly able to breathe.

"Honey, I'm sure it'll pass. I know he loves you. Edward and I think the world of you and always thought you two would get married."

Until that moment, I hadn't had the opportunity to feel ashamed, so this emotion was new. I tried it on like a cloak and found it also fit, along with horror, abject sorrow and listlessness.

Stuart left the day of my last exam. I came home to find the apartment quiet. We'd planned to go out for dinner to celebrate, and at first, I thought I'd messed up our plans. I'd done this before, so I figured I was supposed to meet him at the restaurant instead. I ran into our bedroom to get dressed.

"When I opened the closet, I discovered it was bare—only my clothes were on the hangers," I told him now. "I didn't understand what I was seeing. I honestly had to sit down on the bed and think, Stuart, actually think about what it could mean. Then I got suspicious and started checking around the apartment." Some of his books had been removed from the office, his favourite CDs were missing, and then I saw the scrap of paper.

"It was your handwriting." I looked over at him. He watched me now, allowing me to tell him what that had been like. I began crying. "I didn't get out of bed for two weeks. I couldn't eat. I didn't sleep except when I was so exhausted I couldn't keep my eyes open. Siobhan spoon-fed me ice cream, pleading with me to keep up my strength. She called my parents to tell them, as well as Heather and Grace. Matt and Sarah came up, leaving Daniel with my parents. I'll never forget Sarah, patting my hair with a sponge as I lay in bed. I hadn't showered in days. She was the one who finally got me into the shower, but she had to get in with me."

"I'm sorry," he whispered, looking right into my eyes.

"I lost ten pounds."

"I'm sorry," he repeated, not blinking. "I'm so sorry."

"I got a doctor's note—Sarah's idea—so I had two weeks off from working at the pub. But then I had to go back. I thought I was going to die. Siobhan started looking for an apartment for us. She was fed up with her roommates by then. She called our landlord, which is how I found out about the money you sent him. As angry as she was with you, she said that was a decent thing you did. And then you called.

"I was still angry and hurt, but I was so happy to hear your voice again. I thought you were going to apologize, that you were going to tell me it had all been some huge mistake," I said, wringing my hands together. Stuart rose and brought me the tissue box. He sat down on the bed next to me, holding my free hand. My other contained a balled-up wad of tissue, with which I dabbed my face every couple of seconds, though I couldn't stop the flow of tears from cascading. "And then…"

"Jennifer," he said, in a whisper, exhaling deeply.

Stuart's call had been awful. I was full of hope at its beginning. But it was over quickly when I dropped the phone and lurched to the kitchen sink, where I started vomiting. After just a week in Boston, Stuart had gotten drunk for the first time in his life and fucked—his word—Jennifer, who had stayed in Brookline, attending Boston University.

"Are you together?" I managed to ask before I dropped the receiver.

"Of course not," he said, crying, as bile rose in my throat. "Caitie…"

I could have moved past his indiscretion, especially given my own egregious behaviour. When he said "fucked," I knew the encounter was retaliatory in nature and I forgave him even though it made me physically ill. I believed him when he said he didn't remember what had happened, that it was only when she called Edward's house the next morning that the enormity of what had transpired became clear. I knew he was sincere when he called it the biggest mistake of his life. I'd been drunk many times; I knew how out of control you could spiral. But as he told me, my hand clamped on the phone's receiver, my other hand reaching for a chair as I stood in our kitchen, I saw it all: his mouth on hers, his hands caressing her face, her hands reaching to unzip his jeans, his fingers undoing her bra strap, their hurried copulation in a park near downtown Brookline. And every time I imagined it for weeks afterwards, a wave of nausea rolled over me. Despite that, I would have forgiven everything, but he didn't come back.

"You're going to have to block it out," Siobhan said at the time, shaking her head. "That bitch is not going to win. I'll bet he never speaks to her again. And that fucker, I don't know what he was thinking."

"He was hurt, angry and confused," was all I ever came up with. It didn't matter. My heart was broken, my trust evaporated like water poured on a hot skillet.

Now, sitting on the bed with him, I resisted the urge to grab him and make him hold me, the way I wanted him to comfort me all those years before when he had hurt me. He turned to look at me, put his finger to my cheek and made me look at him. I did.

"Until that point, I hadn't actually thought about staying away," he said. "My plan, if you could call it that, was to go to Boston for the summer and then come back to Ottawa and figure out a way to fix things between us. But that night, I completely lost control. I went out with Jason, and she was there. I started drinking. And I drank so much. I've never done that again. Never. I hardly remembered it the next day. Except I did, you know? I knew what I'd done. I felt so ashamed afterward. I had to tell you that I'd done it because I'd done it to you. I used her—I used her because I knew she wanted me—to get back at you, to hurt you the way I felt you had hurt me when I found out you had been pregnant. And I hated myself for that. I never saw her again. She called me—relentlessly for about a week after—but I told her it was a mistake and we would never be anything past that night. She called me some names, which I totally deserved. And then hearing you cry when I told you, I knew I had really fucked up and could never ask for your forgiveness. But, God, I wanted to go back to you."

"I thought you had moved past the miscarriage," I said,

wiping a few tears that had started to wane. "You seemed to be okay."

"Oh, Caitie," he said, turning his head away from me.

"I mean, Stuart, I was an immature twenty-year-old who had just found out she was pregnant and a couple of weeks later it was all over. During that short time, I was totally freaked out about what would happen between us, but also what it would mean for the rest of my life! I was terrified I would have to drop out of school. What would my parents have said? Yes, I should have told you right away, and I kicked myself over and over for not doing so in those intervening months, but I wish you could have told me how much I hurt you."

"I forgave you, Cait. I did. I didn't understand why you hid it from me, but I forgave you. It wasn't just the baby and it wasn't just all the wedding talk, which you asked about. God this is hard," he said, standing up and walking to the minibar. "I need a drink." Stuart opened the little fridge, took out a bottle and poured a small amount in a short glass tumbler that had been sitting on a paper coaster on the desk. "I mean, it was partially the wedding talk. It was as though everyone we knew was getting married or wanted to. I wanted to marry you and assumed we'd get married, but not then. I was almost thirty when I married Erin, and it was over within two years. Even though you said you didn't want to get married, I guess it was the only thing I didn't believe about you. It seemed impossible that you wouldn't want to. Even Nicole got engaged that Christmas."

"I remember."

"And it was all she and my mother talked about. I was doing well in school, finally; that I had found something I enjoyed didn't seem to matter. Nobody cared about it except my dad. Then, Brandon and Cassandra, your friend Heather and the schoolteacher, it was too much. I called my dad and he told me he knew you and I were headed down that path but to make sure I was ready. I told him I wasn't, and he said ... actually, he told me to come clean to you, but I didn't."

"What do you mean come clean? Had you cheated on me?" I asked, standing up and putting my hands to my forehead. Stuart came over to me, taking another sip of his drink before setting it down on top of the television. Then he took my hands in his and looked at me. We sat back down on the bed.

"No. I never cheated on you, not once. He was talking about coming clean about him and my mother," he said. He broke eye contact to take another sip of his drink and then he took my hand, pulling me to sit back down on the bed. He sat beside me, linking his fingers with me. "And then, you surprised me about the pregnancy."

Stuart looked away, taking several deep breaths before he continued. I touched his chest, letting him know he could tell me. I *needed* him to tell me. I had tortured myself for years after our break up, wondering what I had done, why he no longer loved me. I hated keeping the pregnancy, however brief, from him. If I could have gone back in time, I would have changed that. I would have done several things differently.

"My dad loved my mom," he said, after a few minutes. Then he laughed. "I mean, of course he loved her; he married her. But he really loved her. I don't know how much I've told you about them because by the time we met they had been divorced for years and their relationship was awful. It's not better now, by the way. They met in university. My dad always said my mom knew her mind. She had goals. She was tough. She sounded as though she used to be a lot like you, Cait, to be honest. But she had her issues, and needing to be in control was one of them. After they had been dating for a couple of years, she started hinting to my dad that she wanted to get married. He wasn't ready. He wanted to do a graduate degree and maybe go to law school. While he never planned on leaving her, she hated that instead of talking about getting married like her friends were, he was talking about continuing to go to school. According to my dad, as soon as he started looking at universities other than Western, he felt as though their relationship started changing—and not in a good way. Then, one day she told him she was pregnant. He was thrilled with the idea of being a father. He was still in love with her, so he did the honourable thing in the 1970s and proposed.

"My mom told him she didn't want to be a pregnant bride so they eloped—just went to City Hall and got married. They said they'd celebrate with their family and friends later. My grandmother was hurt and my grandfather was livid. I'm sure you can imagine he lobbed some choice words at his pregnant-out-of-wedlock daughter. Regardless, they were married. My dad decided to axe his grad school plan and head right to law school. He studied hard for his tests, was accepted and planned to work full-time doing whatever he had to to support his family while he continued his studies. Three months after they were married, my dad found a pregnancy test in the garbage. A positive pregnancy test."

Stuart stopped talking and my mind raced to catch up with what he was telling me. I started to ask a question when he gave me the answer.

"She had never been pregnant when they got married.

When he confronted her about it, she told him that she had had a miscarriage shortly after they were married. They never used any birth control because they were married and, my dad assumed, already pregnant. But he kept probing and the truth came out. She had pretended to be pregnant because she knew my dad would marry her. Then, she tried to actually *get* pregnant so he would stay. She was right. That's exactly what he did."

"When did you find out?" I said, stunned. Stuart had been my best friend, lover and holder of all my secrets and dreams when we were together. I was partially crushed to think I hadn't been the same for him.

"My grandfather made some snarky insinuations over the years when he had been drinking. But I just ignored him when he was like that," Stuart said. "It wasn't until I went to live with my dad in Boston. Obviously, he knew that things weren't great between my mom and me and he knew, first-hand, what she could be like. I know I never told you everything that happened at home because when I was away from her, the last thing I wanted to do was talk about her. But you were at the house enough to get a sense of what she was like, how controlling she was. As we started talking, I started asking about what had gone wrong between them. It was really hard for my dad to open up about it and it was difficult to hear it. He kept saying, 'Stuart, no matter how you got here, I love you and your sisters and wanted all of you very much.' I had always thought my sisters and I were the reason why he left. Turns out it was the opposite. We were the reason he *stayed* for so long.

"So, fast-forward. You and I have survived almost-cheating—well, some cheating on your part. I'm just kidding, I didn't *really* care that you kissed that guy—while we were apart for almost a year. We go away to university together and then live together. We're in love. And now everyone we know is talking about getting married. We're broke. We're trying to figure out what we're going to do after university and I'm taking a general arts degree. And then I find out you hid an actual pregnancy from me. I freaked out. I thought you were trying to somehow lay a trap for me the way my father had been hoodwinked," he said, kissing my hand. "It was wrong. You were nothing like how my dad described my mom when they were young. Instead of looking at the situation rationally, as I should have, I thought I needed to get out. I couldn't be a husband. I couldn't be a father. And if that was what you wanted, I was willing to do whatever you needed so you could have that. In my eyes, I was getting out of the way so you could find someone else to have everything with."

"But I wanted that with you," I said, looking down at our entwined hands. I wanted to look at him but didn't trust myself. I felt emotionally drained, exhausted. I'd been so lost after he left. I'd felt entirely alone, as though I'd never be able to trust anyone again.

"If you had only come back..." I said, lying down on the bed. I was so tired. I felt like I'd run a marathon. I just wanted to sleep. "If you had come back, I would have forgiven you and never would have let you go again. We could have moved forward."

"I wish I had come back," he said. "It's the greatest regret of my life."

After more than a decade of wondering, I had my answer. It's the logical train of thought that if we love people, we have to keep them to ourselves. But, sometimes, when we love someone, we have to love them enough to let them be who they want to be. It's that old adage: if you love something, set it free. That's what Stuart did for me. But I wish he hadn't done that. I had only wanted him to come back to me. And, now?

Stuart lay down beside me and we stayed like that for a few minutes. Then he propped up on his elbow, just as he'd done a thousand times when we were together. He brushed a strand of my hair out of my face, and when he leaned in toward me, I wanted him to return to me.

I kissed him back.

seventeen

MARCH 2017

I LEFT Stuart's room at four a.m. and was still asleep while everyone else was congregating for the morning sessions. We'd stopped at kissing, which was slow and careful at times, and hungry and lustful at others. I think we were too emotional and exhausted to consider moving further. And my head felt fuzzy.

I missed Heusten's entire morning session, choosing instead to shower, drink a litre of water and look professional. Stuart texted me to say he'd saved me a seat for lunch. When I joined him, he stood and pulled my chair out. He'd attended the morning sessions and appeared rested. Natasha and the frumpy conservative, looking as though she wanted to be anywhere else, also sat at our table. Natasha's platinum blonde hair was teased high. She wore heavy eye makeup, and I saw a speck of red lipstick on her teeth when she smiled. When she saw me, a flicker of disappointment crossed her face, but otherwise, she remained cheerful and flirtatious with Stuart, calling him Stu, which I knew he hated. My phone buzzed in my purse, and I pulled it onto my lap and checked it under the table.

> **STUART**
> You and me tonight. Wear something sexy. I've got a reservation—and it's my birthday next week so we are celebrating.

> Can't wait. I don't think I can take much more of this one

> What do you mean?

> Peyton

> I love it when you're jealous

After the afternoon session concluded, I rushed to my room, ignoring the plans others had made for drinks and a night on the town. I showered and put on my hunter green sequined shirt, which made me look younger—I was pretty sure I could pass for thirty. To expose the top's plunging V-neck, I wore a long, simple silver chain that held the ring of diamonds Stuart had given me before he'd left for Boston. The original chain had broken while I was at my parents' house the Christmas after we split up. Still reeling from the separation, I threw the entire necklace in the garbage. Sarah found it and kept it, giving it to me a few years later. I thanked her and bought a simple silver chain so I could wear the pendant from time to time.

I pulled on my skinny black jeans, grabbed my slingback heels and applied eyeliner, eye shadow, mascara and lipstick. I sent a quick text to Rob, updating him about my sessions. I told him I loved him and the boys. He texted back, saying he hoped I was enjoying my time alone and that he missed me. I looked at my reflection in the mirror. *What was I doing?* When I was with Stuart last night, I had rationalized our intimacy as the natural ending to my quest. I now knew why he had left. But when I had woken up, a stupid smile played across my face. Then, when Stuart texted me this morning, I thought, *Why not just go with it?* But now, as I was about to head out with him again, I knew I wasn't really that easy-going.

I inhaled deeply. I told myself that I would go out, have one last fun time with Stuart and then leave the story of us at that point. One more quick peek in the mirror and I grabbed my COACH clutch. I looked good. I also looked like someone who had a secret, like someone who was about to get into trouble.

I found Stuart in the lobby and, like a leading man in a movie, he rose from his chair to greet me, brushing a kiss on my cheek.

"You look incredible. I like your necklace," he whispered, as he took my hand and we caught a cab waiting outside.

My resolution evaporated and I felt giddy, like I had back in high school, when he'd waited for me that first time outside the party. I felt free, a sensation I'd missed since leaving The Leg, as though months of worrying about my career, finances and my life, in general, had evaporated, and all that mattered was this minute and the next.

Stuart had reserved a table at Festivita Wine Bar, his favourite Toronto haunt. The cozy restaurant featured exposed brick walls, soft, romantic candles and floral displays in the windows. Large white columns formed a separation of sorts between the bar and dining area, and a large wooden sideboard with glass cupboards held a vast array of wine bottles. The entire dining space was open-concept—I was glad Stuart hadn't selected a restaurant where we could be whisked away to a sheltered booth in the back. Here, in this space, we were wide-open; there were no places to hide. The grown-up part of me knew this needed to end tonight. It was my inner twenty-year-old self who was trying to overrule me.

We ordered and then enjoyed a relaxing and engaging conversation. It was as though, having rehashed the past the previous night, we could move forward, in whatever direction that might be. We talked about old friends. Brandon and Cassandra now had two kids and lived near Stuart's mom, so he saw them when he visited, which wasn't often; although Caroline adored Paisley, she disapproved of Stuart's divorce, which I found ironic. I updated him on my high school friends and Siobhan, who had always been his favourite.

I felt self-conscious at times and caught Stuart looking at me with longing. Though I tried to deflect his desire with a shy smile or by starting up a different conversation, I studied him as well, trying to block out my racing thoughts, which were flipping between *This is how we are supposed to be* and *I will not ruin my marriage.* After my second glass of wine, I decided to just enjoy myself and, with every story Stuart told and laugh we shared, I remembered how he'd captured my heart and soul—his infinite good nature, his readiness to see the best in others, his selflessness. I pushed my final memories of him into the dark recesses of my mind and knew I was falling back in love. I passed on dessert but ordered a tea to match his cappuccino. After two hours, and now that we were completely sated, Stuart paid the bill, fending off my protests with an arched eyebrow.

"Where to?" he asked, and I suggested a walk.

The city felt magical on this warm spring night, as we sauntered along Tank House Lane and Trinity Street, through Gristmill Lane to Parliament, my arm looped through his.

"Caitlin, don't take this the wrong way because I could walk around with you all night long, but would you like to go somewhere?" he asked, as we reached Front Street and stopped at a red light.

"Dancing," I said, surprising both of us.

"All right," he said, laughing, while looking around for a cab. "Dancing it is."

Stuart hailed a ride and, upon the driver's recommendation, we pulled up to Maison Edun, a recently opened club on Adelaide West, ten minutes later. Stuart tipped the driver and paid the cover and we slipped inside the ultra-chic club. It took a few minutes for my eyes to adjust to the fluorescent blue and pink lighting as Stuart led me to one of the long banquettes facing the dance floor. Two couples sat nearby, though neither glanced our way when we sat down. I looked around, feeling old and frumpy. I saw several women wearing tight leather outfits with ample bosoms, some in actual bustiers and high heels. Stuart leaned over and kissed my cheek.

"Quit worrying. They look terrible. They're trying way too hard," he said, before promising to return with drinks.

When we'd been lovers, we didn't frequent clubs. We occasionally went to the Byward Market or across the river to what was then the town of Hull with Siobhan and other friends, but after Stuart and I had moved in together, it seemed unnecessary. The clubs smelled like desperation, and it made me sad that people looked for love while grinding up against someone on a dance floor. The couple sitting next to me was doing some heavy panting and petting and I looked away after seeing him slide his hand under her skirt. The other couple seemed to be in the early stages of a full-blown fight. I tried to listen to what she said, but could make out only the occasional cuss word.

Stuart returned a few minutes later and handed me a Tom Collins while he sipped a tonic water with lime. We flirted as we finished our drinks. Then, not interested in sticking around to see what would happen to the couples around me, I took his hand and led him out to the dance floor. The music thumped and I felt the bass reverberate in the walls of my lungs. I felt exhilarated. I let loose, flailing my arms, swinging my hips, smiling, laughing and flirting with Stuart, which made me feel aroused, sexy and invigorated, a far cry from my usual run-of-the-mill mother-of-two identity. When the light changed and the music slowed, I looked at Stuart, our faces inches apart. Everything moved as in slow motion. Stuart placed one of his hands on the small of my back and used the other to pull me toward him. I felt his breath on my neck as we swayed together. The intervening years melted away, and this was us, dancing barefoot in our Sandy Hill apartment or at one of our high school proms.

He pulled his head back and looked at me, his intensity familiar. He smiled and then lowered his lips to mine. A thousand thoughts rushed through my brain as I kissed him. Images kept coming as we kissed, until I broke our embrace. He didn't move, didn't flinch. I began to turn away, moving toward safety, putting a space between us that wouldn't require explanations, apologies or decisions. But I couldn't ignore the feelings we'd unearthed, that pulsated through me, and I turned back to face him. I grabbed his shirt at his sternum and pulled him toward me. In a matter of seconds, his hands were in my hair, holding me flush against him, his mouth finding mine, not letting up.

"Let's get out of here," he whispered, reaching to hold one of my hands as we fled the dance floor and past the table with the other couples. The fighters were nowhere to be seen, the others oblivious to everything going on around them.

Outside the club, we kissed and huddled together, waiting for the Uber he had ordered. Once inside, Stuart said, "Radisson Blu, please," and then leaned over to me and we made out like the teenagers we'd once been, ignoring what the driver might think. At the hotel, we quickly crossed the lobby, which was crowded with people from the conference. Stuart got caught by Tom and a couple of other inebriated managers who slurred their words. But he escaped, telling them he needed to go over figures. I pushed the button for the elevator and waited, willing it to arrive before I could change my mind. The doors opened and inside was empty. And then, just as I pushed the button to hold the door for Stuart, he darted inside. The doors began closing and I caught our reflection in the mirror, just as his mouth found mine again.

"You're flushing," he said, as the elevator dinged, indicating we'd reached his floor. "I forgot how much I enjoyed seeing you blush." We rushed along the floor to his room, his card key already out. With one quick motion, Stuart opened the door and held it open for me. Once inside, our passion increased, and we fell onto the bed. His hands pulled down my skirt as I unbuttoned his shirt. He started pulling my tights off, kissing me as he lowered them. I reached for the buckle of his jeans as he climbed onto the bed alongside me and began pulling my sequined shirt over my head.

And then everything halted.

One of the sequins caught on my bracelet—the bracelet Rob had given me the Christmas after I was let go from Legandcy. Stuart was working to free the sequin from the link.

And that tug jerked me back into reality.

What was I playing at? For the past year and a half, I had felt adrift, floating in a turbulent sea; a little boat without any oars. Stuart seemed like a solid shore, a place I could safely land. And he would have been if I wasn't Rob's wife and the mother of Aidan and Jacob. But that *was* who I was. And sleeping with my former lover, despite how much I loved him and what he still meant to me, was wrong. This wasn't a situation that would only involve Rob. In my mind's eye, I saw those two smiling faces, those little men Rob and I had created together and who didn't deserve to be shuttled between two parents because their mother wanted to feel desired and carefree? Was I really that selfish? Stuart was an adult now and I believed that if I could go back in time—back to a few months after he left; a couple of years later; even eight years ago—and we found ourselves in this exact place, we would have picked up from where we were and it would be Stuart and I who were married with kids—maybe Stuart would have given me the daughter I always wanted; however, I couldn't bear to think of a life without my sons. I couldn't imagine a life without Rob either. I realized I didn't want to.

Stuart freed the bracelet, but when he looked at me, he felt the shift between us. I didn't move. It was as though all my pent-up desire for him had dissipated because I realized I couldn't do this. I shivered.

"What's wrong?" he said, kissing me.

"I can't," I whispered. "I want to, but I can't. I love you, but I can't."

"I don't understand," he said. "Caitie, I'm in love with you. I don't think I ever stopped loving you, to be honest. I want to be with you and if you want to be with me, we will work through it all together. It would be complicated and messy, but I would be all in."

"I know and right now, at this moment, I want to be with you. But just because I want that doesn't mean I can have it. I gave a promise to someone else and I'm not willing to go back on it. I love Rob; I do," I said, Stuart flinching at the sound of his name. "Rob and I don't have what you and I had, you know, that passionate, all-consuming love, but maybe that's because we're older and married. It's definitely more complicated. When I decided to come to your room, I intended to sleep with you—even if it turned out to be just one more time. You have no idea how much I want to."

"I think I do, Caitie. I want you just as much," he said.

"But if we sleep together tonight, it won't be enough," I said, taking his hand and pleading with him with my eyes. "I'll want more from you and I don't think I can do that to Rob and my boys. We're certainly not perfect, but I love my life with him. I don't want to lose them."

I got off the bed and started gathering up my clothes. Stuart laid back on the bed and was staring up at the ceiling. But then he got up and bent down to pick up my tights. He handed them to me.

"I would give you everything," he said, sitting down

again. I sat next to him. "I'm not looking for or offering a one-night stand here. I'm offering forever."

"Our time passed," I said, my heart breaking. "Don't be fooled by my words. I'm beyond gutted. Being an adult sucks, but this is the right decision. You'll never know how much you've helped me since coming back into my life. I do love you, Stuart."

We didn't touch as he walked me to the door. Then we looked at each other. His hand caressed my face and he gently kissed me.

"I'll always love you, C-A-I-T," he said, opening the door. He watched me walk down the hallway toward the elevator, giving me a wave when I stepped inside. I was thankful he hadn't offered to walk me to my room because as soon as the doors closed, I collapsed into huge, violent sobs, which didn't subside until I crawled into bed and turned off the light.

eighteen

MARCH 2017

I ARRIVED at work on Monday following a busy weekend of laundry, grocery shopping and general organizing, not to mention playing Snakes and Ladders umpteen times with Jake, and G.I. Joe with Aidan. Trevor was frenzied, getting ready for the summer shoe promotions.

"Caitlin, we need to get the new sandals up front, in the window display," he barked, shuffling his feet to propel himself between the backroom and the sales floor, where he was stacking hundreds of shoe boxes. As I stood there watching him, amazed that someone cared enough about organizing white boxes, he snapped, "Are you going to watch me all day or could you bring yourself to help?"

When Rob reached for me in bed Saturday night, I pecked him on the cheek and told him I had a terrible headache. I went into our bathroom, where I cried for the next half hour. When I returned to bed, he was asleep. Siobhan's texts had been non-stop for the past few days.

> **SIOBHAN**
> Caitie-Cat! WTF happened?

> I'm heart broken.

> Do I need to grab a spoon and some ice cream?!

> No. But it hurts.

At eleven-thirty, the store door chimed to alert me to a customer. I looked up and Siobhan sauntered in. As I introduced her to Trevor, she turned on the charm.

"Mr. Murdock, *enchantée*. Caitie has told me so much about you. She boasts about how precisely you run this place, and you should be proud of yourself."

"Oh, you can call me Trevor," he said, chuffed. Trevor never spoke of girlfriends or going on dates. His entire life revolved around Heusten Shoes and shopping on Bay and Bloor in Toronto when he got his quarterly bonus. It never occurred to me that he might have feelings, especially with a past that included two ex-wives he referred to as Satan and Gonorrhea. Of course, his vanity prevented him from seeing Siobhan was sarcasm personified, but no matter, she'd said the magic words. So, when she glanced at me and asked, "Caitie-cat, lunch?" even though it was an hour before I was due for a break, Trevor said, "Great idea—why don't you go now, Caitlin?"

We filled the time walking to her car with idle prattle. Mike was home again after a short tour to the east coast of Canada.

"He's insufferable, Caitie," she said, as I laughed. "He keeps telling me he loves me, that he wants to marry me. He literally said, 'Girl, I've got to be with you.' I started to laugh but then saw his face. The poor thing meant it. Oh, Christ, Cait, what am I going to do? I might have to marry him."

"Well, it's not all bad," I said, feeling the need to stick up for Mike. He was a sweet man. He adored Siobhan, though on her it was wasted. She didn't need to be fawned over.

Siobhan was taking the day off, she said, to regroup after putting a massive issue to bed last week. We drove to a chain restaurant we loved though we would never admit that to anyone else, and both ordered salad with grilled chicken and water with lemon. Though I'd tried to delay answering any of Siobhan's questions until that point, after she ordered and handed her menu to the waitress, she said, "Now, Caitie, we have exactly one hour for you to tell me what the fuck went down on the weekend with Stuart. I'm guessing it's not the end of the world by the simple fact that you're standing, which, I can thank Christ for. Now, what happened?"

I told her about my jealousy when other women looked at Stuart. I recounted the meetings we sat in together, though she rolled her eyes and made a "get on with it" motion with her hand. I detailed our dinners together, updated her on what the cast of characters that belonged to our story were doing until our food arrived. It was appropriate. I needed sustenance to get into what she was really asking about, what I hadn't yet been able to process for myself.

I took a deep breath and then told Siobhan why Stuart said he left. There was silence except for the sound of her chewing and the occasional clank of her utensils on her bowl as she cut her lettuce. Siobhan is the best listener. You could explain how you severed the head of a beloved cat and froze it in the freezer and she'd just sit and listen, without facial expressions betraying how she felt or whether she made any judgments.

"Did you tell him about what you went through? Did you let him know what it felt like to get his phone call about that bitch, what was her name?"

"Jennifer. Yes. He didn't try to skirt anything. It was such a gift. I'd worried for so many years that I hadn't loved him enough, that I wasn't enough to make him happy. It wasn't true. Siobhan, I think, understandably, he got spooked, and acted like a scared twenty-one-year-old. He didn't want us to turn out like his parents. He explained everything. And I can understand it now, at our age. He said he was going to come back and I honestly think I could have moved past it. And that's what's heartbreaking. I don't blame him. It just makes me sad. I wish we could have fixed it."

"Caitie, honey, we're all in repair," she said. "Stuart, you, me, Mike, all of us. The devastating thing about that is most people don't want to get fixed. It's not that we won't make mistakes. That's a given. We will. And we'll keep making them. We'll hurt others. We'll intentionally deceive. We'll misunderstand and cause an inordinate amount of damage to the people around us. But we have a responsibility to ourselves—and especially to those we care about—to own up to the times when we've acted like a complete asshole. That's what helps mend us. And that's what he's finally done. That's how you know he truly loves you."

We ate together in silence after that, and I reflected on what she'd said. We *are* all in repair; Siobhan was right. When I looked at my life, every day, I made decisions concerning the boys, Rob, Stuart, my career path and I realized I was a work in progress—every single damned minute. I just hoped I was getting better. Since I'd left Legandcy, I'd come to understand that people have broken pasts, sad tales, and disappointments they carry around. But we all have choices to make. I could let my circumstances define me and act as though I was powerless to control my life—like I had most of my life—or I could take the reins. It wouldn't be easy, but I needed to put more of an effort into creating what I wanted, what would bring me the most joy and make me whole. In the weeks after I was laid off, I'd felt as though I had fractured into a number of different parts, each operating separately, each with its own agenda. It was time for me to literally pull myself together. Now that I'd closed the door on Stuart—he had texted once since that night, a short, "I will love you always, xo"—I had other things to figure out.

"I love you," I said to Siobhan. "You've always been there for me, letting me just be who I am. You've never judged me. I'll never forget when you came to me that day. You fed me ice cream, for crying out loud. I probably don't say it enough, but I'm grateful for you and I treasure every moment I spend with you."

"No problem, babe. Now, did you fuck him? Tell me you at least slept with him!" she said, arching her eyebrows and pulling her lips up in a half-taunting smile.

"No," I said, thinking of how good it felt to lie with Stuart again, feeling his skin on my skin. I pushed my finished bowl away and put my utensils down. "It was close. I wanted to. Damn, I really did. Just to know what it would feel like one more time. Just to relive that all-consuming passion we'd once had. And he wanted to. But I couldn't."

"I knew you wouldn't. Good for you. Now, if you really meant what you said a few minutes ago, you'll be my bridesmaid, because I think I'm going to have to marry Mike." She rolled her eyes. "Fuck."

As the days moved away from my decision to end things with Stuart, I went through a maelstrom of emotions. I tried to lock up all my feelings and act like the Caitie I had been before he re-entered my life. But that was impossible. I had changed. Stuart's honesty meant what I had believed to be true contained only shades of the truth. Yes, he had left. Yes, he hadn't returned. But the *reason* he stayed away made sense. So now, not only was I mourning the loss of him again, I was mourning what really could have been. Had he come back to Ottawa, I know I would have forgiven him. Without question, he would be in my house. My children would be his children.

I was conflicted. I didn't regret marrying Rob. Far from it. But, once in a while, I resented him. Looking at his shoes, scattered around the shoe rack rather than placed neatly, annoyed me. A stray sock under the bed caused me to clench my fists. I wanted to yell when he texted me to ask what time he had to pick up Jacob from Beavers when I had told him earlier that day. And my anger made me feel guilty because Rob didn't deserve any of my misplaced emotion.

I tried, but I was distracted—at home and at work. I caught Rob looking at me sometimes as though he knew something was wrong, something major had happened to me. Occasionally, he asked, "Caitie, you okay?" to which I'd give a curt, "I'm fine, just dealing with a lot at work," which wasn't a complete lie. After he asked me once if I was pregnant, a comment that earned him an afternoon of silence, he left me alone.

I willed myself with every last bit of energy I had to be upbeat and fun, especially with the boys. I cried when I was home alone or, on occasion, in an empty parking lot I pulled into on my way home from work. I stayed busy. If I was occupied, I couldn't think as much. I rearranged closets, and brought old clothes, household items and the boys' discarded toys to the Goodwill. I started planning a getaway with Rob, though I couldn't commit to a date. I wasn't ready.

At work, I went through the motions. Smile and greet customers, fetch shoes, praise staff, organize boxes, fill out paperwork, order inventory and take deep breaths. But I was slipping. Trevor completely lost his cool with me the following week when I forgot to order a shipment of one of our bestsellers. Trevor barely glanced at me before he headed for the backroom. I shot a questioning look at Caleb.

"The clog order didn't come in," he mumbled.

"Shit," I said, dashing behind the counter to see if the order requisition was still in my inbox. It was. "Shit, shit, shit. I forgot to finalize the order on Tuesday when I was in."

Caleb grimaced. "He's pissed."

"Okay, I'll go talk to him." I found Trevor in the backroom, opening a stack of shoe boxes, searching for something he wasn't going to find. At first, I felt sorry for him because he worked hard and took pride in the store, but that feeling dissipated when he spun around on his heel. "Well, I suppose this is your fault. Ever since you got back from the conference, you've been messing up," he seethed. "Can't do anything right, really."

"I'm sorry," I said, feebly, and then regretted my apology. Trevor was such a control hound, acting as though the company, let alone the store, couldn't function without him. I'd made one mistake, not caused ten thousand dollars of merchandise to be sent for discount after botching an order, as he had the previous month.

"I'm going to have to write you up, Caitlin," he said, giving me one of the pompous, condescending looks he doled out en masse to the part-time staff. Caleb and Kareen, a student we hired to cover the busy summer season, were getting pretty good at imitating him, and the other day we were all in stitches as they kept trying to one-up each other using Trevor-speak, complete with what they termed the "patronizing, snooty look."

"This kind of ineptitude can't be tolerated for long," Trevor said. "I'll send something to Mr. Taylor this afternoon. In the meantime, figure out a way to get these shoes out on the floor. You can forget about taking a lunch, too."

"I don't think Stuart will do anything," I said, without thinking. When Trevor narrowed his eyes at me, I backpedalled. "You know, he's a pretty busy guy. Why don't I save you the trouble and text him to let him know I screwed up the order. That way, you won't need to send him a formal complaint." Trevor wouldn't take the bait to start a huge fight, likely because he knew Stuart and I were friends and he wouldn't win. But we were locked in a juvenile pissing contest. I dared him to be the first to blink.

"Fine," he said. "You text Mr. Taylor. Tell him about the non-existent shipment and how you've messed that up. I'll call him later to figure something out."

I never texted Stuart anymore, unless it was work-related. I had made my decision, as difficult as it was. I didn't want to be in a situation where we started flirting, where we started driving down another emotional dead end —or off a cliff.

> Sorry to bother you, but I forgot to send through an order for a shipment of clogs. Trevor's in a tizzy. Told me to text you. He'll call you later.

STUART
> No worries, Caitie. Tell him to relax. It's fine. Miss you xo.

True to her word, Siobhan and Mike announced their engagement a few weeks after—everything in my life was now classified as before or after the night in the hotel room with Stuart—on a rare sunny day in April and they decided to get married in August, which left just a few months for planning. Siobhan's mother had immediately drawn up a three-hundred-name guest list, hired a live band—"He's a fucking musician!" she yelled to me over the phone, "why is *she* hiring a band?"—and ordered flowers and a cake. That's when Siobhan "lost her shit," as she termed it. Now, there were forty guests invited to a champagne brunch on a Wednesday toward the end of August. But she still needed a dress, so today, on an unusually mild Saturday in mid-May, we scoured boutiques on a high-end street in Toronto.

"No wedding gown, and no white," Siobhan demanded. "If I'm going to do the deed, I'm getting something exquisite that I can wear again."

That morning, I dropped the boys off at Birdie's house. Mike was coming to our house because he and Rob had a tuxedo appointment, while I took the GO into Toronto to go gown shopping with Siobhan. Though she eschewed the traditional in terms of her ensemble, I knew the entire affair would be sophisticated. After "wedding lockdown," as we termed it, Siobhan stopped calling me her bridesmaid and reverted to "witness," which is what Rob and I would be during the City Hall ceremony. Their late-morning reception would be held at an exclusive resort in Niagara-on-the-Lake.

I was excited about the wedding and was looking forward to spending some alone time with Rob. For me, it represented a new start. It had taken me a few weeks before I could have sex again with Rob while I worked through my emotions and grief after making my decision about Stuart. After Rob's pregnancy comment, he had stopped asking me what was wrong, but I think he knew something was up. If he'd pressed me, I would have come clean about everything, but I wasn't ready to. I wasn't sure I'd ever tell him what had almost happened between Stuart and me. To be honest, I wasn't worried that my actions would end our marriage or cause a huge rift between us. I *had* to go through what I did to know it was Rob I chose and would always choose—because I could have chosen differently. Despite not wanting to have my boys grow up in a fractured home, no one forced me to stay.

Siobhan and I ambled by a row of pricey boutiques in Yorkville, and I made a conscious effort not to balk at the prices of the dresses Siobhan was trying on. I told myself not everyone considered sixty dollars to be an expensive shirt.

"What do you make now?" Siobhan asked me as we stopped in front of Holt Renfrew.

"Fifty," I said.

"A year?" she asked, looking alarmed. "You're raising kids on fifty thousand a year?"

"Well, Rob makes close to a hundred," I said, knowing what I sounded like. I got a sense of pride from making my own money and not relying on Rob to be the family's sole provider. While Rob had worked his way up to partner at Cre8tive, he bounced from contract to contract and I had found myself in the position of breadwinner. I revelled in it. Somehow, since I'd left The Leg, I hid, trying to convince myself I was doing the best I could and that well-paying jobs were scarce in Niagara. Compared to others we knew, we were doing well. But when Siobhan looked at me, I knew I'd failed myself.

"I need a drink," she said, looking around.

We located a patio about a block down the street and ordered drinks. I tried to order an iced tea, pleading that we had a lot of work ahead of us and I didn't need to feel sleepy in another hour, but Siobhan was having none of it. "Put vodka in it," she told the server, ordering a Caesar for herself. Then she spoke.

"Caitie, you're killing yourself for fifty grand a year? You let that idiot talk down to you for a couple thousand a month? You're worth so much more." She waved her hands around, agitated. "I thought you were making at least eighty to put up with that shit. What's going on? If I don't make one-twenty, I'll shoot someone."

Just that week, I had almost quit. Trevor had gone from unbearable to insufferable; curt, disdainful and haughty at every turn, it was as though creating snide remarks and trying to belittle me had become a national sport only he participated in. I considered calling Stuart but didn't care enough. I got bolder, trying to match him insult for insult, using sarcasm and irony to make my points, pushing as far as I could. Three days earlier, he played his trump card by freezing my pay, even though I was entitled to another raise, as per the contract I'd signed when I was promoted to store manager. Rob told me to fight it, but I didn't want to get Stuart involved, and he would be the one in management I would have to bring this issue to. Stuart would separate anything personal from what was clearly a business decision, but by digging in my heels and fighting for a raise, I set myself up for a future there. And that was something I was reconsidering.

"You don't understand," I started to say, but she cut me off.

"Don't pull that crap with me. I understand fine. You've gone in the box. Yes, you have," she said. She ignored my protests and clinked my glass with hers when our drinks arrived. But she barrelled on. "You're afraid to go out and look for something better because for some fucked-up reason, you think you don't deserve more. Someone put you in the box of mediocrity and you're taking it. And it's not even about the money, Caitie; it's about what you're doing! I know your job's stressful, but it's not challenging you, is it? It's not demanding. How far are you going to grow? I'm not trying to be mean, but someone's got to say this. You graduated with highest honours, and you were one of two people who got internships at that swanky agency in Ottawa, whatever it was called. And you've won, what, five design awards?"

Seeing that I was about to correct her, she soldiered on, now that she was on a roll. This must be what it sounded like when she chewed out one of her junior editors, chastising them, yet trying to inspire them to do better the next time simultaneously. "Fine, you were nominated, you didn't win. Who gives a crap? Maybe the girl who won was sleeping with the judge. You don't know. Caitie, you're a creator! Why aren't you creating? Get out of the fucking box!"

I remained quiet, turning over what she'd said. She was right about everything. These thoughts rolled through my brain every time I found a spare moment during the day or when I caught a glimpse of myself in the washroom at work, not to mention the nights I couldn't fall asleep.

"I thought I was going to be extraordinary, that I was going to do something special," I said, my voice quiet as I gazed across the street, watching people who seemed to know where they were going. A tall brunette carried a Burberry bag. I felt ashamed—not only because I couldn't afford such a bag, but because I'd tricked myself into thinking I didn't want more. "When I break it down, I make about fourteen dollars an hour. I feel so deflated most of the time. I'm afraid. I worry I'm setting a bad example for my boys. When we went to university, and even when I first started working for peanuts right out of Ottawa U, I felt full of potential, as though I'd take the world by storm. Rob believed in me. I believed in me. But if my twenty-two-year-old self met me today, she wouldn't recognize me. And I'm no fun. I guess the most excitement I've had since I got laid off were those days with Stuart."

I paused as a few tears rolled down my cheek and fell onto the table. Siobhan took my hand but didn't say anything. I knew I had let myself get carried away with Stuart, not just because I loved him. He offered an escape from the ho-hum life I led. Most days, I felt as if I watched from the sidelines. Someone who looked like me went through the motions. I didn't feel alive. I'd been playing a part in the play called "The Life of Caitlin Morissette," instead of having the courage to be my true self. I'd tied so much of my identity to my position at Legandcy, and when it was gone, I felt like I was stranded in a room with the lights turned off. I groped around, trying to find the switch in unfamiliar territory. My fingers brushed along the walls, unsure, searching, but not moving very far ahead. And, instead of forcing myself to reach out, to take a risk, I chose the easy path, using my kids and Rob as an excuse when they were the reason I needed to be strong, to be myself.

"Siobhan, I have to confess, I can't stand feeling so small," I said after a long pause, turning to look at my dear friend. "I watch other mothers and they genuinely seem to be happy doing what they're doing—dropping their kids off, going back home to tidy up the house or going to work, picking the kids up from school, making dinner and putting them to bed. If they work, it's only to get themselves out of the house. When I had my kids, I vowed they'd never be my entire reason for living. They're the most important people in my life, along with Rob, but I always wanted to have something for myself. Something big. I want to do something special. I never wanted to be so...so ordinary."

"Caitie-cat, you could never be ordinary. And you have everything inside you. It's all in there. You just have to be willing to fight and let it out," she said, softly. "Don't hide behind someone you're not because she seems to be who you think you need to be. You can do it. You're a tough bitch, even though you pretend you're this sweet and innocent store manager. I don't want to sound like Tony fucking Robbins, but I believe in you. Figure out what you want and let's go get it."

After the clog debacle in April, Trevor ratcheted up his nastiness. He looked for ways to criticize everything I did, whether it was how I welcomed customers, completed paperwork or cleaned up the lunchroom. Nothing I did was good enough, and I was too exhausted to come up with clever and quick replies to his snide remarks.

I spent most of my free time thinking about what Siobhan had said and scouring websites, trying to figure out what I could do. But I decided to take charge, and I locked myself away in my office—even for just half an hour—and wrote. I let Aidan and Jacob watch TV before they got ready for bed, giving myself a few minutes to write in peace. Though I felt guilty I wasn't spending "quality time" with the boys, I forced myself to ignore the constant mom-shaming advice from articles I found online. There were worse things in life than kids watching television—for instance, having parents who don't love them or any food to eat. And I stopped looking at Facebook. I didn't care what people ate for dinner or the clothes they put on their dogs. Instead, as the words flowed out of me, I began to feel more like myself. I applied for freelance design work; most, I never heard back from—not even a form email rejection—but I did land small projects from three budding entrepreneurs, and felt encouraged. But it was the action of doing something, moving myself along, that felt good. I could deal with the rejection, but I wouldn't accept inaction any longer.

And then, when Trevor sneered at me on a sunny, warm July day, something gave. We had been stacking boxes—again. The clog order, which had then been backordered, arrived and Trevor was in a rush to get them out, reminding me we wouldn't be hurrying if I had, in fact, ordered the shoes when they were supposed to have been ordered two months earlier. I kept quiet, ignoring his digs. I worked as expediently as possible, noticing an eerie quiet settling in the store, as though I was the only one there.

I paused, sitting back on my feet and stretching my neck from side to side. My body reminded me that if I crouched on my knees for long periods of time, I'd pay for it. I could hear Caleb's faint falsetto mimicking Adam Levine from the back. He often wore his iPod while working, a great plan to block out where he was. I stood up and was surprised to see Trevor leaning against the same shelf, his hand on his hips, watching me work. He was enjoying it. Not in a sexual way, but rather the way a king observed serfs harvesting fields in medieval England. It was sick.

Just as I meant to reach to grab another box, I caught a glimpse of his slightly upturned lip. A crease formed at the side of his nose; his left eye narrowed. At any other time, I might not have noticed these subtle changes. And to this day, I have no idea why *that* expression caused me to react the way I did. The weeks of uncertainty and self-loathing that had previously enabled me to tolerate his condescension might have had something to do with it. But that day, I'd had it.

Though the moment could only have lasted a millisecond, I felt like I was frozen in time. And with time standing still, I decided I wasn't going to settle. I was going to start fighting again. I was worth it. I was a thirty-eight-year-old wife and mother of two young boys, with a former successful graphic design career. Trevor was a forty-nine-year-old twice-divorced man with a Napoleon complex and receding hairline. I took in the row of shoes on either side of us. Did I really want to match pairs of clogs or rearrange sandals picked over by tourists and bargain-hunting women for the rest of my life? Did I want to answer to Trevor or whomever would be Trevor's replacement in two years' time every day? Was I willing to sacrifice holidays and last-minute shift changes and never be able to plan a dinner with friends in case I had to work Saturday because a part-timer called in sick (again) to go to a party with her other twenty-something friends?

At that instant, I knew I must make the change I'd tried to avoid for six months.

"Trevor?"

"Um?" he murmured, lifting one eyebrow.

And then, without thinking about it for another moment, those two words, those two beautiful, final syllables were out of my mouth.

"I quit."

nineteen

JULY 2017

I FELT ENERGIZED, almost frenetic, by the time Rob arrived home from work that night. I had cleaned and disinfected the entire kitchen and fed the boys their favourite meal of macaroni and cheese from a box with some potato chips on the side because I was in such a good mood. They gobbled it up in case I took away the junk and replaced it with broccoli and chicken stir-fry. They cleared their plates and mumbled "thanks," before rushing off to play on their video consoles, making sure they spoke as kindly as possible to each other, afraid they would press their luck and my breeze of happiness would turn into gale-force anger.

After I had announced my intentions to Trevor, he, in perfect form, said, "Good riddance," before rushing for the telephone to find someone to cover my shifts. Unlike the time I was let go from The Leg, I sauntered to the backroom of the store to collect my belongings, a sense of peace descending—not panic. When I reached the fridge, I contemplated leaving my egg salad sandwich to go mouldy. I revelled at the thought of Trevor seeing the glutinous mess, ready to ooze out of its plastic wrap and onto his thousand-dollar suit. But on the off-chance that Caleb would end up bearing the brunt of the malodorous trick, I grabbed it, along with my apple, yogurt and water. I threw them into my knapsack and pulled my handbag off the coat tree. When I walked into the showroom, Caleb came over to me and hugged me.

"Caitie," he said. "Did you really quit? Trevor just ran out, all panicked."

"I did," I said, breaking into a smile.

"Good for you," he said, beaming. "Keep in touch."

I opened the front door to the store and strolled out into the thick, humid air. The outlet mall was abuzz, inundated with day trippers from Toronto and New York State. I despised catering to tourists, who were, like most outlet mall shoppers, looking for cheap. They seemed to be much more demanding.

On my way home, I detoured to Starbucks. Instead of rushing out the door to get to the next place, I sat on the patio and enjoyed the warm weather. Summer was my favourite time of year. When I'd lived in Ottawa, I would run along the Canal, enjoy weekend festivals in downtown parks and outdoor patios and treat myself to endless gelato on Elgin Street during summer. In Niagara, summer was also glorious, with roadside fruit stands, myriad places to ride bikes and a beach close to home with a carousel you could ride for just five cents. Then there was the region's natural beauty—rows upon rows of blooming grapevines, tender fruit trees and woodland. As I sat, I thought about what I would say to Rob. He might worry about my lack of a paycheque, but he knew I hated my job and felt I wasted my talent working at Heusten Shoes. He said I could always get another job in retail or the service sector, and he was right.

As I sat in the wrought iron chair, I felt I'd taken my first step on the right path. I was following my heart and what I was supposed to be doing. I resolved not to take another job because I was worried about money or because it was what I thought other people in my unemployed situation would do. And I made a promise to myself to stop worrying about what other people thought. When I'd taken the job at Heusten, I'd planned to be there only a few months—not a year and a half—until something better opened up. Nothing had, and so my entire perspective had become skewed. At university and at the firms I had worked, including Legandcy, people strived for excellence, for more, for ways to get better—and we worked hard. But at Heusten Shoes, I allowed myself to get sucked into the box of mediocrity, as Siobhan had termed it. I bought the line that if I started looking for what would satisfy me then I was a selfish mother and wife. That was horseshit—just a bunch of excuses drummed up by average and ordinary people so they could feel better about themselves and their unwillingness to change. I had believed it because it was easier to follow that path than stick my neck out.

The truth was I had been afraid. In fact, I remained terrified. But, at that moment, I was willing to fail spectacularly for the next five or ten years of my life. At least it would mean I tried, that I went down fighting. And I knew Rob would support me. As I slurped the last sips of my iced tea, I felt my phone vibrate. I looked down and saw it was a text from Stuart.

> **STUART**
> Proud of you. Still in love. Go find what you're seeking. xo

I smiled and then stood up, refreshed and invigorated. I walked next door to the grocery store and selected a ready-made salad and roasted chicken—convenient meals would be a luxury we'd need to kibosh going forward when we'd be relying on only Rob's salary. But tonight, Rob and I would have an easy, yet nutritious, dinner. I'd leave the difficulty to explaining my actions. I grabbed a fresh baguette as I walked to the checkout and then found myself singing along to the radio on the way to our bungalow in the north end of the city.

I loved our house. It was a place of refuge for me, and today was no different. As soon as the yellow siding came into view, I felt calm. It was a lighthouse, assuring those who ventured near shore that land was close, that everything would be okay. My rash decision wouldn't cause my family too much distress. We had this harbour in a tempest.

As I set the table, I kept glancing at the clock, counting down to when Rob was due home. Though I didn't want to admit it, Rob's company's success probably gave me the freedom to quit this afternoon. If Cre8tive had been struggling, I might have thought twice. I believed I would still have made the same decision, but I couldn't be certain. Knowing Rob's role as partner would guarantee a flow of money into our house helped soften my blow of guilt and sense of foreboding.

My phone rang. I saw the name and felt blanketed in love. I answered it just as Rob came through the door.

"Caitie-cat," yelled Siobhan, as I said hello. "What the

fuck did you do today? I got your texts but couldn't call until now."

"Uh, can't talk right now. Can I call you back?" I asked, as Rob placed a kiss on my forehead. I watched as he moved into the dining room, placed his shoulder bag on the floor near the table and looked at the spread I'd laid out. He raised his eyebrows at me in question and then shrugged and picked up a handful of peanuts from a glass jar on the island in the kitchen as he came back in the room.

As I hung up, I wondered how I'd gotten so lucky. Rob was a great guy. He did the little things that made me know he appreciated me, like planting a magnolia bush on our front lawn one Mother's Day with the boys. He was so patient when I told him stories about how my day had gone, never interrupting. He appeared to listen, even though the minutiae of my work at Heusten Shoes must have bored him silly. And he was a full partner in the care of our boys. Since we both worked, there was no slopping most of the household chores onto me or even worse—a cardinal sin in my book—assuming I was the only one who should look after the boys, as some of my friends' husbands did. I remembered one Super Bowl party we went to at Siobhan's house, when I met her friends Dustin and Monika and their three children under the age of five. Monika spent the entire night chasing after the little terrors while Dustin drank seven beers by my count and palled around with the other men. Rob was the one who put a fresh diaper on the baby because the Philadelphia Eagles had the ball in the New England Patriots' red zone, and Dustin couldn't tear himself away from the game.

"You seem to be in a great mood," Rob said, looking around. I wanted to laugh at his expression, which was elation (clean kitchen, quiet surroundings) mixed with a healthy dose of apprehension (why?). He reached for another handful of peanuts. "Did you have a good day? Did everything go up to regular price?"

"Stop eating those peanuts. You'll fill yourself up. Well, actually, I told Trevor to stuff it. I quit," I admitted. My skin prickled as I watched his face for a reaction. Then I felt a tug in my stomach. What if I'd been too rash? What if Rob was furious I had quit? I second-guessed my initial prediction, which was that Rob would be thrilled that he wouldn't have to hear anything more about Trevor.

"You did what?" Rob said, his voice extra loud in the silent kitchen. Then he started laughing. Before he spoke again, I could hear Jakey whoop from downstairs. "Sorry, I didn't mean to shout. I'm not used to being able to hear myself think. No more Trevor? No more stories about anybody's dating life? Actually, scratch that, I'm going to miss those."

"So, you're not mad?"

"Mad? Jesus Christ, Caitie, I'm thrilled. I've been dreaming of bumping into that asshole and telling him off or punching him in the face because of the way he treats you, but I knew this was your battle to fight. Way to go!"

"You're not worried about me sponging off you?"

"Sponging? What does that mean?"

"You know, not making as much money. I mean, I have some freelance that's started coming in, but I won't have a lot coming in for now. Will we be okay?"

"We'll be more than okay, Caitie," he said. Rob stopped crunching and then sighed. He moved over to the fridge so he could lean against it. He looked at me for a beat and I could tell he had more to say so I waited.

"Actually, now that we're being honest, I have to tell you I was starting to get really worried. You zoned out a few months ago, around the time you had that seminar in Toronto. Listen, I knew you were working with Stuart," he said. I stood at the island in the centre of our kitchen, mixing the salad. I froze when he said Stuart's name, not trusting myself to say anything, wondering why Rob was bringing this up now. I hadn't slept with him, but I had not only fooled around with Stuart, I had—maybe this was worse—given myself emotionally to him. I had been unfaithful to Rob. He moved toward me, his gaze locked onto mine. "I knew it was the same Stuart from university because he called here one time looking for you and he introduced himself on the phone, saying you had been friends in university.

"You never told me you were working with your university *friend*," he continued, and I heard the quote-unquote in his voice but didn't say anything. "And that made me wonder. When we started dating, I'm sure you told me about him. You likely mentioned him in that time, early on, when we kind of went through the laundry list of past lovers and hook-ups. I didn't really want to know any details about anyone you'd been with because I didn't think it mattered. I never told you this, but I once asked Siobhan about him."

By this point, I had stopped mixing the salad and was clenching the tongs in my hands. I couldn't believe what I was hearing. My heart thumped in my chest, worry gripping my breath.

"This was shortly after you and I got serious. I heard you say his name a few times when you were sleeping. I didn't want to ask you about it because I wasn't sure if this guy was a friend you had lost or something like that. Siobhan told me you had been together for a few years and it had been really serious. She said you fell apart when he left, but she didn't give me any details."

I started to get my wits about me and was just about to say something to try and deny what he was saying. He took the tongs out of my hands and held my hands in his.

"Don't say anything," he said. "This isn't me fishing for answers. I don't care that you never told me it was because of him you were so cautious when we first met. And, while I wish you might have mentioned something now, even just in passing, that he was back in your life, I'm telling you I figured the reason you didn't tell me that he was your boss or whatever he is...was...is because it was your chance to set things right with him, however that turned out. You seemed upbeat. You took care when you were getting ready to go to work. Don't try to deny it—I'm telling you I understood. We've been married for years. I know I'm not as exciting as I once was. And I wasn't that exciting to begin with."

I tried to interject, but he didn't let me. Rob wasn't a great risk-taker. He was solid and dependable. That's why I loved him. That's why I chose him all those years ago.

"Caitlin, let me speak. I didn't say anything to you about why you weren't telling me about this guy. I knew you didn't work with him all the time at the store. I knew you weren't *seeing* him on the side. And while I can deduce that he must have been in Toronto when you were at that conference in March, and I'm pretty sure *something* must have happened, I don't actually want to know about it. I've watched you over the past couple of months and I've seen you go through *this*," he waved his hands around, "whatever it was. But, Caitie, I'm your husband, not your father. I trusted you would choose our marriage if it came to that. I wasn't afraid of losing you."

I couldn't speak. My throat tightened. I just stared at Rob. If I'd made a different decision that night, the result would have impacted my entire family. I'd chosen correctly. In that instant, I knew I'd never tell Rob what had almost passed between Stuart and me. He raised the subject to let me know he forgave me, even though he was unaware of how close I'd come to throwing everything away. Rob knew that, whatever my battle, he could have lost. But I would have been the ultimate loser. I started crying. He turned around to look for the tissue box we kept in the kitchen, reached over, pulled out a tissue and handed it to me. I blew my nose.

"And then you came back and I knew you had sorted it all out. It was as though you were repaired. And now this? I'm proud of you for taking a stand." He looked at me with his beautiful eyes. His mouth, every inch of which I knew intimately, smiled. He brought my hand to his lips and kissed it and then my wrist, touching the bracelet he had given me. "You're worth more than that job, than answering to that mealy-mouthed moron. You're incredibly strong, smart and ambitious, and I know you can do more. I believe in you."

He wrapped his arms around me and I breathed a sigh of relief, my tears continuing to fall. For the past year and a half, I'd come close to losing my family, my marriage, my ambition and my sense of self. In having the courage to say no to Stuart—even though my heart wanted to follow a different path, at least for a little while—and yes to creating a new life for myself, I was restored.

"Do you want to eat?" I said into his shoulder. I felt weak

in my knees and a bit out of breath. Rob released me from our embrace and then turned his attention back to the peanuts. I picked up the salad bowl and moved toward the table.

"Sounds great! Maybe if they stay downstairs long enough we can have a conversation while we're eating. I'm just going to the bathroom to wash my hands. I'll be back in a second," he said, walking up behind me. He engulfed me in a hug, his hands across my chest, his head buried in my neck. "Do whatever you want to do! I know you can. I love you."

I listened for the running water in the bathroom before I took a few deep breaths and moved to the stove. I paused, my hand on the handle to the oven door, and then I smiled and let out a huge breath.

The next morning, I woke late, sunlight streaming through our bedroom window. I heard Rob and the boys in the kitchen, spoons clinking against bowls. Rob was trying to keep their voices down, to contain their excitement about the impending start to the new school year. Though Aidan was fond of school, he lamented the end of summer camps, soccer and playing outside every day. Jacob wasn't a huge fan of school and tried to figure out how he could remain home with me every day. That wasn't going to happen, especially now that I had to figure out what I was going to do—again. He'd have to learn to live with disappointment, I thought sardonically. Then I thought of how disappointment sometimes leads to great opportunities.

I sat up, swinging my legs over the side of our bed. I felt a huge weight lifted from my shoulders, and the fog I'd been walking around in for the past year or so had dissipated. I freshened up in our ensuite and then pulled on my bathrobe and padded out to the kitchen in my bare feet. One of my favourite things about warm weather was the ability to walk around without socks.

Two little faces turned when they heard me come into the room. Rob, dressed in a dark blue T-shirt and the pressed khakis I teased him about, walked over to me with a steaming mug, kissed my cheek, touched my hair and whispered in my ear, "You're beautiful."

I mouthed the words "thank you" over the brim of my cup. Rob told the boys if they hurried and finished their cereal, he'd walk them to Julie's and then head to work. I nodded my assent, smiling and enjoying the moment. I had a husband who loved me and forgave my imperfections. I knew he'd never mention Stuart again. I didn't know what I would tell him anyway. He was all that mattered. He was my everything.

epilogue

OCTOBER 2019

TODAY, I'm a bundle of nerves as I wait for the delivery truck.

After freeing myself from Heusten Shoes, I began to write. The boys went back to school and we got into a strict schedule. I got up, most days went for a run, returned home to see Rob off to work and then took the boys to the bus stop. Then, I'd write all morning long. After a couple of hours, I'd get up, stretch and crank my neck, maybe grab a tea, and sit back down and bang out more words. I spent afternoons looking for and completing freelance work I was able to find. I designed logos, pamphlets, menus, even the occasional website (but only when the client who wanted the website allowed me to use GoDaddy or SquareSpace as a template). I also carved out some time to volunteer in the boys' classrooms, going on school trips with them, something my mother could never do with me because she was always in school at the same time. I started volunteering every two weeks for a couple of hours at the local food bank. I felt happy and productive. I set goals and achieved small milestones. I began to welcome myself back. I'd missed her.

We discovered that, as partner, Rob had a lot more work, but his new position also gave him greater autonomy. In the summer, he worked the occasional Saturday afternoon in exchange for a Monday off, and we'd day trip to Toronto to see Ripley's Aquarium or go up the CN Tower. Rob's increased cash flow and bonuses—"profits, they're called, Caitie," he said, smiling—plus the money I made freelancing also meant I didn't need to find another job.

"Just write, Cait," Rob told me one night as we lay in bed, his hand caressing my face. "It's who you are."

And he was right.

Siobhan introduced me to Kate, my agent, after I finished my novel. Though we share our name, Kate is nothing like me. This Kate is cute as a button, about five feet tall and whippet thin, with a severe bob cut and bangs. The first time we met, over coffee at Starbucks, she wore a long, fashionable knit sweater, with black tights and black leather boots. I like her no-nonsense manner and knew right away I would never call her Katie or Katie-cat.

Kate said a box would be couriered to my house. The first shipment of my novel was being readied at the warehouse before going out to bookstores across Canada. I agreed to a plain blue cover with the title embossed in dark, sans serif lettering. It's simple, yet eye-catching. "Marketable," Kate calls it. I asked Siobhan's opinion about the cover, and she called it beautiful, saying she would put a brief about it in the books section of her magazine. She was calling it one of the top ten books to watch for.

"Just tell Kate to send over the fucking JPEG as soon as possible, so I can make my deadline," she wailed.

I don't know whether the book will sell. My publisher talked about a book tour, interviews and getting the book reviewed, but to me, it's already a success.

The doorbell rings at eight minutes after eleven. The boys bolt up as fast as I do, but Rob tells them to sit back down on the couch and wait. Everyone stayed home to wait for the shipment.

"Mommy can answer the door and bring the box in herself," he says, as I run upstairs from the family room, where we have been watching *Mary Poppins*. We pause the Broadway version of the movie at my favourite part, when Mary sings "Anything Can Happen."

I take a second to breathe deeply, calming myself before I open the front door. When I do, there's a man wearing black shorts, even though it's a chilly day. I sign the electronic delivery form, fumbling with the pen in my excitement. Then he hands me the box.

"Be careful," he says. "It's heavy."

"I know. It's copies of my book."

"Well, congratulations," he says, smiling, before turning around and running back to his truck, which idles at the curb.

I usher the box into the foyer and rip open the top, the front door still open behind me. I expose four neat stacks of my book; I know there are twenty copies inside. I don't know what else I expected—some beautiful note of congratulations from Kate or something—but there's only the packing slip. It reads, "Twenty copies, *My Favourite Mistake*, by Caitlin Morissette."

I take out one of the books and revel in its smell, the

sound of its spine as I crack it. Up until now, I worried it had all been a dream or that someone was playing a cruel trick on me. However, my bank account was padded when my advance cleared last month.

I flip past the opening pages, including the title page, and find what I'm looking for—the dedications. I wanted to keep it simple but meaningful. It took four days of rewriting; I stopped reworking it only when Kate told me she needed it. The printers were finalizing the page proofs and we had a deadline to meet.

It reads,

For Rob, Aidan and Jacob, whom I love with my whole heart
And S.T. for helping me heal

It's perfect—just as it's supposed to be. I hug the book to my chest, feeling the warm glow of the sun on my back, ignoring the chill in the wind, the beckoning of a storm that may or may not come. As I close the front door, I pause, still holding the book against my heart, grateful I had the courage to be myself, to let myself fail, to allow myself to heal. This book, these words, mended me, preparing me for whatever comes next.

acknowledgments

I started writing *In Repair* more than a decade ago. It might have continued to float around in my imagination were it not for a conversation with one of my best friends, Heather Evens, that went like this. Lori: "I think a novel is trying to come out." Heather: "Well, then let it." Seems so simple. But it wasn't.

This novel you hold now in your hands is here only because many people helped me along the way. I am forever grateful for the many hours Sheryl Loucks spent reading early—and horrible—drafts. Without her repeated guidance and encouragement of the manuscript when it was 106,000 words, I never would have gotten here.

Thank you also to all my early readers, who encouraged me to continue. And thank you to my beta readers Janice Arnoldi, Catharine Lowes and Tia Taylor, who let me know it was time to let go.

I am very appreciative for the deft hand of editor Dee Willson, who dove in and provided guidance on manuscript issues I couldn't identify, and to copy editor Dinah Laprairie, who polished it. I am still wowed by the beautiful cover Jessica Bell created and the lovely layout provided by Jody Skinner. And I am grateful for Andi Cumbo and Caroline Topperman of Mountain Ash Press who have been the ones to answer the question, "Now what?"

Thank you to my husband, Kris, for never asking why I keep buying books when so many remain on the TBR stack, and for encouraging me to keep writing. To my kids for providing an audience for why it's important to chase your dreams. And to the rest of my friends and family for all their support and love over the years for every challenge I took on —even if it seemed ridiculous.

And, finally, thank you to everyone who kept asking, "How's your book coming?" I appreciated every single one of the phone calls, text messages and emails. Now that I've started my second novel, I hope you'll keep wondering.

about the author

Lori Littleton is a former award-winning daily newspaper reporter and magazine editor, and current freelance writer. She holds a B. Journ and MA from Carleton University, is a mother of three and lives in St. Catharines with her husband, Kris. *In Repair* is her first novel.

LoriLittleton.com

 instagram.com/LoriLittleton_1

Manufactured by Amazon.ca
Bolton, ON

45440000R00166